tear here

The Complete Idiot's Refere

Six Tricks for Better Listening

- **Eliminate distractions.** If you know that you'll be having a lengthy discussion at your desk, arrange for someone else to handle your calls or set your voice mail to pick up all calls. Or go to a conference room—the phone there won't distract you.
- **Get rid of excess paper.** If your desk is strewn with paper, you probably sit there and let your eyes skim your papers until you realize that you're reading a letter or memo instead of listening. Get rid of those papers.
- **Don't get too comfortable.** Rather than take a relaxed position when you're in a discussion, sit at the edge of your chair and lean forward rather than backward. This position not only brings you physically closer to the other person but also enables you to be more attentive and to maintain eye contact.
- **Be an active listener.** Ask questions about what's being said. Paraphrase or ask specific questions about key points.
- **Be an empathetic listener.** Listen with your heart as well as with your head. Empathetic listeners not only listen to what other people say but also try to feel what other people are feeling when they say it. In other words, you put yourself in the speaker's shoes.
- **Take notes.** Jot down key words or phrases. Write down figures or important facts—just enough to remind you of the principal points that were made. Immediately after a meeting, while the information is still fresh in your mind, write a detailed summary. Dictate it into a recorder, type it into your computer, or enter it in your notebook—whichever is best for you.

Eight Tips for Making Training Meetings More Productive

- **Treat team members as knowledgeable people, not as schoolchildren.** Team members are adults who are willing to learn.
- **Avoid lecturing.** A lecture is deadly. Make the meeting a participatory experience for all who attend.
- **Don't just repeat what's in the training manual or handouts.** Team members can read it for themselves. You're there to expand, clarify, and elucidate.
- **Prepare for each session.** You should know ten times more about the subject than you present at the meeting.
- **Keep the sessions short.** Keep them short, but not so short that the material can't be adequately covered.
- **Use drama and a sense of humor.** Use your imagination to keep attendees awake, alert, and excited about what they're learning.
- **Use visual aids.** Use appropriate materials to augment what is spoken.
- **Set aside the last five minutes of each session for a summary.** Be sure to clear up any misunderstandings made obvious by participants' questions and comments. If a class lasts more than a day, spend 10 or 15 minutes summarizing the preceding day's discussion.

Three Tips to Ensure that an Applicant Tells You What You Need to Know

- **Use silence.** After an applicant has answered your question, *wait five seconds before asking your next question.* You'll be amazed at how many people add new information—positive or negative—to their original response.
- **Make nondirective comments:** Ask open-ended questions, such as "Tell me about your computer background." An applicant will tell you whatever he or she feels is an appropriate response. Rather than comment on the answer, respond with "Uh-huh" or "Yes" or just nod. This technique encourages applicants to continue talking without giving any hints about what you are seeking to learn. This approach often results in obtaining information about problems, personality factors, attitudes, or weaknesses that might not have been uncovered by direct questions. On the other hand, it can also bring out additional positive factors and strengths.
- **Ask probing questions:** Sometimes applicants can be vague or evasive in answering questions. Probe for more detail.

Four Steps to Help Team Members Learn Their Jobs

- **Preparation.** Preparation is both physical and psychological. *Physically*: All equipment and facilities necessary for training should be in place before training begins. *Psychologically:* Before training begins, trainees should be told what will be taught, why it is performed, and how it fits into the overall picture.
- **Presentation.** These four steps will guide you in showing someone how to do a job:

  Describe what you're going to do.

  Demonstrate step by step. As you demonstrate, explain each step and tell why it's done.

  Have trainees perform the job and explain to you the method and reason for each step.

  If necessary, repeat the step; if the job is performed satisfactorily, reinforce with praise or positive comments.
- **Performance.** When you're satisfied that trainees can do a job, let them do it (go away!). Trainees need an opportunity to try out what they've learned. From time to time, check out how things are going and make necessary corrections.
- **Follow-up.** The follow-up phase is important because people tend to change what they've been taught. Although you should encourage team members to try to find more effective approaches to their job, caution them not to make any changes until they have discussed them with you. Often, they may not be aware of the ramifications of their suggested changes.

Five Tips for Making Praise Effective

- **Don't overdo it.** Praise is sweet. Candy is sweet too, but the more you eat, the less sweet each piece becomes—and you may get a stomachache. Too much praise reduces the benefit that's derived from each bit of praise; if it's overdone, it loses its value altogether.
- **Be sincere.** You can't fake sincerity. You must truly believe that what you are praising your associate for is praiseworthy. If you don't believe it, you come across as phony.
- **Be specific about the reason for your praise.** Rather than say, "Great job!" it's much better to say, "The report you submitted on the XYZ matter enabled me to understand more clearly the complexities of the issue."
- **Ask for your team members' advice.** Nothing is more flattering than to be asked for advice about how to handle a situation. This approach can backfire, though, if you don't *take* the advice. If you have to reject advice, remember the Socratic approach—ask people questions about questionable issues until *they* see the negative aspects and reject their own poor advice (see chapter 5).
- **Publicize praise.** Just as a reprimand should always be given in private, praising should be done (wherever possible) in public. Sometimes the matter for which praise is given is a private issue, but it's more often appropriate to let your entire team in on the praise. If other team members are aware of the praise you give a colleague, it acts as a spur to them to work for similar recognition.

Five Elements of Good Delegation

- **Be sure that the person you choose for the assignment is capable of doing the work.** You know the abilities of each of your team members. When you plan assignments, take into consideration which person can do a job most effectively.
- **Make sure that your instructions are not only understood but also accepted.** Asking the question "Do you understand?" is meaningless. Instead, ask "What are you going to do?" If a team member's response indicates that one or more of your points isn't clear, you can correct it before he or she does something wrong.
- **Set control points.** A *control point* is a key area in a project where you stop, examine what has been completed, and, if errors have been made, correct them. In this way, you can catch errors before they blow up into catastrophes.
- **Give your associate the tools and authority to get the job done.** You can't do a job without the proper tools or the authority to do what needs to be done. Providing resources is obvious, but giving authority is another story. If you want a job to be done without having to micromanage it, you must give the people who are doing the job the power to make decisions.
- **When you delegate, don't abdicate.** Staff members have questions, seek advice, and need your help. Be there for them, but don't let them throw the entire project back at you. Let them know that you're available to help, to advise, and to support, but not to do their work.

The COMPLETE IDIOT'S GUIDE TO Managing People

by Arthur R. Pell

alpha books

A Division of Macmillan General Reference
A Simon & Schuster Macmillan Company
1633 Broadway, 8th Floor, New York, NY 10019-6785

International Standard Book Number: 0-02-861036-9
Library of Congress Catalog Card Number: 95-080490

98 97 96 95 8 7 6 5 4 3 2 1

Interpretation of the printing code: the rightmost number of the first series of numbers is the year of the book's printing; the rightmost number of the second series of numbers is the number of the book's printing. For example, a printing code of 95-1 shows that the first printing of the book occurred in 1995.

Printed in the United States of America

Publisher
Theresa H. Murtha

Associate Publisher
Lisa A. Bucki

Production Editor
Rebecca Whitney

Designer
Kim Scott

Illustrator
Judd Winick

Manufacturing Coordinator
Steven Pool

Production Manager
Kelly Dobbs

Production Team Supervisor
Laurie Casey

Graphic Image Specialists
Clint Lahnen
Laura Robbins
Craig Small
Todd Wente

Indexer
David Savka

Production Team
Heather Butler
Angela Calvert
Kim Cofer
Tricia Flodder
Erika Millen
Beth Rago
Erich J. Richter
Christine Tyner
Karen Walsh

Contents at a Glance

Contents

Foreword

The world of business is constantly changing. How you as a manager plan your activities, make your decisions, and motivate your staff is much different today than it was just a few years ago. To be at the cutting edge of management efficiency, you must be knowledgeable about the innovations in your fields, capable of adapting them to your own operations, and, most important, able to communicate these changes to your associates and team members.

Whether you are an experienced manager or preparing to lead teams, projects, departments, or entire organizations, *The Complete Idiot's Guide to Managing People* is an easy-to-read, easy-to-apply manual. It provides guidelines for every aspect of managing people, from hiring to firing. It includes suggestions for developing creativity, delegating, communicating, motivating, and counseling others. It alerts you to the part you play in complying with the changes in laws that govern management in today's working environment.

The author, Dr. Arthur R. Pell, is particularly well qualified to assist you in learning about these approaches to more effective leadership. In addition to his many years of on-the-job experience in management, the seminars on management methods he has conducted for the Business Education Services unit of the Dun & Bradstreet Corporation Foundation throughout the United States and Canada have been praised not only for their content and presentation but also for the practical suggestions that have been readily implemented on the job. This value is carried forward in this book. Each chapter provides examples that illustrate how the principles presented have been applied in real-life situations and demonstrate how to apply those principles in your work.

Use this book as a guide to bringing 21st century techniques to your job today. Keep this book on your desk as a reference tool to assist in dealing with leadership problems as they occur day by day. You will find it a pragmatic accessory in developing your leadership skills.

William O. Frohlich
President
Dun & Bradstreet
Business Education Services

Introduction

You've read books about management. You've taken seminars, courses, and workshops in your own company and at colleges and universities. You've attended countless meetings at professional and trade associations—all providing tips and techniques for managing people. So why another book?

The world is changing, and management changes with it. Whether you're starting your first assignment as a team leader or have years of experience, you have to keep up with these changes. Ideas that weren't even dreams a few years ago are now part and parcel of the corporate culture. You pick up a business magazine and every other article mentions such terms as "project management," "self-directed teams," "empowerment," and "total quality management." Of course, you know what they mean, but how do they affect the way you manage?

In *The Complete Idiot's Guide to Managing People,* I'll talk about these concepts and much more. I'll not only describe them but also provide suggestions and examples of how you can apply them in the day-to-day situations you face on the job.

Part 1, "What's the Fun in Being a Boss if You Can't Boss Anybody Around?" explores how the team concept enables you to take advantage of the skills, brains, and creativity of every person on your team. This part looks at the myths and misconceptions that have often dictated management style. Then it gets right into the pragmatic approaches to setting goals and developing channels of communication so that you can make sure that your ideas and instructions are understood and accepted by your team members. You'll also learn equally important techniques to encourage team members to contribute ideas and suggestions about every aspect of the work they do.

In part 2, "The Supervisor as Coach," you'll learn how to develop your team for optimum performance. You'll learn about not only the techniques of training and development but also how to get the most from your training buck.

The ramifications of the equal-employment opportunity (EEO) laws are discussed in part 3, "Understanding and Complying with Equal-Employment Laws." It presents a list of pre-employment questions you can and cannot ask. This part of the book pays special attention to the latest developments in this area, including the Americans with Disabilities Act, how to avoid sexual-harassment complaints, and the role of the team leader in affirmative action.

Part 4, "Choosing Team Members," discusses the important issue of choosing team members who can not only do the job but also fit in as part of your team.

The focus in part 5, "Motivating Your Team for Peak Performance," is on methods of motivating your team members. Some of the issues covered in this part are money (does it really motivate?), incentive-pay programs, recognition programs that work, how to motivate people when they have the opportunity for advancement, and what "empowerment" is all about.

Part 6, "Dealing with Employee Problems on the Job," covers the day-to-day problems that leaders face on the job, including dealing with poor performance, stress and burnout, overly sensitive people, and alcohol and drug addiction. You'll learn how to counsel employees and when and how to refer them to professionals for help. This part also discusses how to manage people who don't work on-site, such as telecommuters and subcontractors, and how to work with self-directed teams.

Traditional and nontraditional methods of discipline, up to and including termination, are explored in part 7, "Doling Out Discipline." This part also explores voluntary quits and reducing turnover. This part pays special attention to layoffs and downsizing, including a discussion of the WARN law and the concept of "employment at will."

How to Make This Book Work for You

Reading a book like this one can be interesting, enlightening, and amusing. I hope that this book will be all these things to you. More important, it should provide you with ideas you can use on the job. You'll find lots of these ideas in the following pages.

But it will all be a waste of your money, time, and energy if you don't take what you read and put it into effect in the way you perform your day-to-day managerial functions.

Following these five steps should ensure that this book isn't just a reading exercise but also a plan of action for you:

1. At the end of the first chapter is a section that explains how to create an action plan to implement what you've learned. Create this type of action plan after you read each chapter. Indicate what action you will take, with whom you will take the action, and when you will begin.
2. Share your plan of action with your associates. Get them involved.
3. Set a follow-up date to check whether you did what you planned to do.
4. If not, reread the chapter, rethink what you did or didn't do, and make a new plan of action.
5. Do it, review it, renew it.

Extras

To add to the material in the main text of the book, a series of shaded boxes throughout the book highlight specific items that can help you understand and implement the material in each chapter:

Bet You Didn't Know

These boxes contain little-known information that may add to your knowledge or just amuse you.

Meanings and Gleanings

You may have a good idea of what most of these new expressions mean, but you don't have to guess about their meanings and implications. These definitions will put you in the know so that you won't have to bluff your way through when your boss throws these terms at you.

Leadership Lead

These tips and techniques will help you implement some of the ideas you pick up in the book. Some of them come from the writings of management gurus, and others come from the experience of managers like you, who are happy to share them.

Red Alert

Caution! These Red Alerts can help you avoid mistakes that could cost you time, money, energy, and embarrassment.

Special Thanks

The Complete Idiot's Guide to Managing People was reviewed by an expert in the field who not only checked the technical accuracy of what you'll learn here but also provided insight and guidance to help us ensure that this book gives you everything you need to know to make the most of your management role. The publisher's special thanks are extended to:

Ronald B. Smith, who has had three books published and who has more than 25 years' experience in developing business computer systems on mainframes and on client/server systems for major corporations. He is the president of the Greenspoint Area Toastmasters Club in Houston, Texas. In addition to writing, he enjoys reading, teaching, and racquetball.

Part 1

What's the Fun in Being a Boss if You Can't Boss Anybody Around?

The old boss whose motto was "Do it my way or you're on the highway" has been supplanted by the facilitator who gets things done by developing the skills and coordinating the efforts of a team of intelligent, motivated associates. Being a manager still can be fun—even more fun! There's real joy in observing the results you achieve when you see each member of your team growing, watch the synergy that develops between them, and share their accomplishments with them.

You can learn to mold a team and help your team members develop into creative, contributing, collaborative colleagues. To do this, stop thinking like a "boss." Bosses make decisions and give orders. Today's managers coordinate groups of thinking adults who together work out the problems that face them. Today's managers provide a climate in which their team members are encouraged to make their own analyses of problems, suggest solutions, and participate in decisions.

In this part of the book, you'll see how to begin to make this concept work for you.

Chapter 1

Managing Ain't What It Used to Be

In This Chapter

- Understanding the changing face of management
- Evaluating your management style
- Learning how to lead rather than boss
- Creating and developing productive teams

Management is changing. So what's new about that? Management, like all other aspects of life, is always in a state of flux. Nothing stays the same. You've seen changes and lived with them or adapted to them. So why is changing management of special concern now?

Speed! That's why. Things are changing so fast that it's easy to fall behind. This chapter looks at some of the changes that have taken place in the management of people and how it affects the way leaders lead—and the way people follow. You'll see how these changes affect you and what you can do to integrate them into your management style.

Sound difficult? It really isn't. I've done it, and I've helped my clients do it. During the past few years, progressive managers in many companies have made these changes. First examine your current management style (a quiz will help you). Then take the necessary steps to make the changes that will enable you to excite and motivate the members of your team.

Managing into the Next Century—If I Make It 'Til Then

The world of work has changed radically during the past decade, and it continues to change more rapidly than any time since the industrial revolution. Computers have enabled managers to obtain and incorporate information into their decision-making at a speed unheard of in the past. Men and women moving into management positions today are working in an entirely different culture than the one their parents or even their older brothers or sisters faced.

Meanings and Gleanings
Members of an organization's **management team** must achieve specific results by effectively using the organization's available resources. These tools include money, computers, materials, equipment, information, and employees.

Gone is the old hierarchical structure, under which top management made decisions that were passed down through a series of layers to rank-and-file workers. In its place is a more collaborative organization in which people at all levels are expected to contribute to every aspect of organizational activity.

Many of the intermediate layers of middle management have been eliminated. More and more of the responsibility for getting things done is now concentrated in teams consisting of team leaders and team members who together plan, implement, and control the work.

Hey! What's All This Change About?

Companies are rapidly retooling the processes by which they operate. Many structures that existed for decades are being replaced by new and exciting approaches to take advantage of new technologies and new management thinking. Some of these approaches are shown in this list:

Leadership Lead
Don't be afraid to try new approaches. The management climate is changing. To keep up with it and to make progress, you have to take risks. Don't be afraid to go out on a limb. That's where the fruit is.

- **Flatten the organizational structure.** Removing management layers cuts down on the channels through which orders and information flow.
- **Encourage participative decision-making.** Employees at all levels now participate in every aspect of planning the work and getting it done, including (but not limited to) production scheduling, quality assurance, and establishing performance standards.
- **Use teams to get the work done.** The team leader has replaced the "boss."

- **Implement total project management.** Under this concept, a manager is responsible for supervising an entire project from start to finish. This process involves coordinating with other departments over which the manager does not have direct authority.
- **Outsource rather than employ.** Many companies now find it cheaper to subcontract various phases of a job to other firms. Sometimes the work of several different companies must be coordinated with the work of your own team to accomplish the project.
- **Adopt just-in-time delivery.** Rather than store large inventories of supplies or finished products, companies today arrange with suppliers to deliver supplies and products as needed. A project manager or team leader interacts with suppliers to schedule and ensure delivery of supplies.
- **Reengineer.** Reengineering involves radically restructuring the design of business processes, not just tinkering with isolated methods and procedures. When companies reengineer their processes, its managers have to rethink everything they are doing to take advantage of the changes.

How Do These Organizational Changes Affect Me?

As the style and process of management changes, if you have management responsibilities or are preparing for promotion, you have to reorient yourself to meet the changing requirements of your job.

Now is the time to reexamine the way you are managing or would like to manage and to learn what successful managers are doing to become even more successful.

As you read this book, keep in mind these changes in the management function. You will learn how to deal with the day-to-day problems of managing people, and you will learn that *you can't do it alone.* To achieve success, you must use the talents of all members of your group.

As you read this book, you will read pragmatic suggestions for stimulating the brainpower and expertise of all people involved: your team members as well as others in and out of the organization with whom you're collaborating.

Taking an Eagle-Eye Look at Management Style

You may have been managing people for years. You think that you know the ins and outs of running your department, but your boss says that you're not meeting the company's goals. You're cautioned to "get up-to-date or get out." You think, "I'm doing okay—the *boss* is being unreasonable."

Or perhaps you've just been promoted to your first supervisory job. Your boss congratulates you, shakes your hand, and says "Take over." No training, no advice—just "take over." It's nice to get the promotion, but don't you wish that you could get some training?

What happens if the people who report directly to you or your team members are giving you a hard time? No matter how hard you try to get them to do their work, to meet deadlines, or to comply with quality standards, they do just enough to keep from getting fired.

Stop blaming others. Look to yourself. Are you managing like a 19th century autocrat or like a 21st century leader?

Take a look at how your approach to management shapes up with what the management gurus consider the "right way."

Sure, you're entitled to your opinion, but keep an open mind. You want to do a better job—that's why you're reading this book. Use the list of questions near the end of this chapter to take inventory of how you manage now. Then compare your answers with the answers after the inventory.

Seeing the Manager as Facilitator

Men and women in today's corporate environment do not respond to authoritative styles. Truly successful managers commit themselves to obtaining the *willing cooperation* of all involved. They are facilitators who make every effort to make things go smoothly for their staff or team.

Most people respond best to managers who treat them as adults, encourage them to make suggestions about their work, and listen to their ideas even when those ideas may disagree with their own. Successful managers encourage people to be contributors rather than just order-takers.

Team Members: A Fount of Human Resources

To experience the greatest success in getting people to cooperate willingly, use the team approach.

What is a team? Most people would answer, "It's a group of people working to achieve a common goal." That's a good answer, but not good enough. Even if groups work together to achieve a common goal, it does not make them a team. There's much more to it.

A key word must be added to this definition: A team is a group of people working *synergistically* to achieve a common goal. When people work together collaboratively as a team, each one benefits from the knowledge, work, and support of each of the other team members, which leads to much greater productivity than would be achieved by each person working at top capacity as an individual.

A good example of synergy is a rocket ship, which is made up of a series of components (stages). In order for the ship to function, each component must be in tiptop condition. But even if all components are in A-1 shape, the rocket still won't get off the launching pad unless all components work together interactively, or synergistically.

You are the rocket engineer; your team members are the components. To make that team effective, you must ensure that each member works at optimum capacity and then that they work collaboratively to achieve the synergy that will lift your project from its launching pad to its successful completion.

Melding Your Ragtag Group into a Team

Molding people into a team involves more than just changing each person's title from "employee" to "associate" or "team member." Your own attitude is the key to success. When you act as a facilitator (as a coordinator or leader) rather than as a boss, your staff members begin to feel like—and then act like—team members.

Building your team requires careful planning. No team can just spring up by itself. You must work carefully with team members to explain several factors:

- How they are expected to work.
- How this new method of operation differs from what they are used to doing.
- Where they can go for help.
- How the new team approach works.

Giving just lip service to the team approach doesn't work—you must "walk the talk." You must change

Leadership Lead
Although you may be accustomed to handling many day-to-day work details, force yourself to delegate as many tasks as you reasonably can. Handling certain tasks is no longer your job: You can't do it all by yourself. Help your team members to develop their skills, and then give them the ball and let them run with it.

your way of dealing with problems as they occur. Rather than make decisions arbitrarily, encourage team members to come up with solutions to problems and to implement those solutions. You should guide and facilitate rather than direct the work of your team. The participation of all team members is the key to team success (see chapter 14).

Those Dreaded Myths and Misconceptions

As in most fields, an entire anthology of myths has developed about how managers should supervise employees. These myths range from the simple admonition "Use your common sense" to warnings not to coddle people. They have been perpetuated from one generation of managers to another, and, although they may work in some situations, they generally are ineffective.

Leadership Lead
"By clinging to myths in the face of new realities, we close our minds to new ideas and viewpoints."

— Sen. William Fulbright

Chapter 2 debunks some of the most frequently quoted misconceptions and shows you how following the myths can keep you from meeting your goal of becoming a good manager. Oh, yes, you'll also get some suggestions about how to avoid falling prey to the myths.

Previewing Some Tools of the Management Trade

Okay, you agree that the role of the manager has changed. "Enough of this theory," you may say—you want to learn techniques to help you put all this together so that your goals and the goals of your team will be met.

That's the thrust of this book. Each chapter provides a specific approach to your job as a manager. This list shows you some of the tools you will master and in which chapters you can read about them:

- Assembling a team (chapter 3).
- Establishing a climate of open communication to and from your team members (chapters 4 and 5).
- Developing and using team members' skills and talents (chapters 7 and 8).
- Ensuring that you and others on the team comply with civil-rights laws (chapters 9 and 10).
- Hiring the right people for your team (chapters 11, 12, and 13).
- Helping your associates become self-motivated (chapters 14 through 17).
- Dealing with people problems (chapters 19 through 25).

And there's much more.

Bet You Didn't Know

Which is the higher-level title: manager or supervisor? *You can't always tell by a title.* It depends on the industry or even on the company. In most organizations, supervisors report to managers. In the retail field, however, it's the opposite. The person in charge of a store is its manager; store managers report to supervisors of several units.

Taking Inventory: How Strong Are You as a Manager?

Take the following inventory of your management style by checking the appropriate box beside each question to indicate whether you agree or disagree with each statement. Then compare your responses to the answers that follow.

	Agree	Disagree
1. It isn't necessary for a manager to discuss long-range goals with team-member subordinates. As long as team members are aware of the immediate objective, they can do their work effectively.	❑	❑
2. The best way to make a reprimand effective is to dress down an offender in front of coworkers.	❑	❑
3. Managers show ignorance and risk loss of face if they answer a question with, "I don't know, but I'll find out and let you know."	❑	❑
4. It pays off for a manager to spend a great deal of time with a new employee to ensure that training has been effective.	❑	❑
5. Managers should ask their associates for their ideas about work methods.	❑	❑
6. When disciplining is required, you should be careful to avoid saying or doing something that may cause resentment.	❑	❑
7. People will work best for a tough manager.	❑	❑

	Agree	Disagree
8. It is more important for a team to be composed of members who like their job than of people who do it well.	❑	❑
9. The work gets done most efficiently if a manager lays out a plan in great detail.	❑	❑
10. For a manager to lead an effective team, the feelings, attitudes, and ideas of team members should be kept in mind.	❑	❑

Okay, you've answered all the questions. Now look at the responses based on the advice of successful managers:

1. **Disagree.** Persons who know where they are going—who can visualize the long-range picture—are more committed to reaching those objectives and will work harder to attain them.
2. **Disagree.** Dressing a person down does not solve the problem—it only makes the person feel small in front of coworkers. A good reprimand corrects a problem without humiliating the person. It is best to reprimand in private—*never* in front of others.
3. **Disagree.** It is better to admit ignorance of a matter than to try to bluff. People respect leaders who accept that they don't know everything.
4. **Agree.** The most important step in developing the full capabilities of associates is good training on the part of managers. Managers who invest the time in the beginning will lay the foundation for developing each newcomer into a valuable asset of the organization.
5. **Agree.** Persons directly involved with the job often can contribute good ideas toward the solution of problems they are close to.
6. **Agree.** Resentment creates low morale and often leads to conscious or subconscious sabotage.
7. **Disagree.** Tough is not as important as fair and inspiring.
8. **Disagree.** The happiness and satisfaction of team members on the job are important, but they are secondary to getting the job done.
9. **Disagree.** Psychologists have shown that most people work better when they are given broad project guidelines and can work out the details themselves. An exception is that some people do work better when tasks are given to them in detail.

A good manager recognizes the styles in which people work and adapts to them in dealing with each person.

10. **Agree.** Communication is a two-way street. To manage effectively, it's important to know what team members are thinking and how they feel about the job.

There is no passing or failing score for this inventory. Its purpose is to make you think about how you manage people. You may not agree with all the answers, but at least pay them some heed. Most of what you find here is discussed in detail later in this book.

Creating Your Own Action Plans

Based on what you learn in each chapter, decide what actions you will take. To get the most from this book, identify two or three new techniques to adopt as part of your management style. For each technique you identify, spell out these details on paper:

1. Action (What you will do?)
2. Collaborators (With whom will you do it?)
3. Time (When you will start?)

Periodically review your progress toward completing these action plans.

Do It, Review It, Renew It

As you begin to use the ideas outlined later in working with your team, the phrase "do it, review it, renew it" can help you remember the key steps in planning a task:

Do it. After you've decided what to do, arrange with your team members and set a time for it to be done. The task must be more than a notation made on paper.

Review it. Doing it is only the first step. Next, you must review what you've accomplished. What problems did you encounter, and how did you handle them? What did you and your team learn from this action?

Renew it. Fine-tune new approaches and incorporate them into the methods and techniques your team will use in facing similar situations later.

The Least You Need to Know

- The job of the manager has changed. Bossing doesn't work. You have to lead.
- People respond better to participative rather than authoritarian leadership.

- Give people the opportunity to use their talents, skills, and brainpower.
- A team is more than just a group of people—it's a synergistic, interactive, collaborative family.
- Think of yourself as a facilitator. Your job is to make it easy for people to accomplish their jobs.
- After you read each chapter of this book, develop an action plan to implement the ideas you want to adopt. *Do it,* then *review it,* and, when appropriate, *renew it.*

Chapter 2

"Everything I Know, I Learned from My Old Boss—and Was He Dumb!"

In This Chapter

- ➤ Dispelling myths and misconceptions about managing people
- ➤ Overcoming preconceptions
- ➤ Clearing your mind for positive action

Chapter 1 explored the way the practice of management has changed and how important it is for team leaders to recognize the need for change and to adapt to new approaches in their work. Yet managers are often frustrated in their efforts to change by interference from bosses, colleagues, and associates whose preconceptions about how to manage are so ingrained that they resist *any* attempt to change.

What's the cause of this interference? Like all aspects of life, the field of management is loaded with truisms that aren't true, "facts" that aren't factual, assumptions that aren't challenged, and attitudes based on folklore perpetuated over generations. In addition, policies, practices, and principles that may have been valid in the past no longer work.

Myths and misconceptions that have governed people's thinking for years (for a lifetime, in many cases) are tough to overcome. As a manager, however, you must overcome them if you want to be able to move ahead. This chapter examines some common myths, tells you how they impede progress, and explains what you can do to put them in perspective.

Managing Like a Professional

Some people are reluctant to take on a leadership role. They believe that they have to be born with certain leadership traits, especially charisma, that intangible "something" that enables a person to influence others.

It's true that some of the world's greatest leaders were born leaders who did have that special charm which enraptures the public, but they're the exception. The largest percentage of successful leaders are ordinary people who have worked hard to achieve the qualities that made them what they have become. People management is easier if you have natural talents, but they're not essential. You can *acquire* the skills to manage and lead people.

Many managers like to refer to themselves as "professionals," but is management really a profession?

Many professions require special training or advanced study in a specialized field. Physicians, lawyers, psychologists, and engineers all have to take advanced education and pass examinations to qualify for certification in their profession.

Some managers may have special education (degrees in business administration), but *most are promoted from the ranks and have little or no training in management.* Unlike people in other professions, managers learn primarily on the job.

Although more and more successful managers make an effort to acquire knowledge in a professional manner, most managers pick up their techniques by observing and following the habits and practices of their bosses. The model they follow may be good; too often, however, it's based on concepts that don't have validity but that have been perpetuated over the years.

Debunking Those Darned Myths and Misconceptions

Some of these ideas may have worked in the past but are no longer effective; others never were true. Let's look at some of the many myths and misconceptions that have affected the way people choose to manage others in the workplace.

Management Is Nothing More Than Common Sense

One manager said, "When I was promoted to my first management job, I asked a longtime manager for some tips about how to deal with people who report to me," he said. "He told me, 'Just use horse sense, and you'll have no trouble.'"

Common sense is an important asset, but how is it defined? What appears to be sensible to one person may make no sense to another. Often what is accepted as "common sense" is based on the culture of the society in which it exists. In Japan, for example, it's considered "common sense" to wait for consensus before making a decision; in the United States, this technique is often derided as inefficient and a waste of time.

Cultural customs aren't the only cause for differing ideas about what constitutes common sense. Different people have different views about what is good and what is bad, what is efficient and what is wasteful, and what will work and what will not.

Although what we think of as common sense has been developed from our own experiences, an individual's experience is never enough to provide anything other than limited perspectives. Leadership involves much more than the experience an individual may have. If you want to be a real leader, you must look beyond common sense. Books written by management experts abound. Make a practice of reading those books, subscribing to periodicals, and learning from the experiences of men and women who have been successful leaders.

You wouldn't rely solely on common sense to help with financial or manufacturing problems. You would call on the best possible expertise in these areas for advice and information. Why then should you resort to a less pragmatic base in handling human-relations problems?

You can learn much about what really is effective in the art and science of management by reading books and periodicals in the field, attending courses and seminars, and actively participating in trade associations in your industry.

Accept that you don't have all the answers. No one does. By making friends with people in other companies who have faced similar situations, you can learn a great deal from them. This *networking* process gives you access to these people when you need information or ideas and provides an ongoing resource for obtaining assistance in solving problems.

One of the peripheral benefits of the total-quality movement has been the practice of *benchmarking:* seeking organizations that have been successful in certain areas and learning their techniques. Companies that participate in competitions such as the Malcolm Baldridge Awards (presented annually by the U.S. Department of Commerce to firms that have demonstrated high quality in their work) must agree to share their techniques with any organizations that request this information.

Meanings and Gleanings

One of the fastest-growing phenomena of the past decade is **total quality management.** In this management system, the focus of an entire company is placed on the production of high-quality products or services. It involves statistical processes, training in both technical and intangible aspects of quality management, and the commitment of all levels of employees to work toward continuous improvement.

Follow the "Golden Rule"

When you manage people, the Biblical rule "Do unto others as you would have others do unto you" is sound advice—to a point.

Because people are *not* all alike, treating others as *you* want to be treated is not the same as treating them as *they* want to be treated.

For example, Linda prefers to be given broad objectives and to be allowed to work out on her own the details about how her job should be done. Her assistant, Jason, is not comfortable receiving an assignment unless all the details are spelled out. If Linda delegates work to him in the way she likes to have work assigned to her, she won't get the best results.

Sol needs continuous reinforcement. He's happy on the job only when his boss oversees his work and assures Sol that he's doing a good job. Tanya gets upset if her boss checks her work too often. "Doesn't she trust me?" she complains. You can't do unto Tanya as you do unto Sol and get good results from each of them.

Each of us has our own style, our own approach, and our own eccentricities. To "do unto others" what we want done to us may be the poorest way of dealing with someone else.

To be an effective manager, you must know each member of your team and tailor your method of management to each person's individuality. Rather than follow the golden rule, follow the *platinum* rule: "Do unto others as they would have you do unto them."

Compromises must be made, of course. In some situations, work must be done in a manner that may not be ideal for some people. By knowing that what must be done may cause problems, you can anticipate problems and prepare team members to accept their tasks.

Meanings and Gleanings

An effective way to keep in touch with the way other managers and companies deal with problems similar to yours is **networking**, or making contacts with managers in other companies to whom you can turn for suggestions and ideas. Organizations that have achieved success in a certain area are often willing to share their techniques and methods. They provide **benchmarking** that other organizations can emulate.

Leadership Lead

Keep up with your field:

- Attend seminars and read current books about management.
- Read trade and professional journals.
- Take an active role in business associations.
- Network with other managers.
- Benchmark the best companies in your field.

"Tell 'Em What to Do—If They Don't Do It, Fire 'Em"

Management by fear is still a common practice. And it works—sometimes. People will work if they fear that they might lose their jobs, but how much work will they do? The answer is "Just enough to keep from getting fired." This technique isn't considered effective management. Successful management involves getting the *willing* cooperation of your associates.

Moreover, it's not that easy to fire people. Considering the implications of the civil-rights laws (see part 3) and labor unions (see chapter 25) and in many cases the difficulty and costs associated with hiring competent replacements, firing people may cause more problems than keeping employees with whom you're not satisfied.

Meanings and Gleanings

When you work with your associates, rather than follow the golden rule, remember the **platinum rule**: Do unto others as they would have you do unto them.

You can't keep good workers when you manage by fear. When jobs are scarce in your community or industry, workers will tolerate high-handed arbitrary bosses. When the job market opens up, however, the best people will leave for companies that have a more pleasant working environment. Employee turnover can be expensive and often devastating.

Recently I was retained by a company to help staff an entire office facility. Although its salary scale wasn't any higher than in other companies in the community, it was inundated with applicants from one particular firm, a large insurance company. My immediate assumption was that the other company was shaky and that its employees were seeking more stable employment. The company was in excellent shape, however. Applicant after applicant told us that the company's arbitrary management style made the working environment unpleasant. Despite good pay and benefits, they wanted out.

Bet You Didn't Know

Turnover is usually calculated by dividing the number of people leaving a company each month by the average number of employees on the payroll for that month (multiply by 100 to get a percentage).

The lesson in this example is that you should use positive rather than negative techniques to motivate people (see part 5).

Production, Performance, and Profit: The Manager's Job

Production, performance, and profit are important aspects of your job as a manager, but is that all you have to consider? If a business is to survive, it must produce results. Equally important, however, is its development of the potential of the people in the organization. If you ignore people's potential, your team's ability to attain results is limited. Short-term results are achieved at the expense of long-term success and even survival.

When Lee founded his computer-components company, he was a pioneer in that new and growing industry. Determined to be a leader in his field, he drove the people in his company to attain high productivity and kept his eye carefully on the profit picture, but he paid no attention to the development of his staff. His technical and administrative staff members were given little opportunity to contribute ideas or use their own initiative. Over the years, Lee made reasonable profits for his company, but it never grew to become a significant factor in the industry. By holding his people back, the turnover of technical staff was high. By depending only on his own ideas, he lost out on possible innovations the people working in his company might have come up with.

Management must keep a balance between the *P-factor* (potential of people) and the *R-factor* (results desired). If you put too much emphasis on R, short-range goals may be attained, but long-term goals suffer. On the other hand, if you tilt the scale in favor of P (for example, if you overemphasize training and development and sacrifice results), your company may not be able to continue to stay in business. The P/R balance is shown in the figure on the following page.

Your overall objective is to obtain superior performance of the entire team, which requires keeping the P and R factors in balance. When people are given the opportunity to hone their skills, develop their own professionalism, and grow in their career areas, they are stimulated to work harder to achieve results. When a person obtains desired results, it stimulates a desire to give even more effort to the job—and therefore bring out his or her greatest potential. This in turn pays off in even better results.

Bet You Didn't Know

Most employees have an exaggerated idea about the profits most companies attain. Survey after survey indicates that people think corporate profits are 20 or 30 percent or even higher. True profits for most companies are closer to 5 percent.

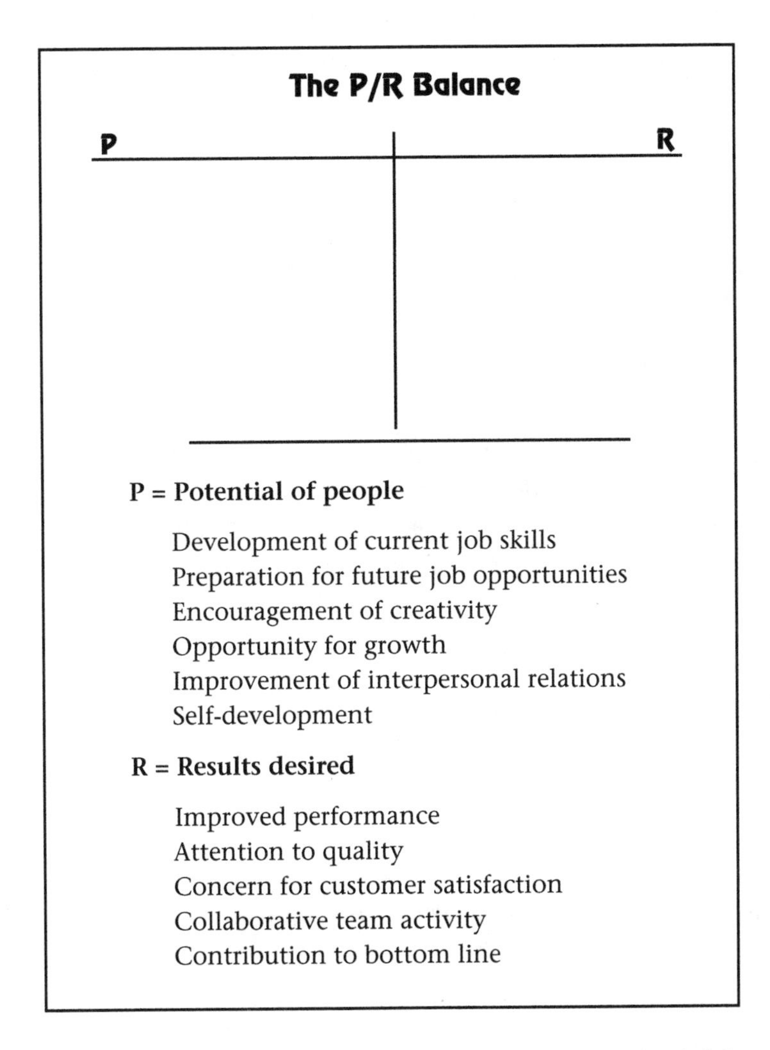

The comparison between performance and people potential. List potential factors on the left and results factors on the right to see whether they are in balance.

"Give Them Some Praise and They'll Ask for a Raise"

People need to be praised. Everyone wants to know that good work is appreciated, yet many managers are reluctant to praise their employees.

What's the reason for this hesitation? Some managers fear that if they praise a team member's work, that person will become complacent and not try to do even better (and some people do react that way). The objective is to phrase your praise in a manner that encourages a team member to keep up the good work (see chapter 16).

Red Alert

Don't promise employees raises or bonuses based on the accomplishment of a specific task. Financial reward should be based on overall performance over time. Never promise a raise unless it's part of a compensation or management-by-objective plan that has been formally approved by your superiors, the human-resources department, and others in your organization who approve changes in compensation.

Some managers are concerned that if team members are praised for good work, they will expect increases in pay in the form of a raise or bonus. And some folks might. But that behavior is no reason to withhold praise when it's warranted. All employees should know how salary adjustments, bonuses, and other financial rewards are determined. If compensation is determined at an annual performance evaluation, team members should be assured that the good work for which they are praised will be considered in the evaluation.

Some managers don't believe in praise. One department head told me, "The people I supervise know that they're doing okay if I don't talk to them. If I have to speak to them, they know they're in trouble."

Praise can be overdone. If people are repeatedly praised for every trivial accomplishment, the value of praise is diminished to the point of being superficial.

"The Best Way to Get People to Work Is a KITA (Kick in the You-Know-What)"

Sure, some managers still kick their employees in the rear end—not literally, but verbally. In a contest held every year by James Miller, a management consultant and the author of *The Corporate Coach,* employees nominate their bosses for either the best or worst boss of the year. Miller reports that he gets many more nominations for worst boss than for best boss. In almost every case, one of the chief reasons for being nominated as a bad boss is that the person continually finds fault with subordinates, expresses sarcasm, gloats over failures, and often hollers and screams at employees—that's verbal KITA.

Meanings and Gleanings

Leadership is an art that can be acquired. You can learn to guide people in such a manner as to command their respect, confidence, and whole-hearted cooperation. **Charisma** is usually inborn—it's the special charm some people have that secures for them the support and allegiance of other people.

No one really knows what causes people to behave in this way. Some people have always been screamed at—by parents, teachers, former bosses—so they believe that it's an effective communication tool.

We all raise our voices occasionally, especially when we're under stress. It takes great self-discipline *not* to yell. Effective leaders, however, control this tendency. An occasional lapse is okay, but when it's your normal manner of communicating, you're admitting your failure to be a real leader. You cannot get the *willing* cooperation of your associates that way.

The Least You Need to Know

- Managers are often influenced by misconceptions and myths. Don't assume that because your old bosses practiced these types of methods, you must follow suit.
- When you deal with people, using your common sense makes sense. No person's experience is broad enough, however, to cover all the bases. Seek out advice from experts to learn about leadership.
- Practice the platinum rule: "Do unto others as they would have you do unto them."
- Don't rule by fear. Earn the respect of your associates, and they'll "knock themselves out" to please you.
- Praise people for work that's well done. Work without praise is like a plant without water. Productivity will wither away.
- Leadership traits aren't necessarily inborn. They can be acquired.

Leadership Lead
When you're angry, when you're exasperated, when you're frus-trated—take a deep breath. Count to 10 or 20 or 100, if necessary, before expressing yourself. Then you can do it calmly and reasonably and achieve your purpose without causing resentment.

Chapter 3

You Gotta Know Where You're Going and How to Get There

In This Chapter

- Setting realistic and attainable goals
- Planning for the long haul
- Scheduling day-to-day activities
- Assembling resources to get the job done

Now that you've cleared your mind of the myths that have held you back, you're ready to take the first steps forward in becoming a modern manager. This process begins when you set goals. Like a good navigator, you determine when you want to go and choose the best route to get there.

Some people like the excitement and novelty of setting out on a journey and following the currents, hoping that it will bring them adventure and fortune—and sometimes it does—but managers can't take those risks. You must know where you want to go, what you want to accomplish, what kind of problems you may meet along the way, and how to overcome them.

This chapter helps you begin the process of setting goals and planning to reach them long-term and along the way. You'll learn about the tools that are available to help and how to use them effectively.

Determining Your Goal Standard

Unless you know what you want to achieve, there's no way to measure how close you are to achieving it. Goals give you a standard against which to measure your progress.

The goals you set for accomplishing your team's mission must be in line with what your company wants you to do. If what you plan to achieve for your job, department, or team isn't coordinated with the goals of your organization, you'll waste your time and energy.

Meanings and Gleanings

Goals and objectives are interchangeable terms that describe where an organization or individual is headed or what long-term results are desired.

Goals are the foundation of motivational programs. By reaching toward your goals, you become motivated, and by knowing the goals of your team members and helping them reach those goals, you help to motivate them.

In most organizations, overall goals are established by top management and filter down to departments or teams, who use them as guides in establishing goals.

Guidelines for Setting Goals

The process of setting goals takes time, energy, and effort. Goals aren't something you scribble on a napkin during a coffee break—you must plan what you truly want to accomplish, establish timetables, determine who will do each aspect of the work, and anticipate any obstacles that may thwart the achievement of your goals.

The suggestions in this section provide a systematic approach to setting goals.

Understanding the Elements of a Goal

Are you ready to set your goals? To ensure that goals are more than just pipe dreams, be sure that they meet the following three conditions:

- **Clear and specific.** It's not enough to state that your goal is "to improve market share of our product." Be specific (for example, "Market share of our product will increase from its current 12 percent to 20 percent in five years").
- **Attainable.** Pie-in-the-sky goals are self-defeating. If you can see yourself getting closer to attaining your goals, the incentive to work harder to accomplish them is much greater than if they seem impossible to achieve.
- **Flexible.** Sometimes you just can't reach a goal. Circumstances may change: What seemed to be attainable may no longer be feasible. Don't be frustrated.

An assistant manager set a goal to become a store manager in two years, but it didn't happen. Rather than quit in frustration, he reviewed his situation. He had based his goal on the premise that his company would continue to open six to ten new stores every year. During the preceding year, business had not been good, and only two new outlets were opened. But business got better, and the company seemed likely to renew its expansion. He recognized that quitting would be the wrong solution and that he had to be flexible in his time goals.

Leadership Lead
"The way to achieve success is first to have a definite, clear, practical ideal—a goal, an objective. Second, have the necessary means to achieve your ends—wisdom, money, materials, methods. Third, adjust all your means to that end."

— Aristotle

Levels Galore: Three-Level Goal-Setting

All of us set goals based on what we anticipate will happen over the time in which a project is extended. Circumstances do change, however, and original goals may have to be adjusted. To anticipate this situation, many companies use a goal-setting program that involves three levels:

- **A main, or standard, goal:** What you plan to accomplish if everything goes well.
- **Alternative 1:** A slightly lower goal. If circumstances change and it becomes obvious that your main goal cannot be achieved, rather than start from scratch in redefining your goal, you can shift to this alternative.
- **Alternative 2:** A higher-level goal. If you're making greater progress than you had originally thought you could, rather than be complacent about being ahead of target, shift to this alternative and accomplish even more.

CSC services and repairs computers in the Philadelphia metropolitan area. Its sales goal for one year was to open ten new accounts. To prevent loss of customers when a national competitor opened a service in the same community, all the company's energies were redirected toward saving its current accounts. The goal for developing new clients then had to be reduced.

On the other hand, if CSC were having a good year, its goals could be accelerated. By the next month, CSC had gained eight new clients. Rather than coast along with a goal of two new openings for the next six months, the goal was raised automatically to the higher level.

Getting Your Entire Team Involved in Setting Goals

At a recent goal-setting seminar, one participant complained, "I have trouble getting people to buy in to the big-picture concept. They're so absorbed in their individual phases of the work that they can't see around their own problems."

> **Red Alert**
> Learn the goals of each team member. If their goals aren't in line with those of your company, department, or project group, work with them to demonstrate that applying their skills to meeting the team's goals enhances their opportunities to fulfill their own expectations.

Here's how you can overcome this type of situation:

- Bring all the people in your department or on your project team into the early stages of the planning process.
- Go over the major points of the plan.
- Ask each person to describe how he or she will fit in to the plan.
- Give each person a chance to comment on each stage of the project.

Breaking a long-term goal into bite-size pieces that people can relate to can help in getting them to see how their part in a project fits together with others. They can also then see how to set overall team or project goals for the long run.

Sopping Up SOPs: The Company Bible

Your company may have a set of standard operating procedures (SOPs), or SPs (standard practices), that detail company plans and policies. Although progressive companies restrict their SOPs to such matters as personnel policies, safety measures, and related matters, many companies either incorporate specific job methods and procedures into their "bible" or publish them in accompanying "instruction manuals." Providing policies and procedures for routine activities obviates the need to plan anew every time they occur. Because SOPs set standards that everyone must follow, all employees working with the manuals can refer to them at any time, which ensures consistency in dealing with particular situations.

If you have to develop SOPs, keep them simple. SOPs too often become complicated because managers want to cover every possible contingency. *It can't be done.* Managers often have to make decisions based on many unforeseeable factors. Cover the usual aspects in detail, but give managers (or nonmanagerial people, where appropriate) the flexibility to make decisions when circumstances warrant.

Don't make SOPs so rigid that they can't be changed when circumstances change. Plans may become obsolete because of new technologies, competition, government regulations, or the development of more efficient methods. Build in to SOPs a policy for periodic review and adjustment.

Not all plans are SOPs. Plans may be developed for special purposes, sometimes to be used only once and sometimes for projects that run for several months or even years.

Leadership Lead

To ensure that standard operating procedures are effective, follow these guidelines:

- Clearly state any actions that are expected.
- Be specific about areas in which no deviations from the procedure can occur.
- Provide guidelines for acceptable deviations.
- Before setting any method as an SOP, test it on the job to ensure that it's "the one best way."

Planning, Planning, Who'll Do the Planning?

Standard operating procedures are just one phase of planning. As mentioned, it's best if SOPs cover only broad policy matters so that specific plans can be designed for projects as they're created.

Your entire team should be involved in developing plans for the team. As team leader, you should lead the process, assign aspects of the planning to the members of the team who are most knowledgeable about each particular phase, coordinate the process, and make decisions that have a significant effect on the entire project.

In some companies, special planning specialists coordinate the development of the plans. The reason is that most managers are so busy with day-to-day operations that they can't divert their time and energy away from what they perceive to be their "real job."

The people who are closest to the work—who will be responsible for implementing the plans—should be directly involved in the planning process. Planning experts can help in facilitating the process, but if the plan is to be realistic and workable, the people who have to make it work should do the planning.

Hands-On: How to Plan

To illustrate how planning works, let's look at how Louise, the owner and manager of Featherdusters (a janitorial service company in Rock Hill, South Carolina), developed a plan to take over a new account to clean a five-story office building. The following list shows you the steps that Louise determined were necessary to implement her plan:

Step 1: List what has to be done. After consulting with her client, Louise made the following list:

Must be done daily

Empty wastebaskets into dumpsters
Carry dumpsters to pickup location
Dust furniture
Mop tile floors
Vacuum carpeted floors
Clean restrooms
Clean lounges

Must be done weekly

Sanitize telephones
Polish brass railings
Wax tile floors

Must be done monthly

Wash windows
Wash glass partitions

Step 2: Determine staffing. Louise hired two teams of three people, one of them a working supervisor. Each team is responsible for cleaning three floors. One of the members of each team is a trained floor waxer, and one window washer is assigned to the job. The owner-manager oversees the entire operation.

Step 3: Acquire supplies and equipment. Louise then acquired these supplies:

Vacuum cleaners, dustcloths, sponges, a waxing machine, floor wax, disinfectant, and window-washing solvent

Step 4: Estimate timing. Louise calculated that the cleaning job would take five hours to complete (from 5 P.M. to 10 P.M.) Monday through Friday. The following list serves as a guide to Louise and the supervisors to ensure that scheduled tasks get done at the scheduled time:

Daily tasks: All daily tasks are performed daily.

Weekly tasks: The supervisor assigns one floor every day to one or more workers for each of the weekly tasks.

Monthly tasks: The owner-manager and window washer schedule these tasks every month. The schedule must be flexible to account for weather conditions.

Step 5: Methods. All work will be performed according to the company's SOP for cleaning methods. Supervisors are responsible for quality of work, and the owner-manager will inspect work on an ad-hoc basis.

Step 6: Budget. Specific figures should be included to cover cost of materials, equipment amortization, labor, transportation to and from the site, and miscellaneous costs.

Step 7: Contingencies. Things don't always work out the way you plan. Unforeseen circumstances can develop that impede the completion of scheduled tasks. Louise anticipated the types of contingencies most likely to be encountered:

Truck or van breakdown: Make arrangements for renting replacement vehicles.

Equipment breakdown: Additional waxing machines are stored in a warehouse.

Personnel: Owner-manager and supervisors have lists of substitutes who are available on short notice.

Step 7: Follow-up. Owner-manager makes periodic visits to site to inspect work and meets at least once per quarter with customer to ensure satisfaction with work.

The following planning worksheet enables you to systematically plan and schedule the projects you undertake. Feel free to photocopy it or adapt it to meet your special needs.

Planning Worksheet

Objective: ____________________

Specific actions to be taken: ____________________

____

____

Staffing: ____________________

____

Equipment and supplies: ____________________

____

Timing (include deadlines where required): ____________________

____

____

Methods and techniques to be used: ____________________

____

____

Budget: ____________________

____

____

Contingencies: ____________________

____

____

Follow-up: ____________________

____

____

Converting Plans into Action

Plans similar to the Featherdusters plan of taking on a new assignment are virtually self-starting. Implementing one of these plans step-by-step is relatively easy. Plans for more complex activities, however, require additional elements.

The introduction of a new product, for example, requires a much more complex plan. It may involve phase-by-phase components spread out over several months or even years.

When Proctor and Gamble (P&G) introduced Crest toothpaste to the market, it set up 12-month plans for each of the main aspects of the project: manufacturing, marketing, and distribution. The product manager who coordinated the entire operation developed, in collaboration with managers in each of these functions, month-by-month phases. All parties involved knew just what each of them had to accomplish in the specified period and were kept informed of each other's progress. Every effort was made to keep the project on target. By following this plan, P&G was able to introduce the product with sufficient supply in the hands of retailers at the same time that advertising appeared in the press and on television and samples and discount coupons were mailed to consumers.

The Daily Grind: Planning for Daily Activities

You've set your goals, and now they have to be converted into day-to-day work schedules. Whether you have participated in the planning or the plan was handed down to you, scheduling the work is essential to getting it accomplished.

Unless the work you do is primarily routine and standard schedules are in the SOP, the next step is for you and your team members to determine what each member will do and when it will be done.

The $25,000 Suggestion

In the early days of this century, Charles Schwab, then the president of U.S. Steel, was visited by Ivy Lee, a pioneer in management consulting. Lee told Schwab that he could help Schwab's company become more effective. When Schwab expressed skepticism, Lee said, "I'll give you one suggestion today, and I want you to put it into effect for one month. At the end of that time, we will meet again, and you can pay me whatever you think that idea was worth to you. If it was of no value, you owe me nothing." Schwab accepted the challenge and implemented the suggestion. When they met again, Schwab handed Lee a check for $25,000. He said, "That was the best advice I ever had. It worked so well for me that I passed it on to all my subordinate managers."

What was Lee's advice? Every morning when you get to work (or you may prefer to do it every night before you go to bed), make a list of all the things you want to accomplish that day and put them in order of priority. Then work on the first item, and don't leave it until you have done all you can before going to the next item. You'll be interrupted, of course—no job is free from interruption. Handle the interruption, and then return to what you were working on. Many people who are interrupted forget what they had been doing and never get back to it.

At the end of the day, you probably will not have completed every item on your list. But the important tasks will have been accomplished. Integrate the remaining tasks with new ones that have developed, and make another list for the next day, again in order of priority. At the end of the month, some items may have remained on your list day after day. That's a sign that they weren't important enough to do. You should either delegate them to someone else or perhaps not do them at all.

Meanings and Gleanings
When you **prioritize**, or put first things first, you determine the degree of importance a matter has in accomplishing your goals on the job or in your life. Keep this process in mind when you take action to ensure that the most important matters take precedence over lesser ones.

So How Do I Set Priorities?

In his book *The Seven Habits of Highly Effective People,* Steven Covey cautions that many managers confuse what is urgent with what is truly important. Urgent matters must be attended to immediately or else serious consequences might ensue, but if you spend all your time putting out fires, your truly important goals won't be met.

Scheduling Team Projects

After team members have planned the actions they will take for a project, develop a plan of action that shows what will be done, who will do it, and when it should be started and completed. This plan can be as simple as making entries on a calendar posted in your office or be more complex, involving the use of specially designed planning charts or computer-based scheduling (these methods are discussed in chapter 6).

Leadership Lead
Color-code your calendar or planning charts so that you and your associates can tell at a glance the status of projects and assignments. This list suggests colors for coding certain tasks:

Red ink: High-priority items for that day.

Blue ink: Deadlines for projects (list for two or three days before actual deadline and print final date in red).

Green ink: Follow-up of other people's work.

Black ink: Routine work scheduled for that day.

The daily planning organizer on the following page breaks down activities into categories.

You can print the planner as a looseleaf sheet and keep it in a binder, or you can blow it up to use as a wall chart. You can also format it for computer use.

When you use this type of planner, identify priorities in each category by number or color-coding.

Computer-based scheduling programs are available for specific types of planning for more complex situations. This and other types of work-assignment programs are discussed in chapter 6.

Enough of This Preparation—Let's Get It Done!

The first step in putting plans into action is assembling the resources necessary to do a job, including obtaining and allocating funds, accumulating equipment and materials, and acquiring pertinent information. One of a company's major tasks—choosing, training, and assigning personnel to get a job done—is discussed later in this book.

Getting the Money

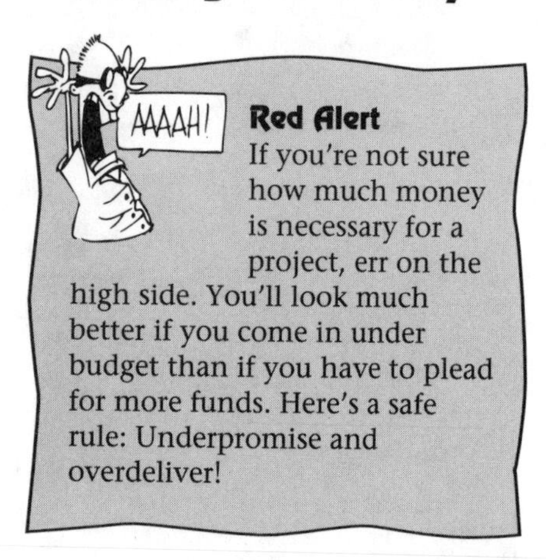

Red Alert
If you're not sure how much money is necessary for a project, err on the high side. You'll look much better if you come in under budget than if you have to plead for more funds. Here's a safe rule: Underpromise and overdeliver!

Without adequate funding, any project is doomed. The most common reason for the failure of start-up companies is lack of capital. Even larger and long-established organizations must determine how much money should be allocated to get a project started and to keep it going until it pays off.

Mike wanted to impress his boss, Sheila. He knew that she watched every dollar spent and was always boasting that she could get work done less expensively than other managers. When he was assigned a new project, he cut corners and came up with a very tight budget. Sheila praised him for his acumen and gave his project the go-ahead.

Mike's lowball figures proved to be inadequate, and, with hat in hand, he had to ask Sheila for additional funds. This mistake not only stalled the project—you can guess how it affected his career.

Our Budget Is Too Low!

You may work in an organization in which budgets are handed down to department heads or project managers and you have no part in determining them. Study your budget carefully before starting a project. If the budget seems unrealistic, discuss it with your manager. Whoever allotted the money for your work may not have been aware of certain factors. By presenting the facts, you may persuade the company to provide a more realistic budget.

There are times and circumstances in which you unfortunately have no choice other than to work with a less-than-ideal budget. That's when you have to sharpen your pencil and calculate in which areas you can save money with a minimum loss of productivity. Check whether some work that's farmed out can be done more cheaply in-house or vice versa. Can some of the work be reengineered so that fewer costly hours are spent on it? Can deadlines be delayed somewhat to eliminate the need for overtime or additional temporary workers? Check all your costs. Saving just a small amount of money on several facets of a job can help you meet a budget.

Daily Planning Organizer

Date: ____________________

Priorities	**Things to Do**	**Phone Calls**
Correspondence	**Appointments**	**Miscellaneous**

A team planning organizer helps you schedule your daily activities and complete your goals.

Everything in Its Place: Lining Up Your Tools

Is any special equipment needed for the job? Most departments have access to machinery, computers, and other hardware that will be used, but problems do occur.

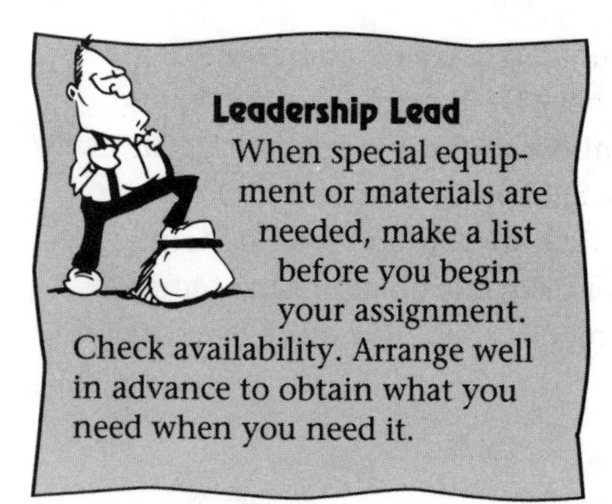

Leadership Lead

When special equipment or materials are needed, make a list before you begin your assignment. Check availability. Arrange well in advance to obtain what you need when you need it.

Angela's assignment was to prepare a long-term market forecast for a proposed new service her company was considering. She created a software program designed especially for the project, but was stymied when she learned that the only computer sophisticated enough to deal with the program was tied up on a higher-priority project. Angela was compelled to use an outside computer firm to run the program, which added both cost and time to her project. *Make sure that the equipment you need will be available when you need it; if it won't be available, consider the alternatives you can use.* Check to see whether another department has equipment you can use. Arrange for work that can't be done in-house to be subcontracted or lease the equipment on a short-term basis. Budget for temporary personnel to augment your staff when necessary.

Information: The Golden Key to Accomplishment

The 19th century brought us the industrial revolution; the late 20th century, the information revolution. Knowledge is now the key to accomplishment. Having an accurate, balanced, and unbiased picture of what is happening in your company, in your industry, and in the economy is essential to sound decision-making.

In the past, managers could wait for weekly or even monthly reports to obtain the information necessary to run their companies or departments effectively. No more. Today, *real time* is the magic formula for success.

Reports tell you what happened yesterday, last week, and last month. They're helpful, of course, because it's useful to review the past, but you have to know what's going on *now*.

You need better and faster information. A report is a snapshot, a still picture of how things were at the time it was taken. You need instead a *telecast*—information that's reported as it happens. The tools are in place, but are you taking advantage of them? Take a look at what they can do for you:

Meanings and Gleanings

Real time refers to the actual time in which a process occurs (what's going on here and now).

- If you're a sales manager, you can immediately get up-to-the-minute sales information from field salespeople and have them enter the results of each sales call from their laptops to your home office.
- In a branch facility, you can e-mail information about production, inventories, and special problems as often as necessary.
- If you need materials, you can contact suppliers instantly by fax or e-mail to order materials, arrange shipments, or solve problems.
- If you're a retail manager, you can get ongoing information about sales and stock of each item in a store from cash-register computers.
- If you're a general manager who needs specialized information, you can use the Internet (a worldwide computer network) to obtain information from anywhere in the world at the time you need it. You can subscribe to services that provide continuous data about weather conditions anywhere in the world, stock-market figures from exchanges worldwide, transportation and shipping schedules, and virtually any type of data you need.

Faster, Faster: Keeping Up with Current Techniques and Methods

The process of obtaining information is not limited to getting facts and figures. Managers must have in-depth knowledge of the most effective methods of getting a job done. All team members—especially team leaders—must keep up with the state-of-the-art in the work they're doing.

You can never stop learning. You've been in your field for many years, you know your job, and you know all the tricks of the trade—or do you? This is a dynamic world in which nothing remains the same. What you're doing works, of course, but is it the best way to do it?

Just because a certain method works is no guarantee that it can't be done better. Equipment that didn't exist a few years ago may improve production or quality. Techniques may have been refined or totally changed, and you have to keep up.

You Can Teach an Old Dog New Tricks

Leadership Lead

To keep up with current information in your field, visit equipment shows, attend seminars on new techniques, read trade journals, obtain literature from manufacturers and suppliers, and learn from your peers, subordinates, and colleagues.

Some of your team members may think that they're too old to learn new things. The old saying "You can't teach an old dog new tricks" may be true about dogs, but it certainly isn't true about humans.

When computers first became an essential management tool, many older managers and workers resisted learning about them. Many times I heard this common complaint: "Computers are for young people; I'll never be able to master them." But they *did* learn. Today you'll find a computer terminal on virtually every desk in an office, whether that desk is used by an executive, a clerk, a secretary, or a technician. They *all* have learned.

The Least You Need to Know

- Make sure that the goals you set are clear, specific, and attainable.
- When you prioritize, determine what's really important: Do first things first.
- Your calendar is a scheduling tool. Plan your day and work your plan.
- Set budgets that will provide the funds necessary to accomplish a job in the specified timeframe.
- Arrange in advance for the equipment, computer time, and materials you need so that you will have what you need when you need it.
- Get data in real time so that you're always on top of a situation.

Chapter 4

Say It Better, Write It Better

In This Chapter

- Getting your ideas across to others
- Understanding why people may not understand you
- Becoming a better listener
- Writing effective memos, faxes, letters, and reports

We live in a world in which *communication*—what you say and how you say it—can determine whether you succeed or fail. Most Americans attribute Ronald Reagan's ability to communicate with people at all levels as the major factor that led to his election and reelection as President.

This skill, shared by top leaders in government, business, and the professions, is a skill you can acquire. With the will to improve and the determination to work at it, you can acquire the tools and techniques that will improve the way you communicate both in your personal life and on the job. You can then better present your ideas to your boss, your peers, your associates, your customers, and others.

In this chapter, you'll learn some strategies for expressing what you want to communicate (orally or in writing), which can be a major step in helping you become a more effective team leader.

What You Say

Suppose that you call a meeting to discuss a new project. You sit down with an associate for a serious discussion about performance, and you're called on to make a progress report to the executive committee. The words you choose and how you say them may make the difference between success and failure.

Communication takes place when persons or groups transmit information, ideas, and concepts between them.

Whether you're addressing a group or having a one-to-one conversation, you should think out your message and prepare in advance what you intend to say. No, you don't always have that opportunity; more often than not, however, when you're required to discuss something with little notice, you *can* prepare.

Know Your Subject

Usually, you're thoroughly familiar with what you want to convey to others. It's about the work you're doing, matters in your area of expertise, or company-related problems. You should still review the facts to be sure that you have all the information and be prepared to answer any questions.

From time to time you may be asked to report on matters outside the area of your regular work duties. Your company may be considering purchasing a new type of computer software, for example, and ask you to check it out. Here are the first steps you should take:

- Learn as much as possible about the subject.
- Know ten times more than is likely to be needed to make the presentation.
- Prepare notes about the pluses and minuses of the proposed purchase, solution, and so on.
- Whether you will make this report to one person (your boss, for example) or to a group of managers or technical specialists, be prepared to answer questions about any subject that might come up.

Know Your Audience

Choose words that your listeners can easily understand. If the people you're addressing all have a similar technical background, the use of technical terminology is appropriate: It will be clear to listeners and readily understood. If a listener doesn't work in the same technical field, however, your message will be lost.

Suppose that you're an engineer whose work involves dealing primarily with other engineers and that you're accustomed to using technical terms. Now you must make a presentation to the finance people in your company to arrange for funds for the project. It's *your* responsibility, not *theirs,* to ensure that your message gets across. If you can explain the matter in nontechnical terms, do so. If you have to use technical language, take the time to explain a term the first time you use it and at least once again if you feel that it needs reinforcement.

Leadership Lead
Unless you're sure that your audience is familiar with the terms, don't use **jargon**—words, acronyms, and initials that are used only in your field.

Don't use *jargon*—those initials, acronyms, or words that are used only in your field or in just your company—and nowhere else. How often have you listened to "experts" on television whose use of jargon left you scratching your head? Everyone has seen a police officer who says, "We booked the perp on a 602A" or a political commentator whose referrals to a series of government agencies by their initials sounds sound like alphabet soup. On the other hand, if an audience consists of people who use this jargon regularly in their work, the terms will be familiar to them and may even add to their understanding of your message.

How You Say It

No matter how well-thought-out your message is, unless you express it clearly and distinctly, it won't be understood by your listeners.

This section discusses the four most common problems of speaking clearly:

- **Mumbling.** Do you swallow word endings? Do you speak with your mouth almost closed? Practice in front of a mirror. Open up those lips.
- **Speaking too fast.** Whoa! Give people a chance to absorb what you're saying.
- **Speaking too slowly.** Speak too slowly, and you'll lose your audience. While you're plodding through your message, their minds skip to other matters.
- **Mispronouncing words.** Not sure how a word is pronounced? Look it up or ask someone who does know.

Red Alert
Do you use "word whiskers," those extra sounds, words, and phrases peppered throughout conversations? You know what they are— "er," "uh-huh," "right!," "okay!," and "y'know" are just a few. They distract from your thoughts. Listen to yourself, and shave off those "whiskers."

- **Speaking in a monotone.** Do you use inflection and modulation? If not, you'll put your listeners to sleep.

Do You Know How You Sound to Others?

You don't hear yourself as others hear you. Listen to yourself. Get a voice-activated tape recorder, place it on your desk, and turn it on. It will record your voice when you talk to others in person or on the phone. Listen to the tape. You'll hear whether you're mumbling, whether you speak too fast (or perhaps too slowly), and whether you speak in a monotone.

Leadership Lead

When you leave a voice-mail message, play it back and *listen* to how you sound. Are you speaking clearly, distinctly, and interestingly?

All you need to do to correct most of these problems is to be aware. If you're aware that you mumble, you'll make an effort not to mumble. If you're aware that you speak too fast, you'll make an effort to slow down; if you're aware that you speak in a monotone, you'll work consciously to speak in a more interesting tone.

Adding Video to the Audio

An old Chinese proverb says that a picture is worth a thousand words. People remember much more of what they see than what they hear, and they remember even more of what they see and hear simultaneously. If people *see* something when you present your message, it makes that message clearer, more exciting, and, most important, more memorable. That's why TV is such an effective tool: It brings together in a *simulcast* both the video and the audio elements of a message. If you want to see a perfect example of how this works, take another look at *Sesame Street* on public television. It shows how children, by taking in the simultaneous combination of words and pictures, are taught to read and expand their vocabulary.

Meanings and Gleanings

A **simulcast** brings together both audio and video elements of a message so that they interact and intensify it.

You don't need a TV camera to be able to simulcast. You can use variations of this technique whether you're speaking to one person or to a group.

These relatively inexpensive and easy-to-use techniques can help you bring your message across more effectively:

- Use graphs or charts to clarify figures.
- Use photos, drawings, or diagrams to illustrate points.
- Use flowcharts to describe processes.

Diane, the claims manager of an insurance company, had a difficult time explaining to new clerks what happened to a claim from the moment it arrived at the company until it was finally completed. She solved the problem by using a flowchart. As she described the process, she drew boxes that illustrated just when and where each step occurred. Diane was *simulcasting*.

Many visual effects are available for you to use in making a presentation to a group:

- **Flip charts and chalkboards:** The least expensive and easiest items to use.
- **Overhead projectors:** Can be used to display prepared transparencies, which can be augmented with additional matters you draw as you talk.
- **Slide presentations:** Colorful and dramatic slides designed to bring out important points.
- **Videos or films:** A much more expensive aid, but worth it, particularly if the presentation will be given on several occasions.

Even if you never make group presentations and usually have to talk to your associates only one at a time, you still can simulcast your messages:

- Flip charts and chalkboards are just as easy to use whether your audience is one person or a group.
- Use your yellow pad (or any color pad you like). Anything that can be drawn on the flip chart can be drawn on a pad of paper.
- Charts, diagrams, and photos can be prepared before any meeting. Emulate salespeople who have used these tools effectively to make sales. Placed in acetate folders, usually in a loose-leaf binder, these items make an attractive visual aid.

Leadership Lead

Provide "takeaway" photocopies of charts or flowcharts or whatever to every person at a meeting to ensure that everyone has a clear representation of the subjects you discuss. These items also serve as permanent reminders of your message; participants can refer to them later if necessary.

Are You Really Listening?

Suppose that one of your colleagues brings you a problem and that you begin listening attentively. Soon your mind begins to wander, however. Instead of listening to the problem, your thoughts are moving on to other things: the pile of work on your desk, the meeting you have scheduled with the company vice president, the problems one of your children is having in school. You hear the words, but you're not really listening.

Does this happen to you? Of course, it does; it happens to all of us. Why? The human mind can absorb ideas ten times faster than a person can talk. While a speaker is talking, your mind may race ahead. You complete the sentence in your mind—often incorrectly—long before the speaker does. You "hear" what your mind dictates, not what's actually said.

This is human nature. You must anticipate that it will happen, and you must be alert and take steps to overcome it so that you can learn to truly listen.

Sorry, I Wasn't Listening

Now suppose that your mind was wandering and that you didn't hear what the other person said. It's embarrassing to admit that you weren't listening, so you fake it. You pick up on the last few words you heard and comment on them. That's good, if it makes sense. But you may miss the real gist of the discussion.

When you're not sure what really was said, you don't have to say, "I'm sorry, I was daydreaming." One way to get back on track is to ask a question or make a comment about the last item you did hear: "Can we go back a minute to such-and-such?"

Another method is to comment this way: "To make sure that I can better understand your view on this, please elaborate."

> **Leadership Lead**
> When you realize that you haven't been fully listening to a person talk (when the words begin to be replaced by a droning sound in your mind), when you hear words but not ideas, or when you realize that you're anticipating what you *think* will be said, stop! Then listen!

Five Tricks to Make You a Better Listener

You *can* become a better listener. You can stop some of the main causes of ineffective listening before they begin. All you have to do is make a few changes in your work environment and in your approach to listening—a small effort with a big return:

- **Eliminate distractions.** The greatest distraction is probably the telephone. You want to give the speaker your full attention—*and the phone rings.* Answering the call not only interrupts your discussion but also disrupts the flow of your thoughts. Even after you hang up, your mind may still be thinking about the call.

  If you know that you'll be having a lengthy discussion at your desk, arrange for someone else to handle your calls or set your voice mail to pick up all calls. If this isn't possible, get away from the telephone. Go to a conference room—the phone there won't distract you. Of course, there's probably a phone in the conference room, but no one knows that you're there, so it probably won't ring. (How many times a day do you call an empty conference room?)

- **Get rid of excess paper to reduce distractions.** If your desk is strewn with paper, you probably sit there and let your eyes skim your papers until you realize that you're reading a letter or memo instead of listening. Get rid of those papers. If you go to a conference room, take only the papers that are related to the discussion. If you must stay at your desk, put the papers in a drawer so that you won't be tempted to read them.
- **Don't get too comfortable.** Some years ago I was discussing a situation with another manager. As was my custom, I sat in my comfortable executive chair with my hands behind my head. Maybe I rocked a little, but, fortunately, I caught myself before I dozed off.

  Ever since then, rather than take a relaxing position when I engage in discussions, I've made a point of sitting on the edge of my chair and leaning forward rather than backward. This position not only brings me physically closer to the other person but also enables me to be more attentive and to maintain eye contact. And because I'm not quite so comfortable, I have less of a tendency to daydream.
- **Be an active listener.** An active listener doesn't just sit or stand with ears open. An active listener asks questions about what's being said. You can paraphrase ("So the way I understand it is that… ") or ask specific questions about specific points. This technique not only enables you to clarify points that may be unclear but also keeps you alert so that you give the speaker your full attention.

  Your body language and nonverbal cues show the other person that you're truly interested in getting the full story he or she is relating and that you take seriously what is being said.
- **Be an empathetic listener.** Listen with your heart as well as with your head. Empathetic listeners not only listen to what other people say but also try to feel what other people are feeling when they say it. In other words, you put yourself in the speaker's shoes.
- **Take notes.** It's impossible to remember everything that's said in a lengthy discussion. Take notes, but remember not to take stenographic transcriptions. If you're concentrating on what you're writing, you can't pay full attention to what's being said.

  Jot down key words or phrases. Write down figures or important facts—just enough to remind you of the principal points that were made.

  Immediately after a meeting, while the information is still fresh in your mind, write a detailed summary. Dictate it into a recorder, type it into your computer, or enter it in your notebook—whichever is best for you.

Learn to Read Body Language

People communicate not only by what they say but also by their gestures, facial expressions, and movements. Wouldn't it be great if you could buy a dictionary of body language? Then you could easily interpret nonverbal language.

Leadership Lead
Study the body language of people with whom you work. You may notice that when John smiles in a certain way, it has one meaning; a different smile, a different meaning. Or maybe when Jane doesn't agree, she wrinkles her forehead. Make a conscious effort to study and remember people's individual body language.

The reason we can't buy this type of a dictionary is that body language differs from one person to another. Some gestures—a nod or a smile—may seem universal, of course, but when you're dealing with a specific person, you can't be sure that he or she is using body language as we have come to expect.

When people nod as you speak, for example, you may assume that they're agreeing with you. However, some people nod just to acknowledge that they're listening. When some people disagree with you, they subconsciously fold their arms. But that's not the only reason people do that—perhaps they're just cold!

What You Send Might Not Be What's Received

Communication works in a manner similar to a two-way radio: The sender sends a message to the receiver, and the receiver responds. At that moment the receiver responds, the receiver becomes the sender, and the sender becomes the receiver.

Sometimes, however, the message that's received may not be exactly the same as the message that was sent. Somewhere between the sender's radio and the receiver's radio, static may have intervened and distorted the message. This static may be generated from either the sender or the receiver.

What causes that "static" in direct conversations? It might emanate from within the minds of either party. Everything you say and everything you hear is filtered through your brain, in which you have built over the years certain attitudes that influence the way you interpret what you say and what you hear, including the ones in this list:

- **Assumptions.** You've seen this situation repeatedly. You have a pretty good idea about what causes a particular problem and how to solve it. In discussing it with others, you assume that they know as much about it as you do, so your instructions are based on their having know-how that they don't have. The result is that you don't give them adequate information. Static!

- **Preconceptions.** People tend to hear what they expect to hear. The message you receive is distorted by any material you have already heard about the subject. If the new information is different from what's expected, rather than actually hear the new message, you hear what your mind is telling you.

  What does this mean to you? Keep your mind open. When someone tells you something, make an extra effort to listen and to evaluate the new information objectively and not block it out because it differs from your preconceptions.

  In communicating with others, try to learn their preconceptions. If they are people you work with regularly, you probably know how they view many of the matters you discuss. In presenting your views, take into consideration what they already believe. If it differs from what you're presenting, be prepared to make the effort to jump over that barrier.

- **Prejudices.** Your biases for or against a person influence the way a message is received. If you greatly admire the person who is speaking, more than likely you'll be inclined to accept whatever he or she says. If you fervently dislike the speaker, you most likely will discount anything that's said.

  Biases also affect the way subject matter is received. People close their ears to opposing viewpoints about matters on which they have strong feelings.

Minimize the Use of Channels

Remember the game of "telephone" we all played as children? One person whispers a message to the next person who in turn whispers it to the next and so on. By the time it gets back to the originator, the message is entirely different.

This happens in real life whenever messages must be filtered through several people. Your company may require that you go through channels. If you want to give information to or get information from a person in another department, you first go to your boss who goes to the supervisor of the other department who in turn goes to the person with the information, gets it, and conveys it back through the same channels. By the time you receive the information, it may have been distorted by a variety of interpretations.

For effective communication, at least minimize the use of channels (you may not be able to eliminate them). Channels do serve a purpose, however. Managers should know what's going on in their company. For routine matters that don't involve policy changes, by enabling people to communicate directly where appropriate, messages don't get distorted and the entire process speeds up. One advantage of flatter organizational structures is that they have fewer channels.

What You Write

Unlike oral communication, written communication tends to be more formal. Most day-to-day communication with team members is done orally. The largest part of communication with our bosses, other team leaders, and even customers and vendors is by telephone or personal contact. Written communication remains an important medium, however. Letters, memos, faxes, e-mail, and reports are major elements in getting and receiving information, ideas, compliments, complaints, and instructions.

Leadership Lead
Clear thinking precedes clear writing.

How often have you sat down to write something (a memo, a letter, or a fax, for example), and you know what you want to say but the right words just won't come? It happens to everyone. Why not just write it the way you would say it? Good idea, but when you put pencil to paper or boot up your computer, your mind goes blank.

Before you begin writing the first word, *TAB* your thoughts (see the TAB Your Thoughts list on the following page). This acronym gives you clues to learning how to clearly think out what you want to write before you write it.

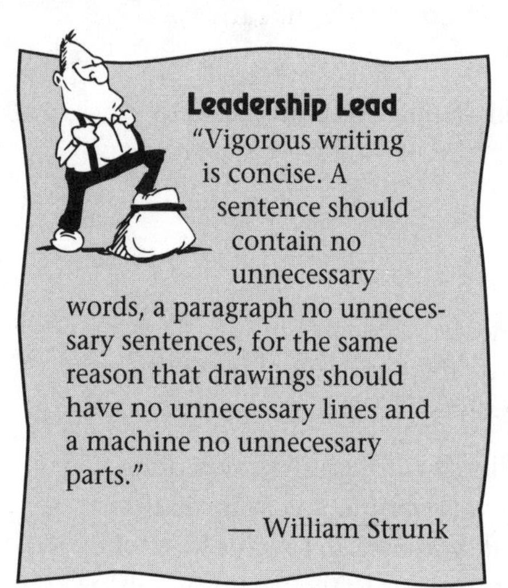

Leadership Lead
"Vigorous writing is concise. A sentence should contain no unnecessary words, a paragraph no unnecessary sentences, for the same reason that drawings should have no unnecessary lines and a machine no unnecessary parts."

— William Strunk

Whether your communication is a letter to a customer, a memo to your boss, or a fax to a branch office, think out the content before you begin to write it.

Ask yourself each of the questions on the TAB Your Thoughts list. Jot down the answers on a scratch pad or use a special form, such as the writing guide that follows the TAB list. By "TABbing" your thoughts before doing the writing, you give yourself a clear guide to what you want to convey. The list helps you organize all the information concerning the situation, indicate what you want done to deal with it, and describe how it will benefit your readers.

The Three Cs

Now that you know what you want to write, you're ready to put it in writing. Whatever you write should be

- Clear
- Complete
- Concise

Suppose that your memo concerns the status of an order. Be sure that you have responded to any specific questions. Include the order number, date of the order, identification of materials, and other pertinent information. Avoid going into extraneous details. Keep to the point.

TAB Your Thoughts

Think about the situation ______

What? ______

Where? ______

Who? ______

When? ______

How? ______

Action ______

What do I want to be done? ______

Benefit ______

How will this help: ______

The company? ______

Readers of this memo? ______

Other people? ______

Me? ______

Use Short, Punchy Sentences

Steer clear of complex, multiphrase sentences. Don't write, "In light of the research in this field, it's our opinion that the program we are offering will facilitate the writing skills of the employees who take the training." Just say, "This program will teach people to write better."

Short and punchy—yes! Simple and dull—no! Rather than write the memo or fax in the usual narrative form, write it in the form of a bulletin:

➤ Headline your main point—use bold print.

➤ Break the story into separate sections for each subsidiary point.

➤ Use an asterisk (*) or bullet (•) to highlight key points.

➤ Where appropriate, use graphs, charts, or other visual aids to augment your words.

Writing Guide

Think about the situation: Why am I writing this?

____

____

____

Action: What do I want to accomplish?

____

____

____

To do this, what do I want to say?

____

____

____

Benefit: How will this be of value?

____

____

____

Watch Your Grammar and Spelling

You can't depend on an assistant to fix up your errors in grammar, sentence structure, and spelling. Today, many managers don't have assistants and write their own letters and memos. Even if you're one of the lucky few who has an assistant, you still have to check what goes out with your signature.

The "spell-check" feature in your word-processing program is a great help with this task. It catches most typos and misspellings, but not all of them. The spelling may be correct, but it might not be the exact word you want. You may mean "break" but instead write "brake." A spell-checker doesn't catch those types of errors. Or you might write "to" rather than "too." Don't depend on the spell-checker for that either.

Leadership Lead
Be precise, be concise. Think of your memo or fax as a cable for which you must pay a dollar a word.

Reread everything you write, whether you typed it yourself or an assistant typed it. The impressions you make from what and how you write affect the image both you and your company project.

Know Your Reader

Your operations manager probably likes details. He or she wants to know facts and figures, statistics and technicalities. When you write a report, include all these elements in it. Your marketing manager may prefer terse, precise reports. He or she usually wants to see graphs rather than tables and to get an overall view rather than specific details. Tailor your style to what's most amenable to your readers.

Leadership Lead
To write right, prewrite, write, and rewrite.

How It Should Be Written

Although there's no ideal report style, this section lists some suggestions for writing effective reports:

- **Briefly state the purpose of your report.** "As you requested, here's the information about the brands and models of forklift trucks displayed at the trade show."
- **Present a summary and some recommendations.** By providing a summary and stating your recommendations at the beginning of your report, whoever reads it gets all the key information at one time. Readers don't have to wade through reams of paper to discover your conclusions.
- **Provide a detailed backup.** A backup is the meat of your report, in which you present all the details that support your summary and recommendations. Use charts, graphs, and tables if they clarify or reinforce the information in the report.

Red Alert
Before submitting a report, proofread it thoroughly. Even a good report loses credibility when it has spelling errors, poor grammar, and sloppy typing. Figures should be checked carefully. Reread it. Have another person who is knowledgeable about the subject double-check it.

How long should a report be? Long enough to tell the whole story—and not one word longer. Your objective is to provide the information—not write undying prose.

The Least You Need to Know

- Whether you're presenting your ideas to a group or to just one person, prepare what you're going to say before you say it.
- Speak clearly and distinctly so that you'll be easily understood. Speak with enthusiasm so that your audience doesn't fall asleep.
- Simulcast. Augment what you say with something that the people you're addressing can see.
- Listen! Train your mind to listen actively and fully and with an open mind.
- To write marvelous memos, fantastic faxes, lovely letters, and readable reports, use the TAB approach before writing and the three *C*s when you're writing.

Chapter 5

Open Your Ears, Open Your Mind

In This Chapter

- Getting people to contribute ideas
- Rejecting bad suggestions without causing resentment
- Developing suggestion programs that work
- Five ways to become more creative

The members of your staff—those men and women who work day after day on the job—have much more insight into what goes on in a company than many managers realize. These people are a resource you should continually tap to obtain ideas about cutting costs, improving techniques, and implementing innovations. No matter how smart you are, there's no way that you can know everything.

My Mind Is Open, but Their Mouths Are Shut

Managers often complain that they're ready to listen to ideas but that no one makes any suggestions. Whose fault is that? It's not likely that team members don't have any ideas—it's more likely that you just haven't established a climate of receptivity.

Leadership Lead

When you solicit ideas from your team members, never present your view first. Because of your position, what you say may influence what team members had planned to say. *Listen with an open mind.* Their comments may give you new insights into the problem and result in a better solution.

At a seminar I gave in Paterson, New Jersey, a participant named Stan came up to see me afterward. "I manage a tax service and have seven skilled accountants working for me. I run meetings at which I ask for their ideas, and I know that they must have some good ideas, but I can't get them to come up with them. What am I doing wrong?"

I arranged to attend one of Stan's meetings, in which he presented a problem, suggested a solution, and then asked whether anyone had ideas that might also apply. He turned from one group member to another, and the typical response was, "No, I go along with what you said."

In a discussion with the accountants after the meeting, I learned that if they had in the past suggested any ideas that were different from what Stan had presented, he had greeted the idea with sarcasm or outright rejection. "Why disagree?" they asked. "It won't do any good."

Keeping an Open Door Open

Barbara supervised 12 clerks and boasted that her door was always open to staff members. They could come and see her at any time with any problems, complaints, or suggestions they had.

Right—they were *allowed* to come, but they didn't. The door was open, but when one of the clerks walked in, the look of annoyance on Barbara's face signaled that visitors were not welcome. It didn't take long for them to recognize that the door was physically open but psychologically closed.

Meanings and Gleanings

People in lower echelons of an organization participate in **upward communication** by making ideas, suggestions, and comments flow to those in decision-making positions.

Some managers say that they want to be available to their associates but that there is so much work to do they can't let people barge in whenever they feel like it.

One solution is to have a *partially* opened door. Set aside certain hours during which anyone is welcome to come in without an appointment to discuss problems, make suggestions, or just kick around ideas. In this way, you can plan your time so that your work gets done and your associates still have the opportunity to bring to your attention any of their concern.

To avoid giving the impression that you feel the work you are doing is more important than your concern for the work of other team members, point out that by setting special hours aside for discussing problems, you are able to give full attention to what they discuss without interruption or distraction.

Managing by Walking Around (MBWA)

You can learn a great deal by walking around. If you never leave your office or stop hiding behind the papers on your desk, how can you expect to know what's going on? You have to get out there with your associates, talk to them, and develop their confidence.

It's not just walking around—it's what you *do* when you walk around. Lou made a practice of walking around the factory floor and stopping to speak to some of his employees—usually the same old-timers whom he had known for years. He asked how they were doing and about their families. It was good for morale, but he never learned anything of real value.

Carmen also walked around her department, but she took a different approach: Before her tour, she reviewed which projects were being performed, the assignments each person had, and the work problems she was particularly concerned about. The questions and comments she presented to her colleagues were specific. She asked whether the new computer program that had just been installed was giving them any problems. She asked whether they had any ideas for change and elicited comments about progress being made and what could be done to expedite the processing of back orders. Her MBWA-style paid off for her: Her associates knew that she wanted to hear their ideas.

Rejecting Ideas Without Causing Resentment

Suppose that Keesha comes to you all excited about a great idea that she believes will help the department but that, in your judgment, isn't practical. You know that she will not only be upset if the idea is rejected but may also wonder why she even bothered to suggest anything. She may even never make another suggestion. Just because that idea wasn't a good one doesn't mean that future ones won't be winners.

Rather than reject a poor suggestion, ask questions about it. With good questioning, you can get people to rethink their ideas and see the weak points they had overlooked. They will then reject their own bad ideas without your having to make a single negative comment.

To see how this technique might work, look at what happens when Don rushes into Lisa's office:

> Don: I have a great idea. We could save time processing these orders if we didn't have to have accounting check them against the invoices. They rarely find discrepancies, and, those few times they do, adjustments can be made later.
>
> Lisa: It *would* save time, Don. Do you know how many orders are returned by accounting with errors in them?
>
> Don: Last week, there were 15. That's only about five percent of the orders we handled.
>
> Lisa: What would happen if those 15 orders had been processed with the errors in them?
>
> Don: They would have been caught down the line.
>
> Lisa: How much time would it take to correct them then?
>
> Don: It *is* time-consuming. I guess that in the long run it would take more time than we would save in the beginning.

Lisa knew that the idea was not practical. By asking questions that made Don reach the conclusion himself, the suggestion was rejected without arguments or resentment.

Make It Easy to Share Ideas

Some people are bubbling with ideas and can't wait to share them. But many people need some prodding to get them to bring their suggestion to your attention.

Various programs have been developed to make it easier for employees to bring their ideas to the attention of the company. Some, such as suggestion boxes, have been around a long time. This section discusses others that have been introduced more recently.

Feeding the Suggestion Box

Suggestion boxes have been around for decades. Do they generate good ideas, or are they just receptacles for gripes and grievances?

Suggestion systems can be as good as you want them to be. All it takes is a sincere commitment and a real effort to make them work. Companies have received from employees many suggestions that have enabled them to solve difficult problems, eliminate waste, improve quality, create new products, and save users millions of dollars annually.

The use of an employee suggestion form (see the sample form on the following page) encourages people to participate.

The following suggestions can help ensure the success of a suggestion program:

- ➤ Make sure that senior management is fully behind the program.
- ➤ Publicize the program with creativity and flair. Place colorful posters promoting the program around the building, and send letters to employees to encourage participation. Some companies have special promotions to increase the number of suggestions made for a specified period.
- ➤ Make awards commensurate with the value of the suggestion. Many companies determine the amount of the award as a percentage of money earned or saved.
- ➤ Acknowledge all suggestions promptly. Unless contributions are acknowledged promptly and contributors kept informed of the status of their suggestions, they lose interest in the program and are loathe to make suggestions in the future.

Suggestion Form

Contributor: ______________________ **Date:** ____________

Department: ____________ **Team leader:** ________________

Situation: ____
____
____
____

Your suggestion (use additional pages if necessary): ____________
____
____
____

Estimate of first year's savings: ____________________________

Other benefits to be derived: ______________________________

Please attach supporting documents to this form.

You will receive acknowledgment and comments from the Suggestion Committee within 10 working days. Thank you for your suggestion.

- Have all suggestions evaluated by a suggestion committee and, where applicable, technical specialists. The suggestion committee should be composed of representatives of various departments and should be chaired by a senior executive, such as the human-resources manager or operations manager. The committee should be empowered to accept or reject suggestions expeditiously with a minimum of red tape.
- Make decisions and notify the contributor as soon as it's practical.
- Give public recognition to persons receiving awards—in the company newspaper, on bulletin boards, and at staff meetings.

Eyeing Ideas for "I" Meetings

The letter *I* in "I" meetings stands for *idea*. Several days before a meeting, the people who will attend are given the agenda (usually only one or two items) and are asked to think about the matters to be discussed and to be prepared to present at least one idea about each item.

Leadership Lead
Make suggestion programs exciting by incorporating some of these rewards:

- Run periodic special-award contests.
- Conduct a lottery. All persons who make suggestions participate in a drawing for a big-screen TV.
- Have a monthly or quarterly luncheon for all winners.
- Send award winners' photos to local newspapers.

At the meeting, the ideas are presented and discussed. Because the participants often approach problems from differing angles, they're likely to offer a variety of ideas.

Unlike brainstorming (discussed later in this chapter), in which the sole purpose is idea generation with no critiques or discussions, suggestions made in "I" meetings are discussed in detail and decisions about their viability are made.

Marty, the owner of a chain of hair-styling salons, adds some excitement to his "I" meetings by handing out crisp ten-dollar bills to anyone who comes up with an especially good idea. Once in a while, if he thinks that an idea has merit but is not well thought out, he tears a bill in half and says to the person who made the suggestion, "I'll give you the other half when you work out the kinks in your concept."

Running Around in Quality Circles

The Japanese people attribute a great deal of the high quality of their products to quality circles. Workers, usually without management participation, are free to discuss any and all aspects of their work. They are given access to any information necessary to give full consideration to whatever they're discussing.

Because the meetings are informal and managers don't oversee them, ideas flow freely and are then passed on to management. A high percentage of these suggestions are accepted and instituted. Although the concept of "quality circles" was conceived to discuss quality problems, these discussions have expanded over the years to productivity, performance, the working environment, and other aspects of business.

Meanings and Gleanings

A **quality circle** is a group of employees who voluntarily meet on a regular basis to discuss ideas for improving the quality of a product or service they produce.

Bet You Didn't Know

The concept of quality circles didn't originate in Japan. It originated right here in the United States in the 1950s, but didn't take off then. When workers were asked to participate in quality circles, the typical response was, "It's not my job. Someone else is responsible for quality." Today, most people recognize that quality is everyone's business.

Stimulating Creativity

"If it ain't broke, don't fix it." Wrong! Today's world is tough and competitive. You no longer can wait for things to break before fixing them. If you don't come up with better ideas—better ways to do things—your competitors will overwhelm you. Use constructive discontent to look at everything you're doing. Keep asking yourself, and encourage other people to ask themselves, "Is there a better way?"

It's easy to get into a rut: You become so comfortable with the status quo that you resist change. Change hurts. If you change the way you physically do something, new muscles are brought into play—and it hurts. If you change a mental process, you get real headaches. That's why so many people resist new ideas—or even try to avoid suggesting new ones.

Five Ways to Stimulate Creativity

Most people don't consider themselves to be creative. They assume that only a chosen few—inventors, artists, and writers, for example—have that talent. But all of us have within us the seeds of creativity. It just has to be developed.

As a manager, you can establish a climate that nurtures those seeds so that creative ideas flow from the people in your department. By becoming aware and helping associates become aware of some of these creative approaches, you and your team members can become familiar with several techniques that bring out their creativity (see the following section).

Looking at It Sideways: Lateral Thinking

Most of the time when you face a problem, you attack it logically—and that's good. Sometimes, though, what's logical may not be the only approach. Often the answer to a problem is not right in front of you, but can be found by looking at it from a different angle.

Alexander Fleming, a biologist, studied certain microbes. Periodically, when he selected a tray in which the microbes were kept for study, he found that the germs were dead. This disturbed him because he had to redo his work. After a number of times, Fleming wondered, "My goal is to find ways to kill germs; these germs are dead. What killed them?" Additional study proved that a mold which had developed in the tray had killed the germs. From this situation came the discovery of penicillin. This story illustrates lateral thinking: Fleming changed his focus from his original objective to facets he hadn't ever considered.

Leadership Lead
The answers to your problems aren't always found by looking at them logically. Learn to think laterally. Learn to look at, over, under, and around a problem.

Training yourself to think laterally isn't easy. By being aware that problems aren't always what they seem to be and that solutions aren't always logical, however, you take the first step. In his book *Lateral Thinking: Creativity Step by Step*, Edward deBono provides a detailed program to help you learn how to think laterally.

Being Flexible: Observation and Adaptation

Every day, as you live your normal life, you observe things happening around you. Sometimes, by adapting what you observe in one context of your life, you can solve a problem you face in another situation.

While Jeff was waiting at a JiffyLube for his car to be lubricated, he thought about his own company. It had a fleet of delivery vans, and whenever one of them needed servicing, a driver had to take it to the dealer's service center and leave it there for the day. Another driver followed along to take the first driver back to the shop, where other work was assigned. In the late afternoon, the process was repeated to retrieve the vehicle.

Jeff realized that, because it took half an hour to get from his shop to the service center, his company lost four person-hours just for transportation every time a van was serviced, in addition to the van being out of service for the entire day. Also, the driver worked on less productive work at his regular rate of pay, and the company had to pay the cost of the lubrication and other incidentals. Jeff knew that if those vans could be serviced at a quick-lube shop, his company could save a considerable part of that expense. He made the suggestion, and it was implemented, which saved his company thousands of dollars and earned Jeff a substantial suggestion award.

Modify, Modify, Modify

By modifying something you already have, you may come up with something new, different, or better. Victor Kiam, the CEO of the Remington Electric Shaver Company, tells this story:

One of the members of his office staff returned to work after undergoing surgery. When Kiam went over to welcome her back, she told him, "Mr. Kiam, when I was in the hospital, I thought of you. Before the operation, the nurse shaved the body hair around the area of my abdomen where the operation was to be performed. She used a double-edge razor and nicked me three times. I said, 'You should use a Lady Remington.'"

Kiam brought that idea to his research people, who developed a modified version of the Lady Remington as a surgical shaver that is now doing well in the marketplace.

Elimination: Getting Rid of Things

Most people think that in order to be creative, you have to invent something new. You can be just as creative by getting rid of things. Because most companies are bogged down with paperwork, a truly creative approach to the paper hassle would save companies considerable time and money.

Evaluate, by asking these questions, every form, record, and report that is generated on a daily, weekly, or monthly basis:

- **Is this paperwork really necessary?** Every month when Susan received a copy of a certain report, she skimmed it briefly and filed it because it wasn't of much value to her. When she mentioned it to a colleague, he agreed that it was no help to him either. A survey of all people on the distribution list showed that although the report had had some use several years earlier, it had outlived its value. By eliminating this report, the company saved time and money.

Leadership Lead
Every time you receive a form or a report, ask these questions: "Is it worth keeping? Can it be eliminated? Can it be combined with another form or made better?"

- **Can it be combined or consolidated with other forms?** Many forms or reports contain similar or even the same data in a different format. In one company a team of clerks spent hours each week compiling a sales report for the marketing manager and then, at the end of the month, more hours compiling the same data in a different form for the controller. At the suggestion of one of the clerks, the computer was programmed to convert the weekly reports to a monthly format, which freed up the clerks' time for more productive work.

- **Can it be improved?** By redesigning a form, you can often make it easier to compile and understand.
- **Review your electronic forms.** Specialized software for creating forms and reports lets you create a form or redesign it.

Brainstorming: Encouraging Group Creativity

A *brainstorming* meeting may be exciting, hectic, and totally chaotic, but it does generate ideas. The goal of brainstorming is to develop as many ideas as possible—not to critique, analyze, or discuss them or to make decisions.

Suppose that you are participating in a brainstorming session in which participants excitedly call out ideas that are hurriedly listed on a flip chart. Some of the ideas seem totally ridiculous, but no one scoffs, rebuts, or comments. No matter how stupid or inane an idea may be, it's listed on the chart.

> **Red Alert**
> Brainstorming isn't appropriate for all types of problems. It works best when you're dealing with specific situations rather than with long-term policies: naming a new product, improving a procedure, probing for new channels of distribution, making jobs less boring, or developing new approaches to marketing a product or service.

Why is the group encouraged to bring out these absurd ideas? The psychological principle behind brainstorming is called *triggering*. Any idea, no matter how dumb it seems, can trigger in the mind of another participant a viable idea. By allowing participants to think freely and express their ideas without fear of criticism, brainstorming frees people to stretch their minds and make suggestions that may be worthless in themselves but that may pave the way for an idea that has value. After the session, a committee culls out for additional analysis the ideas that have some merit.

The Least You Need to Know

- Create a climate of openness to upward communication.
- Rather than reject a bad idea, ask questions. Your questioning will help people who contribute suggestions think more clearly about their ideas and reject those that they realize are inadequate.

- Well-designed suggestion programs generate productive ideas.
- "I" meetings and quality circles can stimulate your team members to think constructively about their work.
- You can develop your own creativity and the creativity of your staff by training yourself and your team to employ lateral thinking, observation and adaptation, modification, elimination, and, when appropriate, brainstorming.

Chapter 6

Assigning and Delegating Work

In This Chapter

- Overcoming your fears of delegating
- Understanding the five elements of effective assigning
- Scheduling the workload
- Managing multiple priorities

Your team has lots of work to do. What will you do yourself, and what will you assign to other team members? When you delegate, you assign to other members of your team not only tasks but also the power, the authority, to accomplish them.

Effective delegation means that a team leader has enough confidence in his or her team members to know that they'll accomplish an assignment satisfactorily and expeditiously.

This chapter looks at some techniques and approaches to help you become a better delegator.

Don't Hesitate to Delegate

Sure, you're responsible for everything that goes on in your department or team, but if you try to do everything yourself, you'll put in 12 or more hours a day. That can lead to burnout, ulcers, heart attacks, and nervous breakdowns.

There are some things, of course, that only you can do, decisions that only you can make, critical areas that only you can handle. That's where you earn your keep. Many of the activities you undertake, however, can and should be done by others. This list discusses some of the reasons you may hesitate to delegate and explains why you should reconsider:

> **Meanings and Gleanings**
>
> **Delegation** enables you to position the right work at the right responsibility level, helping both you and the team members to whom you delegate to expand your skills and contributions. You also ensure that all work gets done in a timely manner by the right person who has the right experience or interest in the right topic.

- **You can do it better than your associates.** That may be the case, but you should spend your time and energy on more important things. Each of your team members has talents and skills that contribute to your team's performance. By delegating assignments, you give them the opportunity to use those skills.

  How often have you thought, "By the time I tell a coworker what to do, demonstrate how to do it, check the work, find it wrong, and have it done over, I could have it completed and go on to other things"? Showing someone how to perform a certain task will take time now, of course, but after your coworker masters the task, it will make your job easier later.

- **You get a great deal of satisfaction from that aspect of the work and hesitate to give it up.** You're not alone. All of us enjoy certain things about our work and are reluctant to assign them to others. Look at the tasks objectively. Even if you have a pet project, you must delegate it if your time can be spent handling other activities that are now your responsibility as a manager.
- **You're concerned that, if you don't do it yourself, it won't get done right.** You have a right to be concerned. The following section explains how to minimize this risk.

Delegating Without Fear

You don't have to be afraid of delegating work to others if you follow the principles described in this section.

Making Appropriate Assignments

You know the capabilities of each of your associates. When you plan their assignments, consider which person can do which job most effectively. If you're under no time pressure, you can use the assignment to build up another person's skills. The more team members who have the capabilities to take on a variety of assignments, the easier your job is for you. If no one on your staff can do the work, then of course you have to do it yourself. Make it a high priority to train one or more team members in this area so that the next time it comes up you can delegate it.

Making Sure That Your Instructions Are Understood

After you give a detailed instruction to one of your team members, your usual question is probably "Do you understand?" And the usual answer is "Yes."

But does the employee really understand? Maybe so, or maybe that person just thinks so but actually doesn't and in good faith says "I understand." Or maybe the person doesn't understand at all but is too embarrassed to say so.

Rather than ask "Do you understand?" ask "What are you going to do?" If the response indicates that one or more of your points isn't clear, you can correct it before the employee does something wrong.

When it's essential for an employee to rigidly conform to your instructions, you should make sure that he or she thoroughly understands them. Give a quiz. Ask specific questions so that both you and your team member completely agree about what he or she will do. When it's not essential for a delegated activity to be performed in a specific manner, you can just get some general feedback.

Tailor the way you make assignments to the preferences of the person to whom you're delegating. Some people like to have responsibilities spelled out explicitly, perhaps in the form of a written list of items. Others prefer a simple, concise instruction. Some people prefer e-mail, and others would rather have you delegate in person.

> **Meanings and Gleanings**
> Some people use the word **assigning** when they're talking about short-term projects and the word **delegating** for long-term projects. The terms are usually interchangeable.

Making Sure That Your Instructions Are Accepted

Your instructions must be not only understood but also accepted by your team member. Suppose that on Tuesday morning, Janet, the office manager, gives an assignment to

Jeremy with a deadline of 3:30 that afternoon. Jeremy looks at the amount of work involved and says to himself, "There's no way." It's unlikely that he will meet that deadline.

To gain acceptance, let your team member know the importance of the work and get him or her into the act. Janet might say, "Jeremy, this report must be on the director's desk when she comes in tomorrow morning. She needs it for an early-morning meeting with the executive committee. When do you think I can have it?" Jeremy may think, "This is important. If I skip my break and don't call my girlfriend, I can have it by 5."

Why did Janet originally indicate that she wanted it by 3:30 when she doesn't need it until the following morning? Maybe she believes that if she stipulates 3:30, Jeremy will knock himself out and finish the report by 5, when the office closes. But most people don't react that way. Faced with what they consider to be an unreasonable deadline, most people won't even try. By letting people set their own schedules within reasonable limits, you get their full commitment to meeting or beating a deadline.

But suppose that Janet really does need to have that report by 3:30 so that it can be proofread, photocopied, collated, and bound. To get the report completed, she may have to assign someone to help Jeremy or allow him to work overtime so that the report will be ready for the early-morning delivery.

Be realistic when you assign deadlines. Don't make a practice of asking for projects to be completed earlier than you need them, because they won't be taken seriously.

Setting Control Points

A *control point* is a spot in a project at which you stop, examine work that has been completed, and, if errors have been made, correct them. In this way, you can catch errors before they blow up into catastrophes.

A control point is *not* a surprise inspection. A team member knows exactly when each control point is established and what should be accomplished by then.

Suppose that, on Monday morning, Gary, a team leader, gives a project to Kim. The deadline is the following Friday at 3 P.M. They agree that the first control point will be Tuesday at 4 P.M, at which time Kim should have completed parts A and B. Notice that Kim knows exactly *what* and *when*. When Gary and Kim meet on Tuesday, they find several errors in part B. That's not good, but it's not terrible. The errors can be corrected before the work continues. If Gary and Kim had not scheduled a control point, the errors would have been perpetuated throughout the entire project.

Providing the Tools and Authority to Get a Job Done

You can't do a job without the proper tools or the authority to get the job done. Providing equipment, computer time, and access to resources is an obvious step, but giving *authority* is another story.

Many managers are reluctant to give up any of their authority. If a job is to be done without your micromanagement, you must give the people doing the job the power to make decisions.

Give people enough authority to get the job done. If they need supplies or materials, give them a budget so that they can order what they need without having to ask for your approval for every purchase. If a job may call for overtime, give them the authority to order it so that the work doesn't get bogged down because you're not around to make the decision.

Meanings and Gleanings
Some managers decide on every phase of an assignment, look over the shoulders of team members to ensure that every *i* is dotted and every *t* is crossed. When you **micromanage**, you stifle creativity and prevent team members from working at their full potential.

Leadership Lead
When people bring you a problem, insist that they bring with it a suggested solution. At best, they will solve their own problems and not bother you. At the least, they'll ask you, "Do you think that this will work?" which is a much better response than "What do I do now?"

When You Delegate, You Don't Abdicate

Team or workgroup members almost always have questions, seek advice, and need your help. Be there for them, but don't let them throw the entire project back at you. Let them know that you're available to help, advise, and support, but not to do their work.

Putting Delegation to Work

Now that you know about the principles of delegation, you're ready to apply them on the job.

To help you systematize your approach to delegation, use the following sample delegation worksheet. You may photocopy it or adapt it to your needs.

Delegation Worksheet

Delegated to: ______________________________

Date of assignment: ______________ **Deadline:** ______________

Brief description of assignment: ______________________________

____

Communication:

Assignee's comments: ______________________________

____

____

Areas that must be clarified: ______________________________

Control points:

First control point will be on __________ at ______________

Phase to be completed: ______________________________

____

Performance standards: ______________________________

____

____

Date this phase completed: ____________

(Use separate pages for each subsequent control point)

Assignment completed: ______________ **Date:** ______________

Comments: ______________________________

____

____

How we can make this person more effective in the next assignment:

____

____

Delegating to Teams

When an organization is structured into teams, work should be delegated and assigned as a team activity. When the people who will do the job have a say in what they're going to do, they approach their assignments with enthusiasm and commitment.

When you receive a complex project, present the entire assignment to your team and together discuss how it should be assigned. Knowing which team members will handle each phase will follow easily. Most members choose the area in which they have the most expertise. If two members want the same area, let them iron it out between themselves. If the issue becomes sticky, step in and resolve it diplomatically: "Abdul, you did the research on our last project, so let's give Carol a chance to do this one."

Certain phases of many jobs are tough or unpleasant, and no one really likes to do them. Have your team set up an equitable system for assigning this type of work.

As team leader, be sure that every member of your team is aware of not only his or her own responsibilities but also the responsibilities of every other team member. In this way, everyone knows what everyone else is doing and which type of support they can give to or receive from others.

Leadership Lead
If you have a difficult task, assign it to a lazy person. He or she will find an easy way to do it.

One way to make this strategy work is to break down the assignments and list them on a chart with the name of the person assigned to each phase, deadline dates, and other pertinent information. Post it in the office for easy referral.

Delegating by Using Teams

Before companies used the team concept, a department manager scheduled production for the department with the assistance of support departments, such as production control, inventory control, and purchasing. The order department processed orders received from customers and sent the orders on to production scheduling, which determined priorities and assigned various aspects of the job to appropriate departments. Each department head then assigned specific aspects of the task to employees. This process often resulted in bottlenecks. Work in one department was often delayed, for example, because the parts being fabricated in another department were behind schedule.

Multidepartmental teams are one way of effectively handling projects that require coordination among many diverse workgroups within a company. An effective team has these characteristics:

- It is composed of representatives of internal departments, such as sales and pertinent production groups. Team members are usually chosen by the team leader in coordination with managers of the various departments from which the members are chosen.
- Outside representatives, such as customers, suppliers, and subcontractors, are invited to participate in team discussions. Although these people aren't members of the team, their input is important in helping the team accomplish its goal.
- Production schedules are determined based on customers' needs. Team members are given detailed information about these needs and are encouraged to deal directly with customers to keep up-to-date on necessary adjustments.

Meanings and Gleanings

In a **multidepartmental team**, also called a **cross-functional team**, representatives from different departments, who are temporarily assigned to work as a team, combine their expertise to work collaboratively on a project.

- Delivery of materials is arranged on a just-in-time basis. To avoid unnecessary inventory costs, arrangements are made for delivery of materials and supplies as close as possible to the time they'll be used.
- Collaborative planning of work assignments are made, and control points are established. Depending on the circumstances, some teams work exclusively on a project and meet daily to coordinate and maintain attention to the assignment. Some projects require only occasional meetings to check on progress and deal with problems.

The key to the success of multidepartmental programs is communication. Team members are encouraged to communicate in person, on the telephone, or by writing, faxing, or sending e-mail to each other on a timely basis. Problems can then be addressed without delay.

Project Management

When companies are faced with special types of projects, usually one-time tasks (such as introducing a new product to the market, moving to a new location, or developing a new product or service), rather than assign it to one or more operating departments, they often create project-management teams.

This new group handles all matters related to the project. Project managers have the authority to obtain from various departments in the company any necessary personnel, equipment, computer time, and anything else to perform an assignment. Project team members are often temporarily relieved of their regular duties for the duration of the project.

The person chosen to be project manager is usually a senior or middle manager who has expertise in the activity the project involves. Some of the project manager's first tasks are shown in this list:

- Assemble a multidepartmental team that includes representatives from various parts of the organization to plan and implement the project.
- Together with these representatives, plan the project and set timetables for each phase.
- Work with team members to coordinate the work of all people involved, from the inception of the design phase to the final distribution to customers, including engineers, production supervisors, marketing and sales staff, and shipping and distribution personnel.

> **Meanings and Gleanings**
> A **project manager** is a team leader assigned to head up a specific project, such as the design and manufacture of an electronic system or the development and marketing of a new product.

The result is that you get cooperation in place of turf wars. Rather than time-wasting red tape, you get fast decisions. By crossing over traditional departmental barriers, project managers can get quick action, shift gears when necessary, and react immediately to urgent problems.

Using the Computer as a Scheduling Tool

As work scheduling becomes more and more complex, it becomes advisable to use a computer to work out scheduling details.

Software is available to help you with your scheduling. One typical program is Microsoft Project, which enables you to define your project tasks and their relationships to one another. You can use Project to create an outline to concentrate on either major phases of a project or on specific detailed tasks. It enables you to allocate and track resources and to set working hours and days for groups or for individuals within your group. Project alerts you to deviations from the schedule so that you can take immediate action.

When you use this type of software, it's easy to see whether your project is progressing as planned. You know which tasks must be given special attention to avoid delaying the completion of a project.

Microsoft Project has a variety of report formats you can use to communicate the progress of your project to your own staff, customers, and others who are involved.

Managing Multiple Priorities

If you're a typical 1990s manager, you're probably loaded down with more work than it seems possible to do—and so are your team members.

Darlene is not only working on a project for you but is also on the quality-assurance team and is involved in the research for a new product. Hans, a member of your functional team, has been asked to work on a special project for another manager. All these assignments are important, but you're responsible for getting the work on your project accomplished.

What can you do when members of your team have other assignments that are equally important or when your team is facing several high-priority tasks that must be completed in the same timeframe?

Communicate, Communicate, Communicate

You can't pull rank. The days when you can force your priorities on others because you're higher in the hierarchy may not be completely gone, but in progressive organizations these types of power plays are discouraged.

Work it out. Talk to team members and to other team leaders to schedule work that will enable all of you to make the best contribution you can to your organization. This process takes diplomacy and a willingness to compromise.

Working Smarter Beats Working Harder

Only a limited number of hours are available for work, and no matter how you look at it, there are only 24 hours in a day—not a minute more. For most men and women in responsible jobs, the 8-hour day is a fading memory. Working 10, 12, or more hours at the office or taking work home is not uncommon. But there's a limit to the amount of time a person can spend working.

Overwork *does* exist. In the past few years, as more and more companies downsize, it has become a serious problem. Employees who remain in an organization after downsizing occurs have had to take on, in addition to their own workload, assignments previously done by their former colleagues. Putting in more hours, bringing more work home, and going to the office on weekends may help, but it often results in stress, fatigue, and low morale, which can reduce performance and productivity. Don't forget that most people have families, other interests, and the need to rest and refuel.

As you learned in chapter 5, you should seek new and creative approaches so that you work smarter rather than harder. Which types of work can be eliminated? Which work processes can be reengineered? Which can be delegated? The time you spend learning about new approaches will pay off in expeditious performance.

Don't Be Afraid to Say No

You can't do everything. At times your team gets so bogged down with work that it's impossible to take on another assignment. How can you turn it down diplomatically?

Sometimes you can't. The project may have a high priority and have to be completed. Reexamine all your other projects. Determine which of them can be put aside so that you can tackle the new assignment. Some projects may be ahead of schedule and can be temporarily postponed; others may not be as important as the new job. Discuss these issues with your boss, and work together to reschedule other priorities.

Often, you can reschedule. The new assignment may not be a high-priority project but one that can wait for a more appropriate time for you. Maybe the project can be done more effectively by another team. It's no shame to admit that your group may not have the necessary background for a project. Know your limitations.

Leadership Lead
When you say "No" to an assignment, show how it will inhibit completion of higher-priority projects and suggest alternative solutions.

The Least You Need to Know

- Overcome any reluctance to delegate. You can't do everything yourself.
- By getting good feedback when you discuss assignments, you can catch misunderstandings before they affect the work to be done.
- You and your team should set control points so that errors can be caught early, before they cause real problems.
- Use multidepartmental teams to tackle assignments that cross departmental lines.
- Purchase computer software to assist in scheduling detailed work assignments.
- When you're faced with conflicting priorities, rethink the order of their importance. Diplomacy and open discussion with all parties involved can help you reach workable compromises.

Part 2
The Supervisor as Coach

Your team is in place. Now comes the real work: molding those men and women into a dynamic, interactive, high-performance unit. That's what a coach does for athletic teams, and that's your job now.

How do you do it? By helping the members of your team develop their talents to optimum capacity. You have to keep your team alert to your organization's goals and to the latest methods and techniques that will enable them to reach those goals. You have to help them learn what they don't know and to perfect what they do *know.*

In this part of the book, you'll pick up some suggestions for the training and development of the people on your team.

Chapter 7

Developing Your Team for Optimum Performance

In This Chapter

- Identifying what your team needs to learn
- Understanding the four-step approach to imparting know-how
- Using your entire team as a training vehicle
- Using techniques that make training fun and effective
- Training people to work under changing conditions

One thing you can be sure of is that things will change. Nothing in this dynamic world stays the same for long. The way we approach our jobs, the way a job is performed, and even the type of work we do changes with the times. As a team leader, you must keep up with these changes and be the focal point for developing your team's capabilities so that team members can learn how to do their jobs and keep up with changes in methods and techniques.

Where Does Training Begin?

Like everything, training starts at the beginning. It's your job to be sure that members of your team have the know-how to do their jobs. Newly employed associates bring with them skills they acquired through education and not experience. It's a plus, of course, if a new team member has done similar work in another company, but it doesn't eliminate the need for training. Every organization has its own way of doing things. To ensure consistency in the way your group works, all new associates should be given training or retraining in performing the basic parts of their job.

But Does It End There?

New people may need basic training, but training and development aren't limited to newcomers. All members of your team need ongoing training. They should continually acquire new techniques and renew established skills. Always encourage self-development.

As a leader and a coach, you are the guide and stimulus to your team's growth. By working closely with each of your team members, you can suggest areas in which additional training will be helpful and skills they should acquire. You can also provide the resources for this process.

How much time, effort, and money should you invest in training? There's no question that well-trained, high-performance teams are major ingredients in a company's success, but (as mentioned in chapter 2), there must be a balance between the P (*p*otential of people) and R (*r*esults desired).

Few companies have an unlimited training budget. Companies aren't universities. People in professional and high-tech jobs must acquire necessary skills before joining an organization. A company's responsibility is to help these people adapt their knowledge to meet organizational needs.

Red Alert

If your new associate has done similar work in another job, don't assume that training isn't necessary. Observe the way a new employee approaches the job, and discuss any differences. To ensure consistency, retrain the person. Always remember to keep an open mind: Your new associate may be able to teach you a better way to do a job.

Some jobs, however, are unique to a company and are the only source for training people to perform them. The amount of time and money a company spends on this training depends on the complexity of the tasks that are performed.

America is moving rapidly from a production to a service economy. Blue-collar jobs are being replaced by jobs in offices, stores, restaurants, and other service industries. The skills required differ, but the need to train the people who perform these jobs presents new challenges to management. Although higher-level positions that have been created call for people with a college- or graduate-level education and a capacity for creative thinking and problem-solving, a high percentage of jobs still require a mastery of the tasks involved. Whether a job calls for skills in computer operations, telemarketing, claims processing, cooking, or customer service, these tasks must be taught. Team leaders and managers who train these people are the coaches who will develop the skills of their team members for optimum performance.

Four Steps That Help Team Members Learn How to Do Their Jobs

Training cannot be a haphazard process. To be effective, it must be planned and systemized. Many organizations have effectively used a relatively simple four-step training program for several years: job-instruction training, or JIT.

Preparation

Preparation is both physical and psychological. All *physical* equipment and facilities that are necessary for training should be in place before you begin. If you're training someone in a computer process, you should have on hand a computer, the software, a training manual, the data, and any other materials necessary to show someone how to use a computer. After you begin, you don't want to be interrupted by having to look for items you need.

Meanings and Gleanings

Job-instruction training (JIT), a systematic approach to training people to perform tasks, involves four steps: preparation, presentation, performance, and follow-up.

In the *psychological* part of the process, you should tell a trainee, before the training begins, what will be taught, why it's performed, and how it fits into the overall picture. When people can see the entire picture, not just their small part in it, they learn faster and understand more clearly, and they're more likely to remember what they've been taught.

Presentation

It's no longer feasible to say to a trainee, "Just watch me, and do what I do." Work today is much too complex to learn just by observation. The following four steps can guide you in showing someone how to perform a task:

- Describe what you're going to do.
- Demonstrate step by step. As you demonstrate, explain each step and explain why it's done (for example, "Notice that I entered the order number on the top right side of the form to make it easy to locate").

Red Alert

Practice does *not* make perfect. If people practice doing things wrong, they become perfect in doing things wrong. *Practice makes permanent.* When you train associates, periodically check out what they're doing. If it's wrong, correct it immediately, before it becomes permanently ingrained as a bad habit.

➤ Have the trainee perform the task and explain to you the method and reason for each step.

➤ If it's not done to your satisfaction, repeat it; if it's okay, reinforce with praise or positive comments.

Performance

After you're satisfied that a trainee can do a job, leave her alone and let her do it. The trainee needs an opportunity to try out what she has learned. She will probably make some mistakes, but that's to be expected. From time to time, check out how things are going and make necessary corrections.

Follow-Up

The follow-up step is important because people tend to change what they have been taught. Careless people may skip some steps in a procedure and cause errors or complications. Smart people may make changes that they believe are better than what they were taught. Although you should encourage your associates to try to find more effective approaches to their job, caution them not to make any changes until they have discussed them with you. They often may not be aware of the ramifications of their suggested changes.

Schedule follow-up discussions of new assignments three to four weeks after the presentation step. At that time, review what the associate has been doing, and, if changes have been made intentionally or inadvertently, bring the person back on track.

Training Is a Team Activity

Just because you're the team leader doesn't mean that you have to train all your team members. The training function should be shared by everyone on the team. Some organizations encourage an entire team to share in the task of training new members; others assign one person to act as a mentor.

Meanings and Gleanings

A **mentor** is a team member assigned to act as counselor, trainer, and "big brother" or "big sister" to a new member.

Determining who will train new members or be assigned to retrain others depends on what the member is being trained to do. ***Caution:*** A person who knows the job best isn't always the best person to train others. It takes more than job knowledge to be an effective trainer.

Job know-how *is* essential for the person who will do the training, but it's only part of the picture. Look for these additional factors:

- **Personal characteristics:** Patience, empathy, and flexibility are good qualities to look for.
- **Knowledge of training techniques:** If a team member has the personal characteristics, training techniques can be taught. Some companies provide "Train the Trainer" programs to build up communications skills in people who will do the training.
- **A strong, positive attitude toward the job and the company:** If you assign a disgruntled person to do your training, that person will inject the trainee with the virus of discontent.

Scheduling Training

When training must be accomplished in only a short time, you should set up a training schedule. Before you can do so, you must determine whether the training will be done on or off the job.

On-the-job training is done at the worksite during regular working hours, usually by the supervisor or another team member. Off-the-job training is conducted in a classroom or a special facility rather than at the regular place of work. It has many advantages over on-the-job training:

- **People learn faster.** Because trainees devote all their time and effort to training, no other work interferes with the learning process.
- **It's usually conducted by a professional trainer.** This person has not only the know-how to train but also no other duties to distract from the training.
- **It doesn't interfere with production.** Because trainees are in a classroom and not on a job site, they don't slow down work in progress or interfere with coworkers' performance.

Despite these major advantages, off-the-job training has a limitation: It isn't cost-effective unless you're training several people at the same time. Because most managers usually train only one or two people at a time, training usually must be done on the job. Another limitation is that you can't really learn the full scope of a job outside the job environment. Therefore, off-site training generally enables you to train only for a particular task or skill, not for the entire job. Many companies use a combination of on- and off-site training.

Setting the Training Schedule

When you prepare a training schedule (see the following on-the-job training schedule), indicate the subjects that must be covered, determine how long it should take an average person to learn the subject matter, and allot the necessary time for the training. A trainer should be given enough flexibility to be able to handle any snags that come up. Indicate the training methods that will be employed and any required training aids.

On-the-Job Training Schedule

Job: ______________________________

Trainer: ____________________ **Trainee:** ____________________

Equipment necessary for training: ______________________________

____

____

Time scheduled Day/hour	Subject	Training methods	Training aids	Completed

Whether you or an associate is assigned to do the training, review the training schedule before you begin. Be sure that everything to be learned is scheduled. The sequence of the subject matter is often a problem, so be sure to check it too. It's tempting to set the schedule for a time that's convenient for you but not consider whether the trainee is ready to receive that material.

Dealing with Problem Learners

Not all people respond in the same way to being taught new things. Some people are slow to learn, some may be reluctant to change their ways and resist training, and some may believe that they cannot learn and therefore give up easily.

Slow Learners

Margaret, the team leader, was about to give up on Mark, who was trying hard to learn new material, but just couldn't quite get it. Margaret asked a colleague for help with the problem: "When Mark worked in your department, did he have difficulty learning new things? "Yes," the other team leader responded, "He's a slow learner, but after he did learn the material, he became one of my best workers." Margaret followed up: "What did you do to help him?" He responded: "I watched his learning patterns and recognized that he needed to have the tasks broken down more into smaller segments so that he could absorb them one by one. Then we worked to bring them together. I also noted that he responded best if I gave him immediate feedback about his performance of each facet of the task and praised him each time he did it well."

> **Leadership Lead**
> Carefully plan the sequence in which you will present the subject. *Begin with the simple stuff, and work up to complex subjects.* Build a foundation before you attempt to construct the framework.

The Learning Curve

Have you ever made great progress in learning something new and realized that your mind suddenly seems to stop? You can't move beyond a certain point, but why?

The human mind can absorb only a limited amount of new information at any time. At some point in the learning process, it has to stop and integrate the new material with what it already knows. While this process is place, you're at a plateau: Nothing new can enter your system. After the new material is absorbed, however, your mind opens again and—boom!—off you go. This process is known as the *learning curve.*

> **Leadership Lead**
> Being a slow learner doesn't mean that a person is stupid. Be patient, and try different approaches! Slow learners often can develop into productive team members.

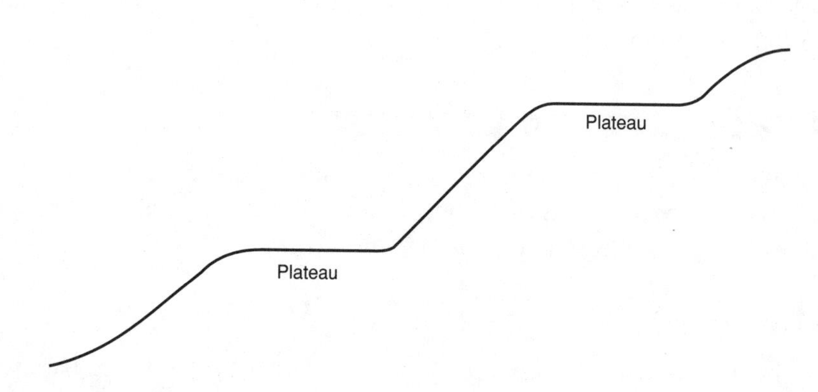

After your mind receives a certain amount of information, it stops and takes a rest on a plateau.

Whether you're the learner or the teacher, keep the learning curve in mind. When you or your trainee seem to be unable to go beyond a certain point, *stop*. Wait an hour or a day or longer. Depending on the complexity of the material and the learner's background, the duration of the plateau varies.

The Know-It-All

You've run into know-it-alls. You can't tell them anything. They believe that they know best and oppose *any* type of change.

But change they must. Because know-it-alls resist learning new things, you have to do some things to overcome their attitude:

- Listen to their objections. Point out the advantages of the new changes and how they will make the system more efficient, less expensive, or easier to maintain.
- Get other team members to back you up.
- Use patience, reinforcement, and diplomacy to make your point.

The Fear of Learning

How often have you heard someone say, "It's too hard for me—I'm too old to learn new things"? Eric, a bookkeeping machine operator for 20 years, was the fastest and most accurate operator in his department. When his company replaced its old Burroughs machines with PCs, he was devastated. "What will I do?" he asked. "I'm 50 years old. I'm too old to learn about computers."

When the computer company's trainer began the training program, Eric froze. He didn't seem to absorb even the basic elements of his work. The trainer spent extra time with him and paid special attention to his efforts. His manager talked to him to build up his confidence, but nothing helped. Eric's request for a transfer to another department was denied because computers are now used everywhere.

When Eric was at his lowest ebb, Lillian, one of the other bookkeeping machine operators, took him aside. "Eric, you *can* learn. I'm older than you, and I had no trouble learning to use the PC. Try it. I'll help you. *All* of us will help you." With the help and support of his peers, Eric made a real effort to learn. Now he's a productive PC operator and proudly boasts about his new skills.

Management Development

Training isn't limited to teaching job skills. Training team members to become team leaders is an important aspect of organizational development.

For many years, training for management positions was limited to people who were on a special management track. They usually were hired as management trainees after graduating from college and went through a series of management-training programs within an organization, often supplemented by seminars, courses, and residencies at universities or special training schools. If you weren't lucky enough to be on the management track, your career in the company was limited.

In recent years the special management track has been supplanted by team development, in which training for management is open to any team member. And why not? Even the military has learned that graduation from military academies isn't essential for top leadership. (The last two Chairmen of the Joint Chiefs of Staff—Colin Powell and John Shalikashvili—aren't West Pointers.) Companies have recognized that latent leadership talent exists in most people and can be developed in them. (Chapter 8 discusses some of the programs that companies have used to encourage people at all levels to prepare to move up in their careers.)

Training and Development Techniques

Today's leaders have available to them a variety of aids and techniques to facilitate their training efforts. Some have been around for years; others are more recent.

Training Manuals

Training manuals, or "do it by the numbers" handbooks, are helpful for teaching routine tasks. They make the training process easy for both trainer and trainees; you can always refer to them when you're in doubt about what to do.

Today's jobs are becoming less routine, however. Training manuals aren't just inadequate—they may even stifle creativity. It's too easy to rely on a book rather than think out new and possibly better approaches.

Interactive Computer Training

Many companies have developed interactive computer programs to train employees in a variety of areas. These programs were designed for use in schools to enable students to learn at their own pace. Slower learners could take their time and repeat unclear sections until they understood them. Fast learners or students who had more background in an area could move quickly ahead, and students could test themselves as they progressed.

Leadership Lead
To provide easy-to-remember shortcuts for various operations in jobs that require the use of a computer, post "Tips and Technique" cards next to the computer or auxiliary equipment.

Because most companies have their own way of doing things, generic programs such as the ones used by schools haven't been of much value. Some generic programs, however, such as those that teach basic accounting skills and various computer operations, can be valuable to any organization. Check any computer-software catalog to determine which programs might be valuable to you.

Some larger organizations have customized programs to meet their own needs. The programs are usually proprietary, however, and aren't made available outside the company.

Case Studies

A *case study* is a description of a real or simulated situation presented to trainees for analysis, discussion, and solution.

Case studies are used in graduate schools, seminars, and training programs to enable trainees to work on the types of problems they're most likely to meet on the job. The studies are often drawn from the experiences of real companies.

Companies that use case studies in their own management-development programs often design cases that simulate the type of situations the trainee will face in that organization. The experience of working out these types of problems in a classroom instead of learning by trial and error after being on the job pays off in fewer trials and less costly errors.

A significant advantage of using case studies in management development is that trainees work on the case collaboratively: They learn how to organize and use teams to solve cases.

Leadership Lead

To make case-solving most effective, design cases that are related to the job. Make them complex and challenging, and make them require collaboration to obtain the best solutions.

Role-Playing

In today's companies, interaction with other people is an essential ingredient in most jobs. Perhaps the best way to train people for this type of interaction is through role-playing.

As in case studies, role-plays should be based on realistic situations a trainee may face on the job: dealing with a customer, resolving a dispute among team members, or conducting a performance review, for example.

Role-plays should be fun, but if they're only fun and not a learning experience, you're wasting your time.

To be effective, a role-play should be carefully structured. Participants should be briefed on the goals of the exercise, and each participant should be given a specific part to play (they don't read from a script). Improvisation makes the exercise more spontaneous and allows for flexibility, but you should establish limits so that participants don't stray from the goal of the exercise.

To get everyone—not just the players—involved, give each role to a group of people. The group studies and discusses how the role should be played. Then one member of the group is appointed to play the role. The other group members may step in to supplement the primary player. For example, if the person playing the role of a personnel interviewer fails to ask a key question, one of the members of that group can intervene and ask the question.

After the role-play is completed, all the groups critique what has transpired and discuss what they've learned from the experience.

Videotaping

Probably the most dramatic innovation in training and development in recent years is the use of video as a training tool.

You can purchase video training tapes to cover a number of situations. Video catalogs list tapes for training people in a variety of types of work.

Tapes are most appropriate for training people to do routine jobs. For situations in which flexibility and initiative are necessary, tapes (like training manuals) can impede creativity. People tend to accept what they see on video as the one correct approach.

Customizing videotapes to meet your own needs is a more effective option. This list describes some ways to use customized video to enhance the effectiveness of your training programs:

- **Tape demonstrations:** For work of a physical nature (most factory or maintenance jobs and some clerical jobs), a good demonstration is an important part of the training. Who does the demonstrating? Either you do it yourself or you have it done by one of your team members. No matter how good a live demonstration is, it can be done only in real time. If the demonstration is videotaped, it can be shown in real time to show the pace and in slow motion to show the steps. When you have a good demonstration on tape, you can show it to all the people you train in that type of work.
- **Tape job performance:** One of the best ways to help people recognize exactly what they're doing on the job is to videotape them at work. Reviewing the tape enables them to see their strengths and weaknesses much better than if you just tell them. An employee who had been performing machine maintenance for many years thought that he was working efficiently. He was amazed at what he learned about himself when he saw a videotape taken on the job. With the guidance of his team leader, he identified where changes were required and what type of training he needed to become more effective.
- **Tape team meetings:** One employee's team leader videotaped several team meetings. By studying the tapes, the employee noticed that she tended to dominate group discussions. She pushed her ideas across, shut off opposing arguments, and was sometimes rude to other team members. She told her team leader that although she was an assertive person, until she saw the tape she didn't realize the way she came across to others and agreed to attend a human-relations training course.

Red Alert

Never purchase a training tape unless you preview it. Most companies that sell tapes charge a fee for the preview, but it's worth it. Catalog descriptions give only a limited amount of information; previewing enables you to determine whether the tape will serve your purpose.

- **Tape role-plays:** Role-plays are an excellent way to develop interpersonal relations. By videotaping role-plays and then reviewing them, they become an even more effective training tool.
- **Tape presentations:** If you make presentations at internal meetings or outside functions, there's no better way of training than to study videos of your practice deliveries.

Audiotaping

One of the best ways to train people who use the telephone as a major part of their job is to tape-record telephone conversations. This technique is most useful in training telemarketers, customer-service representatives, order clerks, credit checkers, and similar personnel.

You can purchase a component that connects the telephone to a voice-activated tape recorder. Some voice-mail and answering machines have this capability built-in.

Red Alert
Some states have laws that restrict the taping of telephone conversations without notifying the other party. Check your state laws.

Tape several conversations, and then review them with each team member. Listen to what is said and how it's said. Pay close attention to the way your associate reacts to what the other party says—and how that person reacts to your associate.

Cross Training

When teams are the operating units in an organization, it's helpful for everyone on a team to be able to perform the work of any other member. The whining comment "It's not my job" is no longer valid.

In cross-functional or multidepartmental teams, this capability isn't always feasible. If your team consists of people from various disciplines, you cannot always expect them to be able to do work in other areas: A team consisting of people from marketing, engineering, and finance doesn't easily lend itself to cross training.

Most teams are made up of people who do similar work, however. One sales-support team consists of order clerks, customer-service representatives, and computer operators. All are trained in every aspect of the team's work and can and do move from job to job as necessary.

Although that team's order clerks spend most of their time processing orders and the customer-service reps are almost always on the phone, if the pressure is on processing orders, customer-service reps work on order-processing between calls. If a customer-service rep is out of the office, any team member can fill in at a moment's notice.

Bet You Didn't Know

In 1994, U.S. organizations spent nearly $51 billion on formal training in the workplace, a jump from $42 billion only three years earlier.

Laying the Foundation for Self-Training

It wasn't long ago that when you were trained for a job, you were considered fully trained after you mastered the skills and functions of the job. This training was augmented by occasional technology updates. Now, just a few years later, however, many formerly routine and highly structured jobs are dynamic and flexible.

Look at the position of "secretary." It used to connote a woman taking dictation, making appointments for her boss, answering the phone, filing papers, and acting as a gofer. Today that secretary is more of an executive assistant. She or he may prepare the agenda for a meeting, supervise clerks, compile information and write reports, and make important business decisions. It's a considerably different job. Traditional secretarial training wasn't adequate preparation for this type of work.

Training must be replaced by learning. The difference between training and learning is that training is a one-way transfer of information from trainer to trainee. Learning involves not only absorbing information but also knowing how to identify potential problems, seeking the knowledge and information that are necessary to solve problems, and creating new concepts. This process is the focus of modern training and development.

Leadership Lead

The National Organization of Executive Secretaries offers periodic seminars on developing management skills for secretaries and executive assistants. They include programs for leadership, communication, human-resources development, and related topics. The seminars are open to both members and nonmembers. For information: 900 South Washington St., Suite G13, Falls Church, VA 22046; phone: 703-237-8616.

Bringing Your Training Activities Up-to-Date

Basic skills training still has its place in the business world. The fundamentals of a job must be acquired as a start, but that's all—as a start. Continued training to learn new technologies is already in place in most companies, but it's not enough. The following list shows five ways to bring your training and development up-to-date:

- Emphasize how to identify and solve problems rather than present specific problems and teach trainees how to deal with them.
- Place the ultimate responsibility for learning on the individual (or, in team learning, on the team). The person who conducts the training is a facilitator: Rather than spoon-feed information to trainees, he or she guides them through the process and summarizes and reinforces the resulting insights.
- Make sure that people who will learn together share a common vocabulary, are trained to use the same analytical tools, and have communication channels available so that they can work together and with other people or teams within an organization. A company, through its training or HR department, should provide these tools.
- Ensure that collaboration across functions is available. To learn to solve problems, trainees may have to tap resources in other departments or from outside sources, such as customers, suppliers, or trade or professional associations.
- Avoid having professional trainers do the training. Let people from all job categories (managers, team leaders, human-resources specialists—technicians in all fields) be facilitators. This technique not only expands a company's training resources but also helps develop future leaders.

Meanings and Gleanings

Training people is a one-way process. The teacher presents information; the student absorbs it (you hope). When training is replaced by *learning,* the emphasis is on developing the capability of trainees to identify and solve problems; seeking knowledge; and taking the initiative in continuing self-development.

Leadership Lead

As jobs change, people must also change. Anticipate the types of jobs you think your company will eventually need. If your company doesn't provide training in those areas, find your own sources to acquire the necessary skills. Take computer training, enroll in interpersonal-relations courses, or learn a foreign language. Take the initiative—your career is in your own hands.

In-House Universities: The Training Medium of the Future

Have you heard of Hamburger University? It's no joke. McDonald's created it to train its management people, and it was the forerunner of many other "company universities." So why was a university created to teach people how to flip a Big Mac? If that was all there was to managing a McDonald's outlet, it would be considered overkill. McDonald's recognized early on that developing managers who know how to lead teams, market products, and increase sales pays off in making its units profitable.

In an article titled "Five Top Corporate Training Programs" in *Successful Meetings* magazine, Robert Carey says that a number of other companies have converted their training departments into autonomous schools with the latest teaching equipment, faculties drawn from both within the company and outside sources, and curricula planned as carefully as (or more carefully than) at many colleges. Most of these organizations call these schools "universities." According to the American Council on Education (ACE), more than 40 of these company universities have been established in the United States.

This section looks at some of the most successful of these "universities."

At Walt Disney, Training Is Show Biz

Disney University isn't a campus, but a process for training all employees of Walt Disney World Resorts. The first week of training includes a workshop called Traditions, in which multimedia techniques are used to give trainees an overview of Disney history and culture and the vision of the organization. Facilitators for the sessions are a variety of "cast members" (the generic term for all employees of Disney theme parks, whether they get into costumes or not). Professional facilitators lead only technical and executive sessions. Cast members share with trainees their own interactions with "guests" (the Disney term for customers).

What makes this program unique is that trainees mingle among the visiting crowds at the parks to observe and study cast members in action. The result is that Disney's front-line attrition rate is only 15 percent compared with 60 percent for the rest of the hospitality industry.

Saturn Company: GM's Training for the Next Century

The key to Saturn's structure is its use of teams. The goal of the Saturn University training program is to teach employees to operate as continuously learning, fully independent work teams. The teams are responsible for their own development. The teams manage their own budgets, order their own materials, and gauge their own educational progress.

Each employee is responsible for creating his or her own training-and-development plan. It may involve brushing up on current skills or acquiring new ones, attending seminars, completing computer-based training programs, or even teaching a training session or cross-training a team member. Half of all Saturn training is in interpersonal relations and communications.

The best example of Saturn's commitment to education is that all executives, including its CEO, teach at Saturn University.

Motorola University

Motorola, an award-winning international electronics manufacturer, is committed to customer service. Motorola University was created to keep all employees at the cutting edge of their technical skills, but that's only the beginning. Motorola programs help trainees develop creativity and leadership, work in teams, and improve customer relations.

The program's success has resulted in Motorola's amazing growth in a highly competitive industry—not just in the United States, but also in the global marketplace. The training program has become a model for other organizations that have also adopted its system for measuring effectiveness.

> **Leadership Lead**
> Motorola University invites other companies to learn about its training. Contact Motorola University, 2 Century Center,1700 East Golf Road, Schaumburg, IL 60173; phone: 708-538-4404.

The Least You Need to Know

- The four steps in systematically training people to perform tasks are preparation, presentation, performance, and follow-up.
- All members of a team should be trained to train. Then you must let them do it.
- Set up training schedules to ensure that everything that must be taught *is* taught.
- Be patient with slow learners. Seek different approaches to which they can relate. These people often develop into a team's best workers.
- Everyone has management potential. Encourage self-development as a step toward career growth.
- Incorporate into your training program techniques such as case studies, role-playing, interactive computer programs, and audio- or videotaping to make the training experience more exciting, more meaningful, and more productive.

- Redesign your training programs to meet the changing challenges of today's jobs by emphasizing the processes of problem solving and creative thinking and by helping participants become self-learners.

Chapter 8

When Do You Graduate? You Don't!

In This Chapter

- Understanding that continuing learning leads to continuing growth
- Developing your team's skills, talents, and potential
- Ensuring career development
- Conducting effective training meetings

"So many books—so little time." I recently saw this phrase on a T-shirt and thought, "How true that is, not only of books but also of all the things we want to learn." Even if we limit what we learn to material that's relevant to our jobs, there's no way we can ever learn it all.

But we must continue to learn. Successful people make a practice of allocating time, no matter how busy they are, to keeping up with developments in their fields.

This chapter discusses some of the things you can do to help yourself and your team members upgrade job skills and develop personal skills that will help in your current job and prepare for career growth.

The need for training never ends. The following list of reasons can help you understand why:

- As technology changes, you have to keep up with the state of the art in your field.
- Changing circumstances in your company or industry require your team to acquire new knowledge in areas in which they had not previously been involved.
- You and your team members want to strengthen your weaknesses and add to your strengths, not only to do a better job now but also to prepare for career advancement.

Upgrading Current Job Skills

It's essential for job survival that you keep up with the latest developments in your field. You must not only be on the cutting edge of technology and other developments but also ensure, as team leader, that your team members are trained in those areas.

Enhancing Skills

Set up a program for yourself and for your team members to continually develop current skills and acquire additional ones. In your program, make sure to do the following:

- Identify the skills of each team member.
- Investigate new equipment and methods.
- Determine which additional skills are necessary.
- Arrange for training in these areas.

Upgrading Personal Skills

Managers often are asked what they look for when they choose people for promotion. They acknowledge that the technical or specialized aspects of a job are important and also realize that personal skills are much more important on the job. These skills include the ability to communicate both orally and in writing and the ability to interrelate with other people both within and outside an organization.

Making Presentations

In the participative atmosphere in which most companies operate, the ability to communicate is essential to getting work done (see chapters 4 and 5).

You or another member of your team may be called on to make a presentation to another team, to a vendor or customer, or even to a higher-level management committee.

People who communicate well one-on-one often freeze when they have to speak to a group. Others may do well when they're talking to their own team, but are on tenterhooks when they have to address others.

Leadership Lead

"The recipe for perpetual ignorance is to be satisfied with your opinions and content with your knowledge."

— Elbert Hubbard

Overcoming a fear of public speaking is best accomplished by getting up and doing it. One man learned this the hard way: After researching the potential market for a new product, his assignment was to present his team's findings to the executive committee. He was so nervous that he rushed through the report, fumbled for words, and—even though he knew the answers—was unable to respond to their questions.

Leadership Lead

Learn how to make dynamic and exciting talks by reading *The Complete Idiot's Guide to Speaking in Public with Confidence*, by Laurie Rozakis, Ph.D.

A manager who attended the meeting called the man aside and said, "When I had to make my first presentation, I was just as nervous as you. But I did something about it. I joined Toastmasters."

Toastmasters International is a worldwide organization created to give people the opportunity to speak in front of audiences. It isn't a formal training program—it's just a group of men and women who meet weekly. Each one gives a short talk about any subject he or she chooses. The experience of speaking in public, augmented by support and helpful hints from others, has helped countless people overcome their fear of public speaking. Toastmasters has many benefits, including networking, discipline, leadership skills, and thinking fast on your feet. You can obtain the address of the Toastmasters Club nearest you by calling Toastmaster's International at 1-800-993-7732 or by looking in your phone book for the number of a local chapter.

More formal training is also available. Most universities and community colleges have public-speaking courses. In many communities, public schools offer adult-education programs in public speaking. Some companies have retained private training organizations, such as Communispond, to run in-house programs to improve their employees' public-speaking skills. Classroom presentations are often videotaped and followed up by critiques. Some organizations have experts who personally coach managers or associates in how to best prepare actual presentations.

Learning a Language

If your company is expanding into the global market, knowing a foreign language can be a significant asset. Although businesspeople in most countries speak English, Americans who sell to and buy from these countries and who coordinate work with them realize that knowing the language of their overseas contacts is an important advantage.

Pioneered by the U.S. State Department, intensive language-training programs have been developed to immerse participants in a knowledge of most languages. These programs are usually conducted at a university or special training center.

In preparation for a tour of duty in Jordan, a man enrolled in a program to learn Arabic. After the first few days, in which he was given an intensive grounding in the Arabic language, the remainder of the program was conducted in that language. All English-language signs in the area were replaced with Arabic signs, and the instructor spoke only Arabic. Participants were at first requested and later instructed to speak only Arabic among themselves. Arabic texts, newspapers, and magazines were distributed. At the end of the three-week program, the man had mastered enough of the language to be able to converse in Arabic.

Leadership Lead

When continuing learning is an integral part of a company's culture, employees seek out opportunities to hone their skills for doing today's job as well as to develop their talents and obtain the knowledge necessary to meet tomorrow's challenges.

In addition to learning the language, members of the class learned about Near East customs, foods, religion, and history—helpful knowledge in doing business with the residents of that area.

If you have the discipline to work on your own, audiotapes and CD-ROM language programs can teach you a language. The availability of a teacher and the advantages of interacting with classmates, however, are much more effective methods.

Using Other Programs

A variety of training and development programs can be valuable to you and your organization. The following list shows some of the types of available programs:

- **Computer training.** As a team leader, you may realize that you and your team members would benefit from receiving training to use certain new computer software. Arrange for it to happen.

- **Writing skills.** One of your team members may express an interest in improving his or her writing skills. If your company provides an in-house writing program or if a local school has a similar course, send the person to it. Your company's tuition-reimbursement plan may pay for this type of program.

- **English-language skills.** If one of your team members is a new immigrant and better English skills could increase his or her value to your team, help the person locate a suitable program.
- **Dale Carnegie course.** If the aggressive behavior of one of your team members is affecting your team's work, discuss the matter with the person and suggest this or a related program to improve his or her interpersonal relations.

Examining Career Development

As a result of the flattening of organizational structures, career paths that were formerly a common road to company advancement have changed radically. A young person used to be hired at an entry-level position, and—with diligence, hard work, and a little luck—could move gradually up the company hierarchy. Career-oriented people joining a relatively large company in the 1970s could expect to move up three to four steps in their first ten years with a company. Their offspring or younger brothers and sisters entering the workforce in the 1990s don't have such an easy a path into management, however.

With fewer layers of management in the reengineered company, opportunities for vertical advancement have been severely curtailed. Opportunities for career growth are still available, but the road to management is much different now.

More Money

Although it's not the only reason, many people seek advancement as the financial reward that goes along with increased responsibility. With fewer management-level positions required in a flattened structure, many companies—to keep good people from quitting and to encourage good work for all team members—have adjusted their compensation systems.

The traditional method of paying employees was to establish base pay for a job. Employee performance was evaluated annually, and most workers received some type of raise, either a cost-of-living adjustment or a higher amount for good performance. Employees usually continued to receive this salary until their next review. One of the inequities of this type of system is that long-term employees are paid significantly more than newer—and perhaps more productive—people. These people were rewarded for longevity rather than for performance.

Meanings and Gleanings
Most companies give employees an **annual raise** if they meet minimum performance standards, and many employees consider it an entitlement. The amount of the increase is usually based on the cost of living. A more meaningful system is based on a **merit raise**, which is determined by each person's performance.

This system is being replaced in many organizations by a system of pay based on performance. All team members, regardless of tenure, are paid a basic salary. Additional income comes in the form of bonuses or profit-sharing. This amount is measured in some companies by a team's productivity: The entire team shares in bonuses commensurate with increased production, and bonuses are based on monthly calculations. Although the base pay doesn't change, total income may vary significantly from month to month.

Red Alert
Profit-sharing plans are sometimes based on formulas so complex that employees cannot understand them and often feel frustrated.

A more common system is some variation of profit-sharing. If a company makes a profit, all employees share in it. If they don't, no one receives a bonus. Bonuses based on profit are distributed either quarterly or annually to serve as an incentive for employees to be concerned about production, quality, waste, and customer satisfaction.

A growing form of the profit-sharing plan is an *ESOP,* or *employee stock-ownership plan,* in which employees are given the opportunity to buy shares in the company and become its true owners. Among the better-known are TWA, United Airlines, and Avis. These companies play up this ownership in their advertising, by letting the public know that, inasmuch as their employees are in a sense their own bosses, they'll knock themselves out to satisfy customers. (And they do!)

Money is the primary reason that some people seek advancement. They're satisfied as long as they have the opportunity to make as much or more money through the compensation system as they might have made by upgrading their position.

Blocks to Advancement

Karen's goal was to move into a leadership position. An outgoing, ambitious, and capable marketing specialist, she was a valuable contributor to her team's success. Her bonuses were more than satisfactory, but that wasn't enough: She was ready for team leadership. Looking around, she noticed that her team leader and others in marketing were doing fine work and weren't about to move up in or out of the organization. It seemed that she was stalled in her career—and she was only 32 years old.

Unusual? Not at all. One of the major challenges to management is what to do with high-potential, ambitious people such as Karen, who are frustrated because of a lack of upward mobility.

If you can't look to moving step by step up the ranks in your current department or job category, you have to seek other channels that may help you reach your goal. Two successful approaches are horizontal growth and outsourcing.

Horizontal Growth

Karen asked her team leader and her human-resources manager what she could do to move into a more responsible role. The company fortunately had a career-development program for people with Karen's goals. After meeting with a career counselor, Karen took additional training in aspects of the business outside marketing because people able to function in several areas have more career opportunity than people who specialize in only one. She was given in-house training in operations and enrolled in outside classes in computer technology and finance. She was then assigned to a cross-functional team in which she was able to interrelate with specialists in other departments.

By expanding outside her specialty, Karen participated in *horizontal growth,* opening several doors that may lead her into higher management spots.

Leadership Lead
If opportunities for vertical growth in your company are limited, encourage team members to acquire skills in other areas. By helping people broaden their background, you help them grow in their career and become even more valuable to your organization.

The Outsource Option

Part of the restructuring process has involved *outsourcing.* In this process, a company subcontracts work that formerly had been performed in-house to outsiders who not only can do the work less expensively but also free company management to concentrate on the areas in which it is most competent.

Robert had been in the traffic department of his valve company for 17 years. He had moved up to the number-two position in the department and reported to the vice president for distribution. One day he heard a rumor that the company was planning to eliminate the traffic department and subcontract it to an outside source.

Panicked, Robert confronted his boss, who verified that the company was seriously considering that option. "But what will happen to me?" Robert asked. His boss responded that the move was at least a year away and asked him to consider being the subcontractor. Because Robert knew as much about traffic as anyone in the company, the boss suggested that the company would probably become Robert's first customer and that he was then likely to get additional customers. The boss also suggested that Robert continue in his present job during the transition period but begin the process of developing his new company on his own time. In this way, he could keep things moving smoothly during the transition and be ready to begin functioning as a subcontractor immediately when the new system went into effect.

Companies planning to outsource are often happy to assist one of their own employees in becoming a subcontractor. They can then work with someone they know and trust and who knows their special problems. This process offers to ambitious men and women a career opportunity the company cannot provide internally.

Being an independent entrepreneur isn't for everyone. Risks are involved: You have to raise capital, lease work space, purchase equipment, and hire staff members. And there's always a risk that it won't work out. Being your own boss may sound appealing, but it often involves longer hours and harder work than being employed by a company. In addition, you have to provide your own benefits. Contractors aren't covered by a company health plan, pension fund, or group insurance. People who feel more comfortable under a corporate umbrella may find it difficult to adapt to being in business for themselves.

Developing Team Leaders

Organizational flattening has led to the elimination of many middle-management positions and has reduced the number of layers within many companies. But companies will always have a CEO, senior officers, and some middle managers. And the chief source for filling these openings will be team leaders.

Any member of a team is a potential team leader, and any team leader is a potential higher-level manager. The selection and development of team leaders can therefore be the single most important personnel activity a company undertakes.

Identifying Potential Team Leaders

As a team leader, *you* are the most important source for identifying potential team leaders in your company. This list shows some things you should remember as you evaluate your fellow team members:

- Be a keen observer of their behavior, skills, and personalities.
- Know the goals of each person, and help each one clarify his or her career goals.
- Give each person an opportunity to lead a project, make a report, or chair a meeting.
- Encourage them to take in-house training and enroll in seminars or educational courses.
- Keep your managers aware of your team members' abilities and goals.

Leadership Lead

If your goal is upper management, prepare for it now. Tomorrow's leaders won't be specialists—they'll have experience in several management functions and probably in more than one industry. They'll be comfortable working with computers, statistics, financial and marketing figures, and international business relations. They'll also have superior communication and public-relations skills.

Preparing People for Advancement

As mentioned in chapter 7, the restricted "management track" approach to promotion has been supplanted in most organizations by a more open attitude.

To accomplish this openness, most companies have instituted management-development programs or arranged for management candidates to take outside training. Some programs begin with career-counseling sessions, in which employees meet with human-resources specialists who have been trained in career counseling. Using in-depth interviews, aptitude testing, assessment centers, and discussions with managers and peers, career counselors can evaluate your team members' strengths and limitations. They develop a plan of action to provide internal training and recommendations for outside schooling.

This list mentions some types of management-development programs that are available:

- **Special skills.** Training in areas such as statistics, computers, and specific technical fields.
- **Leadership.** Seminars and courses in psychology, applied leadership, and management techniques through either in-house or outside sources.
- **Problem-solving and decision-making.** Effective seminars and special programs such as the ones offered by Kepner-Tregoe (Princeton, New Jersey).
- **Graduate degrees in management or a technical specialty.** Tuition reimbursement.

Red Alert
Many "development" programs develop little else than income for their promoters. Before you subscribe to a program, send team members to a course, or purchase audio- or videotapes, ask for references from current users. *Check it out.*

Another way to facilitate training for yourself or team members is to purchase materials that people can study on their own time, such as audio- or videotapes or CD-ROM programs (and, although it may seem old-fashioned, books).

You have no assurance that any of these programs by itself will guarantee success, but companies that have invested large sums of money in this type of training continue to do so, which is one indicator that they work for at least those companies.

Introducing the T&D Meeting

A team meeting for T&D (training and development) can be an easy and effective vehicle for ongoing learning—or it can be a complete waste of time. A well-thought-out training

Leadership Lead

A team leader's role in T&D includes the following tasks:

Communication: Ensure that team members are made aware of information that affects their jobs.

Observation: Keep tabs on team members to identify training needs.

Assessment: Measure accomplishments against goals.

Counseling: Work with team members to shore up strengths and strengthen weaknesses.

Helping: Train team members to develop their full potential.

Leadership Lead

Distribute handouts or other reading materials far enough in advance of a meeting to enable team members to study them. The focus of a meeting should be on expanding, demonstrating, and clarifying information; it's not a good place to introduce brand-new concepts, particularly technical or complex material.

meeting can be an effective way to reinforce old knowledge and introduce new ideas. It can serve as a means of getting feedback about how earlier training has been applied and as a guide to what changes should be made. It also gives team members an opportunity to participate in the training process.

Prepare for training meetings by following these suggestions:

- **Set clear objectives.** State clearly the purpose of the meeting: to teach participants a new method, perfect a technique, or develop skills, for example.
- **Choose the method to be used.** You can choose a demonstration followed by practice, a participative workshop, or a problem-solving discussion, for example.
- **Assemble training aids.** Use flip charts, an overhead or slide projector and slides, handouts, videos, computers, and other items to make your meetings more "user-friendly."
- **Use your team members as trainers.** Take advantage of the expertise of your own team members. Assign one or more team members to lead the discussion about different aspects of the material. This technique not only provides information and expertise you may not possess yourself but also leads to a more participative atmosphere.
- **If it's helpful, arrange for backup instructors.** If your background in what's being taught isn't adequate, bring in an expert to conduct the meeting or at least to assist. When you train people in the use of a new piece of equipment or computer program, have a representative from the supplier lead the meeting.

Tips for Conducting Better Training Meetings

Conducting a training meeting is a challenge to a team leader. It must be informative: Participants should leave with more knowledge about the matters that were discussed than they had before the meeting. It should be exciting: Everyone should participate, by asking questions, expressing their agreements and disagreements, and sharing their ideas. It should be motivating: Attendees should leave a meeting eager to put into practice what they have learned.

Here are some suggestions for making your meetings more effective:

- **Treat team members as knowledgeable people, not as schoolchildren.** Team members are adults who are willing to learn.
- **Avoid lecturing.** A lecture is deadly. Make the meeting a participatory experience for all who attend.
- **Don't just repeat what's in the training manual or handouts.** Team members can read it for themselves. You're there to expand, clarify, and elucidate.
- **Prepare for each session.** You should know ten times more about the subject than you present at the meeting.
- **Keep the sessions short.** Keep them short, but not so short that the material can't be adequately covered.
- **Use drama and a sense of humor.** Use your imagination to keep attendees awake, alert, and excited about what they're learning.
- **Use visual aids.** Use appropriate materials to augment what is spoken.
- **Set aside the last five minutes of each session for a summary.** Be sure to clear up any misunderstandings made obvious by participants' questions and comments. If a class lasts more than a day, spend 10 or 15 minutes summarizing the preceding day's discussion.

The Least You Need to Know

- Training never ceases. It's an ongoing part of every job.
- Job skills and personal skills are essential for success. Skills you should develop include the ability to make public presentations, knowledge of a foreign language, and improved interpersonal relations.
- Organizational flattening and restructuring have lessened the opportunity for advancement. Rather than take the direct vertical route, ambitious people must find

new approaches, such as the acquisition of skills outside their current specialty or becoming independent contractors.

- Well-designed career-counseling programs can help team members assess their future opportunities and prepare for them.
- Seek out college courses, seminars, and special training to supplement in-house programs to develop your own leadership skills in addition to those of your team members.
- Periodic training and development meetings, if they're well-planned and conducted effectively, are an excellent way to establish a climate for continuing education.

Part 3
Understanding and Complying with Equal-Employment Laws

You're not a bigot. You believe in fair treatment of everybody regardless of their color, gender, ethnic background, or age. But you are concerned that somewhere along the line you might inadvertently make a comment, ask a question, or do something in good faith—and be accused of violating the law.

Like all laws, the laws governing equal employment opportunity are subject to interpretation. What appears clear and simple, therefore, easily becomes vague and complex.

This part of the book looks at these laws and provides you with some suggestions and guidelines to help you cope with some common problems, such as questions you can and cannot ask an applicant, how to prevent sexual harassment, and making accommodations for people who have special challenges.

Chapter 9

What You Have to Know About Equal Employment Opportunity

In This Chapter

- Hiring under the civil rights laws
- Avoiding age discrimination in hiring, firing, and retiring
- Adhering to the ADA: Abilities, not disabilities
- Understanding the penalties for violating the laws

Your efforts to comply with any law aren't as simple as just reading and understanding the statute. Administrative rulings and various interpretations of the law based on court decisions determine how a law should be applied.

As a manager, the laws governing equal employment opportunity affect most of your decisions that relate to the way you hire, supervise, compensate, evaluate, and discipline personnel.

This chapter looks at these laws and discusses some of the problems you may have in applying them in your job. It explores some of the problems that have plagued employers and what you can do to avoid trouble.

The Laws: An Overview

The laws governing equal employment affect every aspect of your job as a manager. It begins even before your first contact with an applicant and governs all your relations with employees: how you screen candidates, what you pay employees, how you treat employees on the job—all the way to employees' separation from the company, and sometimes even after that.

The main federal laws that apply to equal employment are shown in this list:

- The Civil Rights Act of 1964, as amended, prohibits discrimination in employment on the basis of race, color, sex, religion, or national origin. The section of the law that covers employment (Title VII) is the Equal Employment Opportunity (EEO) law and is administered by the Equal Employment Opportunity Commission (EEOC). The EEOC also administers the Age Discrimination in Employment Act (ADEA) and the Americans with Disabilities Act (ADA).
- The Age Discrimination in Employment Act of 1967, as amended, prohibits discrimination against individuals 40 years of age or older. Some state laws cover all persons over the age of 18.
- The Americans with Disabilities Act of 1990 prohibits discrimination against people who are physically or mentally challenged.
- The Equal Pay Act of 1963 requires that an employee's gender not be considered in determining salary (equal pay for equal work).

Most states have similar laws. Because some state laws are stricter than the federal laws, make sure that you know what your state requires.

In addition, several Presidential executive orders require that certain government contractors and other organizations receiving funds from the federal government institute affirmative-action programs to bring more minorities and women into the workplace (see chapter 10).

Red Alert
The interpretation of EEO laws comes from both administrative rulings and court decisions. As in many legal matters, what seems simple is often complex. It's strongly recommended that you consult an attorney to clarify any actions you take under these laws.

It's important to remember that an employer isn't obligated to hire an applicant just because he or she is in a protected category (such as a person covered by the ADA). An employer can still hire another, better-qualified candidate—it just can't use discriminatory information to *exclude* a candidate who otherwise is most qualified for a job or promotion. A manager must therefore avoid doing, asking, or saying anything discriminatory, to avoid the appearance of discrimination, which can be misinterpreted regardless of whether it was a factor in a hiring or promotion decision.

The Hiring Process

Suppose that you have an opening in your department and you ask your personnel or human-resources department to line up some applicants for you and other team members to interview. You describe the type of person that you believe will fit in best with your team:

> "We're an aggressive, hard-hitting bunch of young guys. Get me a sharp, up-and-coming recent college grad. Most of my boys are Ivy Leaguers, so that will be an asset. And, oh yes, no hippies—get me a clean-living churchgoer."

How many violations of the equal-employment laws are in that statement? Let's review it:

- "Young guys." Violates the prohibition of both age and sex discrimination. Avoid terms that even hint at gender, such as "guys" or "boys."
- "Recent college grad." "Recent" usually means "young." Of course, some people graduate from college in their 40s or older, but they're still the exceptions to the norm. Specifying *or even implying* that a candidate be "young" violates the age-discrimination laws.
- "Ivy-Leaguer." Discriminates against people who, because of their race or religion, have chosen to attend primarily minority colleges or religion-sponsored schools. Also, because minorities are likely to be less affluent and attend less expensive schools, hiring only "Ivy Leaguers" has the effect of discriminating against minorities.
- "Churchgoer." This phrase violates the prohibition against religious discrimination. It can be interpreted as discriminating against people who choose not to belong to any organized religion or as "Christian only" because members of other religions may not attend "church."

What Happens if You Didn't Know That a Question Was Illegal?

Who does the interviewing? In today's companies the human-resources department does preliminary screening, but team leaders and often other team members interview applicants (see part 4, "Choosing Team Members"). Every team member must be thoroughly familiar with EEO laws because an improper question from any interviewer can lead to a formal complaint.

To test yourself, take the following quiz.

What Do You Know About EEO?

To function as a manager today, you must be thoroughly familiar with various state and federal laws concerning equal employment opportunity. To help you measure your knowledge of these laws, we have prepared the following quiz. It covers only a few of the key factors in the laws but should give you some insight into understanding this important area.

Answer Yes or No:

On an application form or in an interview, you may ask:

1. "What are the names of your nearest of kin?" ____
2. "Do you have a permanent immigration visa?" ____
3. "Have you ever been arrested?" ____

Indicate whether each of these help-wanted ads is legal:

4. "Management trainees: College degree; top 10 percent of class only" ____
5. "Accountant: Part-time opportunity for retiree" ____
6. "Sales: Recent college graduate preferred" ____

Other areas:

7. Companies may give tests to applicants to measure intelligence or personality as long as the publisher of the test guarantees that it is nondiscriminatory. ____
8. A company may refuse to employ applicants because they are over 70. ____
9. A company may refuse to employ an applicant if she is pregnant. ____
10. A company may ask whether a woman has small children at home. ____

A company may indicate an age preference if:

11. It is for a training program. ____
12. Older people cannot qualify for the company pension program. ____
13. The job calls for considerable travel. ____

Miscellaneous questions:

14. A company may specify that it requires a man for a job if the job calls for travel. ____
15. The company may specify that it requires an attractive woman to greet customers and visitors. ____

The following quiz answers are based on federal law, but some states have interpreted the laws somewhat differently. In addition, because new laws, administrative rulings, and judicial interpretations are promulgated from time to time, the reasoning on which the answers are based may change. Keep in mind the job-relatedness of the questions and whether the questions asked of applicants have a disparate effect on minorities. These are key factors in determining the legitimacy of the questions.

1. **No.** You cannot ask about next of kin because the response may show national origin if the name differs from the applicant's. You may not even ask whom to notify in case of emergency until after you hire an applicant.
2. **Yes.** Immigration laws require that aliens working in the United States have a permanent immigration visa (green card).
3. **No.** Courts have ruled that because minorities are more likely than nonminorities to be arrested for slight causes, asking about an arrest record is discriminatory. You *can* ask about convictions for felonies (see the section "Criminal Records," later in this chapter).
4. **No.** Unless you can substantiate that students from the top ten percent of their class have performed significantly better than students with lower grades, this ad isn't job-related.
5. **No.** Because most retirees are over the age of 60, specifying a "retiree" implies that persons between the ages of 40 and 60 are not welcome. The Age Discrimination Act protects persons older than 40 against discrimination because of their age.
6. **No.** The phrase "recent college graduate" implies youth. As noted, even the implication of "youth" violates the terms of the ADEA.
7. **No.** The Supreme Court, in Griggs vs. Duke Power Co., upheld the EEOC's requirement that intelligence and personality tests must have a direct relationship to effectiveness on the job for the specific job for which the test is used. Because only the company using the test can verify this relationship, it must be validated against each company's experience.
8. **No.** The Age Discrimination in Employment Act prohibits discrimination against people who are 40 years or older. There is no top age limit.
9. **No.** Pregnant women may not be refused employment unless the work might endanger their health (such as heavy physical work or exposure to dangerous substances). Employers cannot ask an applicant whether she is pregnant or comment that the company doesn't hire pregnant women. If a pregnant woman is rejected, she would have to prove that the reason for the rejection was her pregnancy.
10. **No.** Because men aren't usually asked whether they have small children at home, it has been interpreted as a means of discriminating against women.
11. **No.** Training programs may not be limited to young people.

12. **No.** Participation in a pension program is not an acceptable reason for age discrimination.
13. **No.** Ability to travel is not related to age.
14. **No.** Ability to travel is not related to gender.
15. **No.** A company's desire to have an attractive woman as a receptionist doesn't make it a bona fide occupational qualification (see the following section).

Every manager who hires people should, ideally, score 100 percent on this quiz. Failure to comply with any one of these rules may result in complaints, investigations, hearings, and penalties.

Using Bona Fide Occupational Qualifications (BFOQs)

There are some positions for which a company is permitted to specify only a man or only a woman for the job. Clear-cut reasons must exist, however, for why a person of only that gender can perform the job. In the law, these reasons are referred to as *bona fide occupational qualifications,* or *BFOQs.*

If a job calls for heavy lifting, for example, is it a BFOQ for men only? Not necessarily. Certain strong women may be able to do the job, and certain weak men may not. It's legitimate to require that all applicants—both men and women—pass a weightlifting test.

And that's not all. Suppose that a job calls for driving a forklift truck and that the operator is occasionally required to do heavy lifting. A woman applicant may be able to drive the truck but not be able to do the lifting. If the lifting is only a small part of the job, you cannot reject her. She is capable of performing the major aspect of the work, and other people can be assigned to handle the lifting.

> **Meanings and Gleanings**
> The only undisputed bona fide occupational qualifications are (for a woman) a wet nurse and (for a man) a sperm donor.

Suppose that you have always had an attractive woman as your receptionist and that the job is now open. Is this a BFOQ for a woman? Of course not. There's no reason that a man—with the personality for the position—cannot be just as effective.

"But I Really Need That Information!"

To make sure that the person you hire will, in your judgment, be effective, you believe that there are certain questions you *must* ask. Although civil rights laws vary somewhat from state to state, federal law governs all organizations doing business in the United States. The "lawful and unlawful" questions in Table 9.1 are presented as general guidelines that apply under federal laws and the laws of the strictest states. To ensure that you're in compliance with legal requirements and interpretations in any specific state, however, check with local authorities and an attorney specializing in this field.

(Note that questions which would otherwise be deemed lawful may in certain circumstances be deemed as evidence of unlawful discrimination when the question seeks to elicit information about a selection criterion that isn't job-related and that has a disproportionate effect on the members of a minority group and cannot be justified by business necessity.)

Table 9.1 Legal and Illegal Preemployment Questions

Subject	Lawful	Unlawful
Race or color	None.	Complexion, color of skin, coloring.
Religion or creed	None.	Inquiry into applicant's religious denomination, religious affiliations, church, parish, pastor, or religious holidays observed. Applicants may not be told "This is a Catholic (or Protestant or Jewish) organization."
National origin	None.	Inquiry into applicant's lineage, ancestry, national origin, descent, parentage, or nationality. Spouse's nationality. "What is your native tongue?"
Gender	None.	Any inquiry about gender on application form or interview. "Do you wish to be addressed as Mr., Miss, Mrs., or Ms.?"
Marital status	None.	"Are you married, single, divorced or sepated?" Name or other information about spouse. Where spouse works. "How many children do you have?" "How old are your children?" "What arrangements have you made for child care when you're at work?"
Birth control	None.	Inquiry into capacity to reproduce or advocacy of any form of birth control or family planning.

continues

Table 9.1 Continued

Subject	Lawful	Unlawful
Age	"Are you 18 years or older? If not, state age."	"How old are you?" "What is your date of birth?" "What year did you graduate?"
Disability	"Do you have any impairments (physical, mental, or medical) that would interfere with your ability to perform the job for which you have applied?"	"Do you have a disability?" "Have you ever been treated for any of the following diseases?" (followed by list of diseases).
Arrest record	"Have you ever been convicted of a crime? (Give details.)"	"Have you ever been arrested?"
Name	"Have you ever worked for this company under a different name?" "Is any additional a change of name or use of assumed name or nickname necessary to enable a check of your work record? If yes, explain."	Original name of applicant whose name has been changed by court order or otherwise. Maiden name of married woman. "If you have ever worked under a different name, state name and dates."
Birthplace	None.	Birthplace of applicant Birthplace of applicant's parents, spouse, or other close relatives.
Birthdate	None. (After person is employed, proof of age for insurance or other purposes may be requested.)	Requirements that applicant submit birth certificate, naturalization, or baptismal record. Requirement that applicant produce proof of age in the form of a birth certificate or baptismal record.
Photograph	None.	Requirement or option that applicant affix a photograph to employment form at any time before being hired.

Subject	Lawful	Unlawful
Citizenship	"Are you a citizen of the United States? If not a citizen of the United States, do you intend to become a citizen of the United States? If not a citizen of the United States, have you the legal right to remain permanently in the United States?" (see chapter 10). "Do you intend to remain permanently in the United States?"	"Of what country are you a citizen?" Whether applicant is naturalized or native-born citizen. "On what date did you acquire citizenship?" Requirement that applicant produce naturalization papers or first papers. "Are your parents or spouse naturalized or native-born citizens of the United States?" "On what date did your parents or spouse acquire citizenship?"
Language	Inquiry into languages applicant speaks and writes fluently.	"What is your native language?" or any inquiry into how applicant acquired ability to read, write, or speak a foreign language.
Education	Inquiry into applicant's academic, vocational, or professional education and schools attended.	None.
Experience	Inquiry into work experience.	
Relatives	Names of applicant's relatives other than spouse already employed by company.	Names, addresses, number or other information concerning applicant's spouse, children, or other relatives not employed by company.
Notify in case of emergency	None.	Name and address of person to be notified in case of an emergency. (This information may be asked only after an applicant is employed.)
Military experience	Inquiry into applicant's military experience in the Armed Forces of the United States or in a state militia. Inquiry into applicant's service in specific branch of United States Armed Forces.	Inquiry into applicant's general military experience (for example, a military unit of another country).

continues

Table 9.1 Continued

Subject	Lawful	Unlawful
Organizations	Inquiry into applicant's memberships in organizations the applicant considers relevant to ability to perform job.	"List all clubs, societies, and lodges to which you belong."
Driver's license	"Do you possess a valid driver's license?"	Requirement that applicant produce a driver's license prior to employment.

Marriage and Children

In your desire to obtain as much information as you can about an applicant so that you'll make the right hiring decision, you may ask questions that seem to be important but that violate equal employment opportunity laws. The most frequently asked illegal questions relate to marriage and child care. "But this stuff is important," you might say. "I *need* to know."

Suppose that your team puts in a great deal of overtime—often on short notice. One applicant is a married woman (you noticed the ring on her finger), and you think that you have to know whether she has children at home. You reason that everyone knows that women with children have to pick them up at day care and can't work overtime. Another applicant isn't wearing a ring. Maybe she's divorced. Maybe she has children. You have to find out in order to know her availability, right?

Leadership Lead

In choosing interview questions, ask yourself whether knowing the answers to those questions is necessary to determine whether applicants can do the jobs for which they have applied. Steer clear of questions that even hint at relating to a person's race, religion, national origin, gender, age, or disability.

Wrong, in both cases. Of course it's important to know whether applicants can work overtime on short notice, but you cannot assume their availability to work based on their marital status. In many families the father picks up a couple's children from a day-care facility. The inability to work overtime isn't limited to child-care matters. Anyone—single or married, man or woman—may not be able to work overtime and for many reasons.

How do you deal with this issue? You tell both men and women applicants about the overtime and then ask whether that will be a problem.

Here's a good rule of thumb: Don't ask questions of one gender that you wouldn't ask of the other. "Okay," you think, "I'll ask both men and women about their children, and then I'll be safe." Nope, even this method can be interpreted as discrimination.

If you ask a male applicant how many children he has and he says that he has four, your reaction may be, "Good, here's a stable family man. He'll work hard to support his family."

If you ask a woman applicant the same question and she gives the same answer, do you have the same reaction? Usually not. Managers often think that a woman will stay home from work every time one of her children gets sick, but you can't make that assumption. In many families, both spouses share child-care responsibilities or make arrangements for it.

Don't ask applicants any questions about marriage or family. These types of questions elicit information that may be used to discriminate against women.

Criminal Records

You cannot ask applicants whether they have ever been arrested. Surprised? You shouldn't be. In our judicial system, after all, a person is innocent until proven guilty. Because police are often tougher and more likely to make arrests in minority neighborhoods, asking about arrests has an adverse effect on some minority groups.

You can ask about *convictions* for a felony; however, you cannot refuse to hire a person solely on the basis of a conviction—unless it's job-related. A shoplifting conviction may be a legitimate reason for disqualifying an applicant for a cashier's job, but not a conviction for disorderly conduct.

Lie-Detector Tests

In many companies, because employees handle cash or work with confidential information, you want to do your best to weed out dishonest people. For years companies used polygraphs in screening applicants for these sensitive jobs, but no more! A federal law now restricts the use of these tests.

Employers who are exempt from this law are government agencies, defense contractors, companies providing armed security guards, and a few others.

Although lie-detector tests are not legal in the hiring process, they can still be used as a part of an investigation for theft, embezzlement, industrial espionage, and similar offenses. Before using polygraphs for any purpose, check with your attorney to ensure compliance with federal laws and with any state or local laws that apply.

Age Discrimination

The one area covered by the equal-employment laws that will eventually cover you and everyone else is age discrimination. Despite federal and state laws, the accent on youth in many companies has kept productive men and women from getting and keeping jobs or from functioning at their highest levels in a job. Study after study has shown that mature people are at least as productive and creative as their younger counterparts are and that they are more reliable and make better judgments and decisions.

Bet You Didn't Know

In 1994 more age-discrimination complaints were filed with the Equal Employment Opportunity Commission (EEOC—the federal agency that enforces equal-employment laws) than in any other category.

Avoiding Age Discrimination in Hiring

Even though most company application forms don't ask a person's age or date of birth and most people omit that information from their résumés, it's still easy to guess an applicant's age range within a few years. A team leader who prefers that young people join his or her team may overlook, just because of age, potential members who could be of great value to the team.

When you interview older applicants, avoid the stereotypes that may keep you from hiring highly qualified people for the wrong reason:

- **"The applicant is overqualified."** The term "overqualified" is often a euphemism for "too old." Some people may have more know-how or experience than a job requires, but that doesn't necessarily mean that they won't be productive. Discuss the details of the work with the applicant. It may be an opportunity for the person to learn new things, or he or she may be able to contribute to the job some expertise that makes it more challenging. Judge the person as an individual, not as a member of an age group.
- **"The applicant made more money in the last job."** People with many years of experience often have earned more money than those with less experience. If the amount of salary your company can offer is a factor in your hiring decision, discuss

it with the applicant—he or she should be the one to determine whether the salary is satisfactory. You may worry that if a better-paying job comes along, the new member will jump to it. That may happen, of course, but a younger person would probably do the same.

- **"This person won't fit in with my team."** Being of different age levels isn't necessarily a barrier to cooperation and collaboration. Make that determination on the basis of the candidate's personality, not on his or her age.

Early Retirement

One method companies use to cut costs when they downsize is to compel higher-paid workers (who are most often older men and women) to retire before they had planned. Under current law, employees cannot (with a few minor exceptions) be forced to retire, no matter how old they are, unless they're not capable of performing their work.

Although forcing out older workers is illegal, companies often persuade people to retire by offering them bonuses, benefits, or other rewards. You can use this strategy as long as you do it in good faith and according to the law. Because it's a legal matter, an attorney should prepare the appropriate documents.

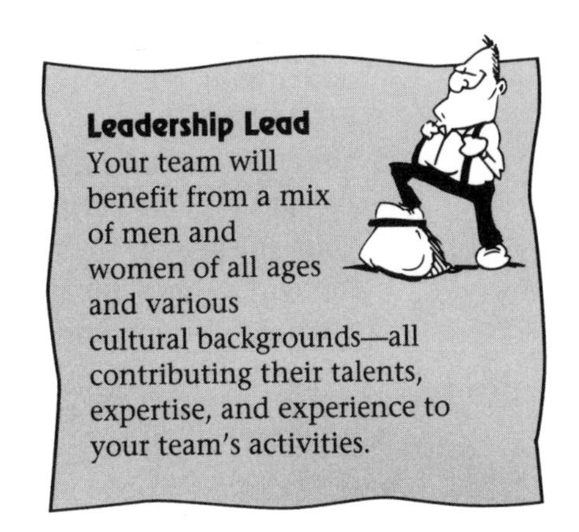

Leadership Lead
Your team will benefit from a mix of men and women of all ages and various cultural backgrounds—all contributing their talents, expertise, and experience to your team's activities.

The Americans with Disabilities Act (ADA)

The newest and probably least understood civil rights law is the Americans with Disabilities Act (ADA). This section discusses some of the highlights of the law and how it applies to you as a manager. Your company must adhere to this law if it has 15 or more employees.

Reasonable Accommodation

The ADA makes it illegal to discriminate in hiring, in job assignments, and in the treatment of employees because of a disability. Employers must make *reasonable accommodation* so that these people can perform the essential duties of their job.

This accommodation can vary from building access ramps for wheelchair users to providing special equipment for people who are seeing- or hearing-challenged, unless this type of accommodation is an undue hardship for the company. Undue hardship is usually defined in monetary terms. If an applicant who uses a wheelchair applies for a job with a small company, the cost of building an elevator or a ramp to give access to the floor on which the job is located may be a financial hardship. Because of this undue hardship, the company could reject the applicant or provide a less expensive accommodation if possible. If the same applicant applied for a job in a more affluent company, however, it may not be considered undue hardship to do the necessary construction.

Accommodation doesn't always require expensive construction. The hypothetical examples in this list examine some other ways to meet this requirement:

- The small company you work for wants to hire someone who uses a wheelchair as an accountant, but the accounting department is on the second floor of your building. The building has no elevator or ramp, and providing one would cost more than the company can afford. Must you do it? No. That would be an *undue hardship* for your company. There may be other ways to accommodate this person, however. Use your imagination. Why not let him work on the ground floor? His work could be brought to him. It may be an inconvenience, but it would qualify as reasonable accommodation—and it would enable you to hire this particular competent accountant.

- A highly skilled word-processor operator is legally blind and walks with the aid of a white cane. She can transcribe from dictated material faster and more accurately than many sighted people can. You want to hire her, but you're concerned that in case of a fire or other emergency she would be a danger to herself and others. The accommodation you can make is to assign someone to escort her in case of an emergency.

- An assembler in a factory was badly injured in an automobile accident, and his job requires him to stand at a workbench all day. When he was ready to return to work, he was unable to stand for long periods. His supervisor sent him home and told him that, until he was able to perform the work as he did before, he could not return. The supervisor was wrong. Accommodations should have been made. Perhaps a high stool could have been provided so that the employee could reach the workbench without having to stand. If that option wasn't feasible, his hours might have been adjusted so that he could work part time on that job and do other work that didn't require standing for long portions of the day.

Alcohol and Drug Abuse

Alcohol and drug users are considered disabled under the ADA. If a person can perform a job satisfactorily, a previous record of alcoholism or drug addiction is not reason enough to refuse hiring or to discipline or terminate a current employee. If an applicant is still addicted, however, and it's manifested in a recent history of poor attendance or poor performance, you can reject or discipline the person—not because of the addiction, but because of poor work habits.

It's legal to discipline employees who use drugs or alcohol in the workplace or who report to work under the influence of an illegal substance.

Red Alert
If you suspect that an employee cannot perform a job because of alcohol or drug abuse, have the person tested. Employees should be made aware that this policy will be followed, and it should be clearly stated in the company's policy manual.

AIDS in the Workplace

You may be concerned about hiring people who have AIDS (acquired immunodeficiency syndrome) or retaining employees who have become infected with this disease. The courts have ruled that AIDS is covered by the ADA.

If your team members see this policy as a problem, point out that all medical reports show that AIDS is not spread by casual contact. To overcome this unjustified fear, follow the example of many companies that have instituted AIDS-awareness programs: Using videos, pamphlets, company newspaper articles, and talks by doctors, they teach their employees the facts about how AIDS is spread.

People Who Are Mentally Challenged: An Overlooked Source

Even in this day of computers and technological sophistication, many types of work are still routine and repetitious, resulting in high turnover among workers who are assigned to that work.

Many companies have found that people who are mentally challenged can do this work and are not bored by it. These people are often capable of learning much more than you might expect. It takes more patience, and some tasks may have to be simplified, but trainees who master these tasks retain the skills and often improve on them. Coaches who are

Leadership Lead
When you interview a candidate for a new job or consider someone for a promotion, don't focus on disabilities. Concentrate on that person's *abilities*.

specially trained to work with people who are mentally challenged are available in many communities. Your local mental-health association can tell you whether this type of help is available in your area.

What Happens if You Violate the Laws

If, after hearings before state or federal agencies responsible for enforcing civil-rights laws, a company is found to be in violation of these laws, any or a combination of the following penalties may be invoked:

- If the complainant is an applicant, you may be required to hire that person with back pay to the date of the interview. If no job is available, a financial settlement will be negotiated.
- If the complainant is a discharged employee, you may have to reinstate that person with back pay from the date of termination.
- If the complainant has been denied a promotion, raise, or other benefit, you will be required to make that person "whole" (promote or give him or her the raise or benefit retroactively).
- If it's a class action, in which a pattern of discrimination is found, all parties to the class action may be awarded a financial settlement (frequently hundreds of thousands of dollars).
- In addition to financial penalties, companies have been required to institute an affirmative-action plan to correct imbalances of minorities or women in the organization.
- Government contractors who violate the law or executive orders may lose their contracts or be banned from receiving future contracts.
- Companies that don't comply with orders from administrative agencies can be prosecuted in the courts and fined. Executives who defy the orders can be jailed.

Bet You Didn't Know

When the Civil Rights Act of 1964 was introduced in Congress, it covered only race, color, religion, and national origin. An opponent of the act added sex discrimination to it because he believed that such a radical provision would make the law unpassable. As they say, the rest is history.

The Least You Need to Know

- Equal employment opportunity laws prohibit discrimination in employment based on color, race, religion, national origin, gender, age, and disability.
- Job specifications should be determined by what's necessary for success on the job, not by preconceived stereotypes.
- Don't ask either men or women applicants questions relating to their marital status or family.
- You cannot refuse to hire or force to retire anyone over the age of 40 just because of age.
- In screening people for hiring, transfer, training programs, or promotion, focus on their abilities, not on their disabilities.

Chapter 10

EEO Problems on the Job

In This Chapter

- Preventing and dealing with sexual harassment
- Making accommodations for religious requirements
- Working with people from diverse cultures
- Complying with affirmative-action laws
- Understanding the family-leave law

Chapter 9 discussed the various laws that relate to equal employment opportunity. This chapter explores some of the major issues you face in applying these laws in the day-to-day management of your team.

In the first 20 years these laws were in effect, most complaints were made in the areas of hiring and firing. Although complaints in those areas are still prevalent, more and more complaints in the past 10 years have involved on-the-job problems, such as sexual harassment and treatment of minorities and women in the workplace.

Sexual Harassment

You read it in the paper; you hear it on television: The president of a famous cosmetics company is accused of sexually harassing 15 female employees, and the company pays the women $1.2 million in an out-of-court settlement. Then a U.S. senator is forced to resign because he is accused of sexually harassing at least 26 women who worked for him.

It's not only company presidents and senators who are accused of sexual harassment. Organizations of all sizes and in every aspect of the working world have had charges brought against them by both female and male employees who claim sexual harassment by managers at all levels and even by nonmanagerial employees.

Bet You Didn't Know

Although sexual harassment on the job has been illegal since 1965, relatively few cases were filed until the sexual-harassment charges made during hearings on the confirmation of Supreme Court Justice Clarence Thomas made the public aware of this aspect of the law. In the three years preceding these hearings, 18,300 sexual-harassment complaints were filed with the EEOC. In the three years following the hearings, 40,800 cases were filed.

The commonly accepted definition of sexual harassment isn't always the same as the legal definition of the term. The legal definition of sexual harassment covers much more than just demanding sexual favors for favorable treatment on the job (naturally, these types of demands are included).

Here's the way the courts and the EEOC define sexual harassment: Any unwelcome sexual advances or requests for sexual favors or any conduct of a sexual nature when:

- Submission is made explicitly or implicitly a term or condition of initial or continued employment.
- Submission or rejection is used as a basis of working conditions including promotion, salary adjustment, assignment of work, or termination.
- Such conduct has the purpose or effect of substantially interfering with an individual's work environment or creates an intimidating, hostile, or offensive work environment.

But what does this mean in plain English? This section looks at how this concept works on the job.

"Explicit" Is Clear, but What's "Implicit"?

You would think that a corporate president or a senator would have enough common sense to refrain from making explicit sexual demands, but it still happens. Some men (and a few women) in positions of authority make it clear to subordinates that if they want to get favorable treatment or even keep their jobs, they must submit to these demands. But the harassment is often much more subtle. Even if no actual demands are made, implication by references to other employees who benefited by being "more friendly" or comments about a person's physical attributes and similar remarks can be interpreted as harassment.

"Wait a minute," you say. "If I tell a woman that she's attractive, *that's* harassment?" It depends on what you say and how you say it.

The comment "That's an attractive dress" is much different from the comment "That dress is sexy." The statement "I like your new hairdo" is also acceptable, but the statement "Wearing your hair like that excites me" is not.

Randy is a "toucher." When he greets men and women, he grasps their hands, pats them on the back, and gives them hugs. That's his way of expressing his personality, and he has been doing it for years. He also is a kisser. He doesn't kiss his male associates, but when he greets his female colleagues, he often pecks them on the cheek. Randy was shocked when he was called into the human-resources office and told that some of the women in his department had complained about his hugging and kissing. In Randy's eyes, these acts were acts of friendship with no sexual connotation, but to the women who complained, they were unwelcome.

Leadership Lead
Unless you know someone well, other than the traditional handshake, don't hug, don't pat, and certainly don't kiss. Remember the platinum rule (refer to chapter 2): "Do unto others as they would have you do unto them."

Dealing with an Intimidating, Hostile Work Environment

As noted in the legal definition, sexual harassment isn't limited to demands for sexual favors: It also includes conduct that creates an intimidating and hostile work environment.

Ken's team has always been all-male, and now two women have been added to his group. Some of the men resent this "intrusion" on their masculine camaraderie and make life unpleasant for the female team members. The men make snide remarks, give the women wrong information that causes them to make errors, and exclude them from work-related discussions. No actions are taken that can be interpreted as "sexual" in nature, but it still qualifies as sexual harassment. The men have created a hostile work environment for the women.

Tina works in a warehouse. She is offended by the street language some of the men continually use. When she complains, she is told, "That's the way these guys talk. They talked this way before women worked here, and they're not going to change now. Get used to it."

Many men are just as offended by this kind of language as women are. Because people may find that this language creates "an offensive work environment," offensive language does create legal grounds for a complaint.

If you're faced with a similar situation, talk to the people (or person) using the inappropriate language. Diplomatically point out that this behavior offends both women and men and that it isn't appropriate to use it in a business environment. Inform them that it can cause legal problems for the company and for them as individuals. Tell them that if they continue to use street language they will be subject to the same type of disciplinary action as what is given for violating other company work rules.

Dating, Romance, and Marriage on the Job

Cathy was perplexed. Dennis, one of her team members, had gone out a few times with Diane, who worked in another department. It never developed into a romance, but Diane kept bugging Dennis to go out with her again. Diane came into Dennis' office several times a day to talk with him, but Dennis didn't welcome her visits. It interfered with his work, and he wasn't interested in seeing her. The next time Diane came into the office, Cathy called her aside and told her that social visits were not permissible. She didn't go back, but she continued to harass him by telephoning him after work.

Is the company off the hook? Not yet. Even though the harassment has ceased on the job, because both Dennis and Diane are employed by the same company, the company has an obligation to stop Diane from bothering Dennis. Cathy should discuss the situation with Diane's' manager and, if necessary, with the human-resources department. If Diane continues her harassment, appropriate disciplinary action should be taken.

Dating isn't always unwelcome. Many romances that start on the job develop into marriages. But what effect does it have on your team when two associates become romantically involved? This situation can be a delicate one. Some companies, fearing that close relatives working together will lead to complications, prohibit parents, children, siblings, and spouses from working on the same team or even in positions in which they must interrelate.

Relationships other than spousal relationships are not covered by law and are left to the discretion of companies. When it comes to marriage, additional complexities are possible.

If a company prohibits married couples from working together and two team members marry, which one should leave the team? Some companies base their policy on rank (the lower-ranking spouse leaves) or salary (the lower-paid spouse leaves). Because it may be more likely for the man to be the higher-ranked or higher-paid employee, this policy discriminates against women. If this type of policy exists in your company, the best way to deal with it is to let the couple make the determination about which one will leave.

> **Leadership Lead**
> Why lose productive workers because of an archaic rule? Most married couples work well together and have enough control over their own lives not to bring their personal problems into the workplace.

Discrimination based on marital status isn't expressly prohibited by federal law, but it is barred by administrative interpretation of the sex-discrimination clauses. Some states do have specific laws prohibiting discrimination based on marital status.

Harassment from Outsiders

Suppose that one of the salespeople who comes into your office makes a point of telling off-color jokes to the women who work there. Some of them think that he's hilarious, but you notice the look of disgust on the faces of others. Although no complaints have been made, you see that the behavior is creating an offensive work environment. The salesperson doesn't work for your company, but you still have an obligation to do something about it.

The courts have ruled that an employer is responsible for the offensive behavior of all its employees (regardless of whether they're in management) and even non-employees when the employer or its agents (that's you, in this case) know about it *or should have known* about it.

> **Leadership Lead**
> Companies can protect themselves from charges of sexual harassment by clearly notifying all employees that the behavior will not be tolerated and by establishing and publicizing a procedure for dealing with complaints. This policy should be administered by a senior executive and all complaints, if true, investigated and quickly corrected.

Speak to the person on whom that sales rep calls. Tell him or her to discuss the matter with the sales rep. If the undesirable behavior continues, the company has an obligation to tell the salesperson that it cannot continue doing business with him.

Note that your company is responsible not only when it knows about the offensive behavior but also *when it should have known* about it. This point is a delicate one. How are you supposed to know about everything that might happen?

You can't, of course, but if you're observant, you should know a great deal about what transpires.

Religion in the Workplace

The law requires you to make reasonable accommodation for a person's religious practices unless it results in undue hardship on your company.

Sometimes accommodation is easy. Suppose that your company is open seven days a week and that members of your team take turns working on Saturdays and Sundays. David can never work on Saturdays, but you can schedule him for Sunday work. If you're not open on Sunday and you have other employees who can work Saturdays, you're required to excuse David from Saturday assignments. The other employees may resent having to work on Saturday, but the unhappiness of other employees doesn't qualify as "undue hardship."

Meanings and Gleanings

According to the EEOC, religious practices include not only traditional religious beliefs but also moral and ethical beliefs and any beliefs an individual holds "with the strength of traditional religious views."

If your business is small and there aren't enough people qualified in the work to be done to cover the Saturday shift, it may be considered an undue hardship, and you would not have to hire David.

Here are two other religious considerations in the workplace:

- **Religious holidays:** Employees must be given time off to observe their religious holidays, although you're not required to pay them for these days. These holidays usually are considered excused absences and are charged against personal or vacation days.
- **Proselytizing on company premises:** Margaret, a devout member of her denomination, believed that it was her mission to convert people to her religion. She continually pressed her religious beliefs on her coworkers and distributed tracts and other religious literature. At the request of team members, her team leader asked her to refrain from this behavior. She refused, claiming that the religious accommodation law and the First Amendment gave her the right to proselytize. Margaret was wrong. Just as a company can prohibit political campaigning on company premises and during working hours, it can restrict religious behavior that disturbs other people in the workplace.

Other Areas of Concern

Suppose that you're upset that some of the young people on your team come to work dressed in clothes that are more appropriate for leisure activities. The women wear shorts and tank tops; the men, shirts open to their navels. What can you do about it?

It's not illegal to require people to obey a *dress code* as long as it doesn't discriminate. If women were prohibited from wearing shorts, for example, but nothing was done about the men's open shirts, it would not be considered equal treatment under the law. Prohibiting a Muslim woman from dressing as prescribed by her religion or an Orthodox Jew from wearing a yarmulke would also violate the law's religious provisions.

Dress codes may vary within a company depending on the type of work that's done. Dress codes for factory and warehouse workers are different from those of office employees and employees who deal with the public.

Don't overdo it. Even IBM has dropped its requirement that male employees wear dark suits, white shirts, and blue ties and that women wear dark dresses or suits. As long as what an employee wears is in good taste, it should be acceptable.

Another area of concern is smoking: If you want to stop employees from smoking in your work area, can you do it?

Despite the surgeon general's warning and increasing evidence of the dangers of secondhand smoke, no federal law prohibits smoking on the job. Several states and local communities have laws, however, that restrict smoking in commercial buildings.

Even in areas in which no local laws apply to this situation, many companies have either prohibited smoking or restricted it to specific areas.

In some companies that have no company-wide policy, team members determine the smoking policy for their work area. These policies vary from total prohibition to restricting smoking places and times to no restrictions.

Bet You Didn't Know

Unless the need to speak English is job related, you cannot require that employees speak only English in the workplace. Employees who normally speak a different language and are more comfortable conversing in their native tongue cannot be compelled to speak English among themselves.

Employing Non-U.S. Citizens

You're worried. You continually read about companies that get into trouble for hiring undocumented aliens (no, not Martians—people from foreign countries). You're almost afraid to hire anyone who has a foreign accent.

Not hiring someone because of this fear is illegal. You cannot discriminate against a person because he or she isn't an American. But you must ensure that an applicant is legally allowed to work in this country.

To ensure that your company doesn't inadvertently fall afoul of immigration laws, follow these guidelines:

- **Have all new employees (not just those that you suspect are foreign) fill out an I-9 form.** You can obtain copies from the Immigration and Naturalization Service. This form should not be completed until *after* a person is hired. When a starting date is agreed on, the employee should be advised that he or she must submit proper documentation before being put on the payroll.
- **Have new employees provide documents to prove their identity.** You have to be sure that a new employee isn't using someone else's papers. Acceptable documents include a driver's license with photo, a school ID with photo, and similar papers.
- **Have new employees provide documents to prove citizenship.** These documents include a current U.S. passport, certificate of naturalization, birth certificate, or voter-registration card.
- **Noncitizens must have documents that authorize employment.** The most commonly used authorization is INS Form I-551, commonly called the "green card" (it originally was green, but now it's white). The employee's photograph is laminated to the card. Other forms are acceptable for students who may work while in school and some other exceptional cases.

The Diverse Workforce

If your team consists of men and women who come from different cultures, it can lead to misunderstandings and conflicts. As a team leader, you cannot ignore this situation. Your job is to make your team a smooth-running, collaborative group. It isn't always easy to change a person's deeply ingrained perceptions. Newcomers to America must be taught American ways, and Americans must learn to understand the attitudes and customs of newly arrived immigrants.

Digital Equipment Corporation (DEC) has set up a program to address this situation. Small groups of employees meet regularly to explore assumptions and stereotypes about their own culture and those of others. This list shows some of the goals of DEC's program:

- To identify and eliminate preconceptions and myths about new ethnic groups in the company.
- To overcome the tendency of people to fraternize with people of only their own ethnic group. All DEC employees—Americans and new immigrants—are encouraged to make friends with people from other backgrounds.
- To become aware of assumptions that cause differences in the perception of other cultures and to take steps to correct them.

A large company such as DEC has resources you may not have available to you, but, with a little imagination and sensitivity, any team leader can adopt a similar program.

Affirmative Action

Under current civil rights laws, you're not required to give to women or minorities any preferential treatment in hiring or promotion. Companies with government contracts or organizations that receive federal funds, however, fall under an executive order requiring them to establish formal affirmative-action plans (AAP).

If your firm has an AAP, it was probably drawn up by a specialist in the legal or human-resources department. You don't have to worry about the technical aspects of this plan: All you have to know about is the company's goals for various minority groups and women for your department so that you can make every effort to comply with them.

If your department isn't in line with the affirmative-action goals of your company, you should make an effort to hire or promote a person from the group in which the deficiency exists. This advice doesn't mean that you must hire unqualified people just because of their minority status. If you have two candidates with relatively equal qualifications, you're expected to give preference to the minority candidate even if he or she needs more support or training to become productive.

At the time this book went to press, both Congress and the President were contemplating changes in affirmative-action requirements. As new regulations are approved, the EEOC or the Department of Labor will publicize them through the media and send formal notification to companies who have filed plans.

Meanings and Gleanings

Companies that have government contracts in excess of $50,000 and more than 50 employees must have a written **affirmative-action plan** committed to hiring women and minorities in proportion to their representation in the community in which the firm is located.

Bet You Didn't Know

If your community has a population made up of Italians, Hungarians, Slavs, and Poles, you don't have to have an affirmative-action plan to staff your company with a proportionate number of employees from each of these groups. Affirmative action is required only for African-Americans, Hispanics, Asians and Pacific Islanders, Native Americans, and women.

Twelve Ways to Keep Alert to Your EEO Responsibility

Go along with the spirit as well as the letter of the law.

Offer women and minorities opportunities that were previously denied to them.

Open training programs to minorities, women and the physically challenged, and encourage them, by offering counseling and support, to complete these programs.

Discipline should be administered equitably and should be carefully documented.

Be aware of your own biases and work to overcome any influence they may have on your job decisions.

Use everyone's abilities optimally. Don't base your views about a person's abilities on age, sex, or race. Judge people not on what they cannot do, but on what they *can* do.

Set realistic performance standards based on what a job really calls for. Do not specify, for example, that a job calls for heavy lifting when most of the lifting is done mechanically.

Ignore stereotypes and judge people by their individual abilities, strengths, and weaknesses.

Never use racial epithets or slurs—even in jest.

Encourage all people to deal with their coworkers as human beings, whether they're black or white; Hispanic, Asian, or Anglo; men or women; physically challenged or able-bodied. Mold them into a team.

Sex life and job life must be kept separate.

Support your company's equal-employment and affirmative-action programs fully in every aspect of your job.

Follow these suggestions. They add up to good business.

The Family and Medical Leave Act

Congress passed the Family and Medical Leave Act (FMLA) in 1993, which requires companies with 50 or more employees to provide to eligible employees as much as 12 weeks of unpaid leave in any 12-month period for the following reasons:

- The birth or adoption of a child or the placement of a child for foster care.
- To care for a spouse, child, or parent with a serious health condition.
- The employee's own serious health condition.

To be eligible, the employee must have been employed by the company for at least 12 months and must request this leave at least 30 days before the expected birth or adoption of the child. When this notification isn't possible, such as the onset of a serious illness of a family member, employees are required to provide as much notice as possible.

Both men and women are eligible for leave under this law. If both husband and wife work for the same employer, however, the total amount of leave is limited to 12 weeks for the couple.

The key provisions of the law make these requirements:

- The company must provide the employee, after returning from the leave, with the same position or with a position with equivalent pay, benefits, and other conditions of employment.
- Health insurance must be continued during the leave period and paid for in the same manner as though the employee were still on the payroll.

As with most laws, variations apply in special circumstances. For example, Dick's mother receives outpatient chemotherapy every Tuesday, and Tom brings her to the hospital on Tuesday and stays with her on Wednesday while she regains her strength. Although the law primarily calls for continuing periods of leave, special arrangements can be made so that Dick can take off the time he needs. If the type of work Dick does makes this arrangement unfeasible, however, the company has the right to transfer him temporarily to another job with the same pay and benefits that enable him to take the days off.

To obtain the details about how this law may affect you or a team member, check with your human-resources department, legal department, or local office of the Wage and Hour Division of the U.S. Department of Labor (listed in the U.S. government pages of most local telephone directories).

The Least You Need to Know

- Sexual harassment isn't limited to demands for sexual favors: It also includes permitting a work environment that is hostile or offensive to employees because of their gender.
- Protect your company from sexual harassment situations by having a strict policy that that type of behavior will not be tolerated—and then enforce it.
- Companies must make provisions for employees to observe their personal religious practices.
- Encourage employees from different cultural backgrounds to get to know each other as people—not as members of an ethnic group.
- If your company has an affirmative-action plan, you're required to seek out members of protected minority groups and women for hire and promotion.
- Be aware that employees may take as much as 12 weeks off (without pay) to care for a family member with no loss of benefits and the guarantee of returning to the same or equivalent job.

Part 4
Choosing Team Members

It's your dream—to build a dream team. Team leaders rarely have the opportunity to choose a full team, but from time to time new members are added—either as replacements for people who have left or because the team expands.

Choosing a new team member can be one of your most important acts as a team leader. You'll probably have to live with this person for a long time, so do it carefully, do it systematically, and use all the tools available to help you make the best decision.

This part of the book provides you with the know-how you need so that the next time you have a vacancy on your team, you'll get one more chance to hire that man or woman who will bring you closer to making your team the team of your dreams.

Chapter 11

Creating Realistic Job Specs

In This Chapter

- Identifying the skills necessary to do a job
- Reevaluating existing jobs
- Making a job analysis when you create a new job
- Matching job specs to a job description
- Pricing a job

Suppose that you have an opening in your department. You want to fill that position with a person who has the necessary skills to perform the required duties of a job and who can contribute to the success of your team. Before you can even begin searching for this person, however, you had better have a clear and realistic concept of what you need.

The job you're seeking to fill may be a replacement for a person who has left your team, and you may have a job description for that job. The easy way is just to use the existing job description, but that's not necessarily the best way. This is your chance to review the description in light of the changes that may have developed since it was originally written. Reanalyze the job. Treat it as though it were a brand-new position. In this way, the new job description will reflect the current duties and activities of the job.

Creating a Good Job Description

Job descriptions are important. Even if you know the job requirements as well as you know the back of your hand, however, you still need a written job description in order to begin the hiring process. This description serves many useful purposes:

- **Hiring.** Develop realistic job specifications that enable you to seek out candidates who can do what a job requires them to do.
- **Training.** Determine what knowledge has to be acquired and which skills have to be developed in your training program.
- **Reference.** Devise a permanent source of reference concerning job duties for team leaders and members.
- **Performance.** Create a list of standards against which performance can be measured so that everyone knows just what is expected in a job. Each person can measure his or her own performance against those standards.
- **Appraisal.** When a formal performance appraisal is made (see chapter 19), the job description becomes a touchstone against which performance can be evaluated.

Critics of the use of job descriptions are concerned that the descriptions stifle creativity and innovation. They fear that many people will take it too literally and be unwilling to do anything not specifically listed.

How often have you asked someone to do something other than their routine work and heard the response, "It's not in my job description"? All job descriptions should include the phrase "and any other duties that are assigned." The inclusion of this phrase doesn't mean that you have a servant who can be ordered to do any job that pops up. It means that you can assign duties that are at least job-related.

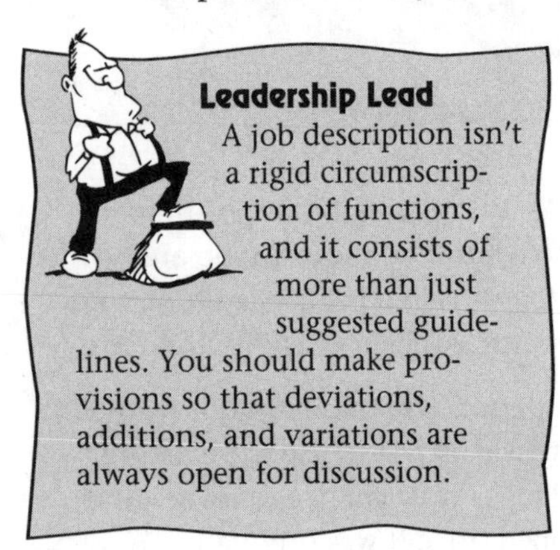

Leadership Lead

A job description isn't a rigid circumscription of functions, and it consists of more than just suggested guidelines. You should make provisions so that deviations, additions, and variations are always open for discussion.

Suppose that Don finishes typing a document and you ask him to please take it to the purchasing department. He refuses and says, "I'm an executive assistant, not a messenger. Delivering papers isn't in my job description." That's true: It's not specified, but it *is* a related duty.

On the other hand, if you say, "Don, you're not busy now; please wash the windows," you're out of line. Your request falls under the phrase "other duties," but it isn't a reasonable extension of his regular work.

Replacing Someone Who Has Left Your Company

Meg was a great customer-service representative. Before she left your company, she was not only a good worker but also a contributor to your team and a pleasure to work with. You want to hire another Meg, so you study her background. Because Meg had a liberal arts degree, you believe that the person you hire should have a liberal arts degree. Meg had previous experience in the theater, so you think that a theatrical background would be good. Meg learned computer operations on the job, so you intend to train your new employee to use computers.

> **Meanings and Gleanings**
> When you perform a **job analysis**, you determine the duties, functions, and responsibilities of a job (the **job description**) and the requirements for successful performance of that job (the **job specifications**).

Stuart was a difficult person to work with—he wasn't a team player. You want someone quite different from Stuart. Because he had a degree in marketing, you don't want any marketing majors. Stuart had been active in politics; no politicians. Because Stuart had IBM experience and you had to train him to use the Macintosh, you definitely don't want anyone with IBM experience.

The background of people who have been successful as well as those who have not been successful in performing a particular job should be a factor, but not the primary factor, in determining which qualities you should seek in the new person you employ.

Meg's liberal arts degree and Stuart's political background aren't necessarily related to what a job does or does not require. To learn the key requirements, make a thorough *job analysis*.

Creating a Brand-New Position

> **Leadership Lead**
> Don't base your job specifications on your version of an ideal team member. That person probably exists only in your mind. Be realistic. Your specs should reflect those factors the new member should bring to the job that will contribute to the team's successful performance.

Suppose that you have *finally* persuaded your boss to authorize the hiring of an additional member to your team. Because this position is a new one, what exactly do you want it to cover?

If the new position is for another person who will just perform exactly the same duties as other team members, you can use the same job description and specifications used by team members. In our ever-changing business world, however, a team's functions constantly expand and new functions and responsibilities require different talents and abilities. You have to create a completely new job analysis.

Making a Job Analysis

The specialists who perform job analyses may be industrial engineers, systems analysts, or members of your human-resources staff. If your company employs these people, use them as a resource. The best people to make an analysis, however, are those closest to a job—you and your team members. A job analysis should include a written description of the responsibilities that fall within a job (*job description*) and a written description of the skills and background required to perform a job effectively (*job specification*).

Four Techniques for Developing a Job Description

To make a realistic job description, follow the guidelines in this list:

- **Observe.** For jobs that are primarily physical in nature, watching a person perform the job will give you most of the material you need to write the description. If several people are engaged in the same type of work, observe more than one performer.

  Even a good observer, however, may not understand what he or she is observing. Sometimes it involves much more than meets the eye. In jobs that are not primarily manual, however, there is little that you can learn from observation alone. Just watching someone sitting at a computer terminal, for example, isn't enough to learn what's being done.

- **Question the performer.** Ask the people who perform a job to describe the activities they perform. This technique fleshes out what you're observing. You must know enough about the work, of course, to be able to understand what is being said and to be able to ask appropriate questions. It's a good idea to prepare a series of questions in advance.

- **Question the supervisor or team leader.** If you are the team leader, review in your mind how you view the position, what you believe the performer should be doing, and the standards that are acceptable. If you're analyzing a job other than the ones you supervise, speak to the team leader or supervisor to obtain that person's perspective of the position.

- **Make it a team project.** When work is performed by a team, job descriptions cover the work of the entire team. The best way to develop a complete job description is to get your entire team into the act.

The job-description worksheet on the following page is a helpful tool. Tailor the form you use to the type of job you're analyzing.

Job Description Worksheet

Job title: ____________________

Reports to: ____________________ Dept.: ____________

Duties performed: ____________________

____

____

Equipment used: ____________________

____

Skills used: ____________________

____

Leadership responsibility: ____________________

____

Responsibility for equipment: ____________________

____

Responsibility for money: ____________________

____

Other aspects of job: ____________________

____

Special working conditions: ____________________

____

Performance standards: ____________________

____

Analysis made by: ____________________ Date: ____________

Understanding the Components of a Job Specification

After you know just what a job entails, you can determine which qualities you seek for the person who will be assigned to do the job.

The job specifications in some situations must be rigidly followed; others may allow for some flexibility. In civil-service jobs or in cases in which job specs are part of a union contract, for example, even a slight variation from job specs can have legal implications. In some technical jobs, a specific degree or certification may be mandated by company standards or to meet professional requirements. For example, an accountant making formal audits must be a certified public account (CPA); an engineer who approves structural plans must be licensed as a professional engineer (PE). On the other hand, if there's no compelling reason for the candidate to have a specific qualification, you may deviate from the specs and accept an equivalent type of background.

Leadership Lead

When you set up specs for a job, ask yourself, "What must the applicant be able to do that I either cannot or do not want to train him or her to do?" Keep in mind that your team will be stronger if it includes people with different but complementary skills (as opposed to a number of people who all have identical strengths, weaknesses, and capabilities).

Most job specifications include the elements in this list:

- **Education:** Does a job call for college? Advanced education? Schooling in a special skill?
- **Skills:** Must the candidate be skilled in computers? Machinery? Drafting? Statistics? Technical work? Any of the skills necessary to perform a job?
- **Work experience:** What are the type and duration of previous experience in related job functions?
- **Personal characteristics:** Does a candidate have the necessary skills in communication, interpersonal relations, and patience? Does he or she have the ability to do heavy lifting?

Eliminating Good Prospects for the Wrong Reason

One of the most common problems in determining the specifications for a job is having the requirement of a higher level of qualifications than is really necessary, thus knocking out potentially good candidates for the wrong reason. This problem frequently occurs in these areas:

- **Education.** Suppose that certain job specs call for a college degree. Is that degree necessary? It often is, but having the degree just as often has no bearing on a person's ability to succeed in a job. Requiring a higher level of education (or, for that matter, any qualification) has more disadvantages than advantages. You may attract smart and creative people, but often a job doesn't challenge them, which results in low productivity and high turnover. More important, you may turn away the best possible candidates for a position by putting the emphasis on a less important aspect of the job.

Leadership Lead
To ensure that the person you hire can do a job, the job specs should emphasize what you expect the applicant to have *accomplished* in previous jobs—not just the length of his or her experience.

- **Duration of experience.** Your job specs may call for ten years' experience in accounting, but why specify ten years? No direct correlation exists between the number of years a person has worked in a field and that person's competence. Lots of people have ten years' on a job but only one year's experience (after they've mastered the basics of the job, they plod along, never growing or learning from their experience). Other people acquire a great deal of skill in a much shorter period.

  It's not that years of experience don't count for anything, however. Often, the only way a person can gain the skills necessary to do a good job, make sound decisions, and make mature judgments is by having extensive experience. Just counting the years, however, isn't the way to determine that ability.

  Rather than specify a number of years, set up a list of factors a new employee should bring to a job and how qualified the person should be in each area. By asking an applicant specific questions about each of these factors, you can determine what he or she knows and has accomplished in each area.

- **Type of experience.** Another requirement job specs often mandate is that an applicant should have experience in "our industry." Skills and job knowledge often can be acquired only in companies that do similar work. In many jobs, however, a background in other industries is just as valuable and maybe even better because the new associate isn't tradition-bound and will bring to a job original and innovative concepts.

- **Preferential factors.** Some job specs are essential to perform a job, but other factors, although not critical, would add to a candidate's value to your company. In listing preferential factors, use them as *extra assets* and don't eliminate good people simply because they don't have that qualification.

  It may be an extra benefit if a candidate already knows how to use a certain type of computer software, for example, but because that knowledge can be picked up on the job, eliminating a person who is otherwise well qualified might be a mistake.

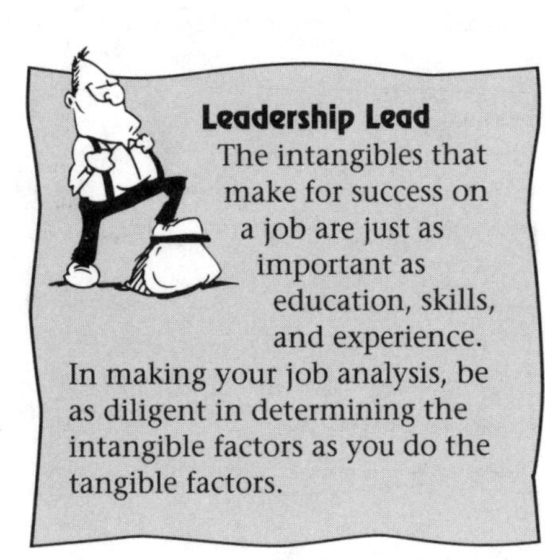

Leadership Lead
The intangibles that make for success on a job are just as important as education, skills, and experience. In making your job analysis, be as diligent in determining the intangible factors as you do the tangible factors.

- **Intangible factors:** Intangible factors can be as important (or even more important!) than some tangible requirements.

  Of course, you want to hire people with high intelligence, creativity, integrity, loyalty, and enthusiasm and who have a positive attitude. When you list the intangible requirements for a job, however, put them in proper perspective as they relate to a job.

  If a job calls for communication skills, specify exactly which communication skills you need: for example, one-to-one communication, the ability to speak to large groups, innovative telephone-sales methods, or creative letter-writing skills.

  If a job calls for "attention to detail," specify what type of detail work. If a job calls for "the ability to work under pressure," indicate what type of pressure (for example, daily deadlines, occasional deadlines, round-the-clock sessions, difficult working conditions, or a demanding boss).

Ensuring Built-in Flexibility

Job specs can be so rigid that you're unable to find anyone who meets all your requirements. Sometimes you have to make compromises. Reexamine the job specs and set priorities. Which of the specs is nonnegotiable? These requirements are the ones a new team member must bring to a job or else there is no way the job can be done. For example, a candidate must have a degree in electrical engineering or else the work she performs cannot be approved by the government; unless the candidate is a certified public accountant, he cannot conduct audits; unless a candidate can do machine work to precise tolerances, the work will not pass inspection.

Some of the specs may be important but not critical. For example, although having a CPA degree may be a good credential, an internal auditor doesn't have to be certified; or, although the specs for a job require knowledge of certain software, experience with different but similar software might do almost as well.

Suppose that your specs call for sales experience but that an applicant has no job experience in selling. As a volunteer, however, she was a top fund-raiser for the local community theater. That person may be able to do the job. In seeking to fill a job, a team leader should make every effort to meet the job specs but should also have the authority to use his or her judgment to determine when deviation from the job specs is acceptable.

Determining How Much to Pay

Another part of job analysis involves determining the pay scale for a job. Most organizations have a formal job-classification system in which various factors are weighed to determine the value of a job. These factors include level of responsibility, contribution of a job to a company's bottom line, type of education, and training and experience necessary to perform the job. Notice that the classification applies to a *job,* not to the person performing a job.

Knowing What to Do When You Have No Formal Pay Program

The pricing of a job in smaller organizations is often done haphazardly: You pay what you have to pay in order to hire the person you want. But you must have some guidelines about what a job is worth so that you don't pay more than necessary or offer too little and not attract good applicants. You have to determine the "going rate" for a job you want to fill.

This list shows some of the sources for obtaining information about the salary scales in your community or industry:

- **Trade and professional associations.** These groups conduct and publish periodic salary surveys. Members of these associations can discern how their pay scales compare with other companies in their field and in their geographic area. These surveys are best used when you seek salary information for specialists in your industry or profession.
- **Chambers of commerce.** Some chambers of commerce publish salary surveys for their locations. Because these surveys include a variety of industries, you can obtain salary information about jobs that exist in a variety of companies, such as computer operators and clerical personnel.
- **Employment agencies.** These agencies can inform you about the going rate for any type of position in which they place employees.
- **Networking.** Ask people you know who are managers in other companies in your community or industry. They often are willing to share information about going rates.

Meanings and Gleanings

To attract and keep good employees, your pay scale must be at least as high as the **going rate**, which is the salary paid for similar work in your industry or community.

The Least You Need to Know

- Base your job requirements on job factors, not on the background of people currently doing the job.
- When you analyze a job, observe the people performing the job and discuss with them and their managers what they do.
- Job descriptions are more than just guidelines. You should take them very seriously. To avoid stagnation, provisions for flexibility should be built-in to the description.
- Base job specifications on the job description. This technique enables you to choose people for a position who are capable of doing the job.
- By overqualifying a job, you eliminate otherwise qualified people for the wrong reasons.
- Know the going rates for your jobs so that you don't overpay or underpay your associates.

Chapter 12

Choosing Mr. or Ms. Right

In This Chapter

- Choosing between insiders and new hires
- Studying applications and résumés
- Preparing interview questions that provide meaningful information
- Conducting an interview

You have a job opening on your team, and you've prepared the job description and job specs. Now you're ready to screen applicants.

The first thing you should do is contact your human-resources department. The HR team is composed of experts in recruiting and choosing personnel and usually takes care of most of the initial steps in the hiring procedure. The HR department can provide you with advice that can save you the time and effort involved in the part of the hiring process you do yourself. An important part of their responsibility is that they're aware of all the legal implications involved in this delicate area and can help you avoid problems.

Applicants can come from many sources. People working in other positions in your company may fit your needs—look there first. In addition, you can seek people from outside your organization through a variety of channels.

This chapter explains how to recruit personnel and provides some tips for evaluating application forms and résumés and conducting interviews that will give you meaningful information on which to base your hiring decisions.

The First Place to Look: Within Your Own Organization

People who already work for your company may make valuable members of your team. They may work at jobs in which they don't use their full potential, or they may be ready for new challenges. Joining your team would be a move up for them. Even if an opening isn't an immediate promotion, a lateral transfer might enable that person to take a step forward in reaching her or his career goals.

Taking Advantage of Internal Transfers

Not every transfer is a promotion, but it's often an opportunity for someone to learn, gain experience, and take a step forward in preparing for career advancement.

Seeking to fill a team vacancy from within a company has many advantages:

- People who already work in your company know the "lay of the land." They're familiar with your company's rules and regulations, customs and culture, and practices and idiosyncrasies. Hiring these people rather than someone from outside your company saves time in orientation and minimizes the risks of dissatisfaction with your company.
- You know more about these people than you can possibly learn about outsiders. You may have worked directly with a certain person or observed him or her in action. You can get detailed and honest information about a candidate from previous supervisors and company records.
- Offering opportunities to current employees boosts morale and serves as an incentive for them to perform at their highest level.
- An important side effect is that it creates a positive image of your company in the industry and in your community. This image encourages good people to apply when jobs for outsiders do become available.

Realizing the Limitations of Promoting Only from Within

Although the advantages of internal promotion usually outweigh the limitations, there are disadvantages to consider:

- If you promote only from within, you limit the sources from which to draw candidates and you may be restricted to promoting a person significantly less qualified than someone from outside your company.
- People who have worked in other companies bring with them new and different ideas and know-how that can benefit your team.
- Outsiders look at your activities with a fresh view, not tainted by overfamiliarity.

Red Alert

The practice of restricting promotions to current employees tends to perpetuate the racial, ethnic, and gender makeup of your staff. Companies whose employees are predominantly white and male and who rarely seek outside personnel have been charged with discrimination against African-Americans, other minorities, and women.

Searching for Applicants Internally

You can't possibly know everyone in your company who might be qualified for a position on your team. But your human-resources (HR) department should.

If a job is a promotion or a position that will give an applicant a raise in pay or more challenging work, look first at your own team. You know these women and men best, and one of them might fit the bill.

If no one on your team is suitable or interested in the position, discuss the opening with someone from your HR department. Go over the job specs with that person. He or she can suggest possible candidates from within your company.

Some companies have formalized this process by using these two methods:

- **Job banks.** A search of this computerized list of the abilities of all employees should turn up qualified candidates for your screening.
- **Job postings.** Many companies post the specs for available positions on bulletin boards and sometimes on electronic bulletin boards. Any interested employee can apply. After preliminary screening by the HR department, anyone who meets the basic requirements is sent to you to be interviewed. In addition, by doing this, companies inform women and members of minority groups, who might not have been considered, about the availability of these jobs.

Recruiting and Selection

In addition to searching for candidates within your company, the HR department may help you *recruit* from outside sources. It may advertise the opening, contact employment services, visit colleges (for trainees), or use executive recruiters (often called "headhunters") for higher-level positions.

Before the actual recruiting begins, the team leader and the members of the HR team review the job specifications to coordinate the process. As expert as HR people may be in their specialty, however, they cannot do the job alone. A team leader's knowledge of the job and the team's personality is necessary to ensure that the best-qualified candidates are sought out and considered.

Evaluating Applications and Résumés

Except for positions for the most routine jobs, most applicants provide résumés of their background and experience. In addition, most companies require all applicants to complete an application form.

You may wonder why an application form is necessary when you have a résumé. You need it! Résumés are an applicant's sales pitch—designed to make you want to hire him or her. A résumé can hide undesirable aspects of a person's background or overplay positive factors. Many résumés don't list every employer—only those the candidate wants you to know about. Others don't give dates of employment, salary history, and other information you may need. An application form provides you with the information *you* need to know, not what the applicant wants you to know.

Because all the information requested on the application form is the same for all applicants, it complies with the equal-employment opportunity laws. In addition, it helps you compare applicants' backgrounds when you make your hiring decision. Make sure that all applicants complete the form, even if they provide a detailed résumé.

> **Meanings and Gleanings**
>
> **Recruiting** is the process of seeking candidates to be considered for employment. The **selection** process involves screening applicants to determine their suitability, usually by reviewing résumés and then conducting interviews.

Be sure to study an application to get a better idea about a candidate's background before you call the person in for an interview.

Like every aspect of the hiring process, an application form must comply with equal-employment laws. In today's litigious society, you would think that most companies would be conscious of this situation and have these forms reviewed carefully by legal experts. As a consultant, I have had the opportunity to see countless company application forms. I'm amazed that even now—30 years after the EEO laws went into effect—I still see application forms that ask for age, marital status, number of children, dates of schooling (which can identify age), and other illegal questions.

Leadership Lead
Use a résumé as a *supplement* to an application, not as a *substitute* for it.

The sample application form on the following page is typical of those used by many companies. You have to use the form your company provides, of course, but if you plan to revise it, the sample may give you some guidelines. In addition to the questions asked in the sample, companies often add questions that are of particular concern to them. Companies hiring technical and professional people ask about membership in professional societies, awards earned, and papers published. Some companies ask about felony convictions. Remember that the form should meet your needs as well as comply with appropriate laws. (The terms of employment and other matters discussed at the end of the employment application are discussed in chapter 25.)

Preparing for an Interview

Too often it happens that you have a pleasant interview with an applicant and learn little more than basic information. An interview shouldn't consist of just a casual conversation: You should be prepared to ask questions that enable you to judge an applicant's qualifications and give you insight into that person's strengths and limitations for a job.

To ensure that you get the information you want, make a list of pertinent questions *before* you meet with a candidate:

- **Review the job description.** Prepare questions that bring out an applicant's background and experience in the functions of that job.
- **Review the job specifications.** Prepare questions to help you evaluate whether an applicant's background and skills conform with what you're seeking.
- **Review a person's application (if available) and résumé.** Some of the information you need may be gleaned from these documents. Prepare questions that expand on what's in those documents.

Red Alert
Make sure that your application form meets EEO guidelines. Questions that you assume are acceptable may have illegal connotations. Have your legal department or an attorney who specializes in labor law review your application before you have it printed.

Application for Employment

Date: ____________

Name: ____________ Social Security number: ____________

Address: ____________

City, State, ZIP: ____________ Phone: ____________

Position sought: ____________ Salary desired: ____________

EDUCATION

Level: ________ School/Location: ____________ Course: ____________

Number of years: ______ Degree or diploma: ____________

College: ____________

Other: ____________

____

EMPLOYMENT RECORD

1. Company/Address: ____________

   Dates: ________ Salary: ________ Supervisor: ________

   Duties: ____________

   ____

   ____

   Reason for leaving: ____________

   ____

2. Company/Address: ____________

   Dates: ________ Salary: ________ Supervisor: ________

   Duties: ____________

   ____

   ____

   Reason for leaving: ____________

   ____

3. Company/Address:

Dates: ______________ **Salary:** ______________ **Supervisor:** ______________

Duties: ____

____

____

Reason for leaving: ____

____

How were you referred to this company? ______________________________

Are you 18 years of age or older? ______________________________

If you're hired, can you provide written evidence that you are authorized to work in the United States? ______________________________

Is there any other name under which you have worked that we would need in order to check your work record? (If so, please provide.) ______________

APPLICANT'S STATEMENT:

I understand that the employer follows an "employment at will" policy, in that I or the employer may terminate my employment at any time or for any reason consistent with applicable federal and state laws. This employment-at-will policy cannot be changed verbally or in writing unless authorized specifically by the president or executive vice president of this company. I understand that this application is not a contract of employment. I understand that the federal government prohibits the employment of unauthorized aliens; all persons hired must provide satisfactory proof of employment authorization and identity. Failure to submit such proof will result in denial of employment.

I understand that the employer may investigate my work and personal history and verify all information given on this application, on related papers, and in interviews. I hereby authorize all individuals, schools, and firms named therein, except my current employer (if so noted), to provide any information requested about me and hereby release them from all liability for damage in providing this information.

I certify that all the statements in this form and other information provided by me in applying for this position are true and understand that any falsification or willful omission shall be sufficient cause for dismissal or refusal of employment.

Signed ______________________________

Bet You Didn't Know

A survey published in *The Personnel Administrator* reported that 88 percent of human-resources managers indicated that they spend less than three minutes reading a résumé. You can make the most of this time by highlighting key facts and asking about them during an interview.

Questions You Should Ask

Structure interviews so that you don't forget to ask important questions. You usually should explore the five areas in this list:

- **Education.** Does an applicant have the requisite educational requirements or other background that would provide the necessary technical know-how?
- **Experience.** Inquire about the type and length of pertinent experience. Ask not only "What did you do?" but also "How did you do it?" You can determine from an applicant's answers whether he or she has the type of experience that's necessary for a job.
- **Accomplishments.** It's important to learn what an applicant has done that makes that person stand out from other qualified candidates.
- **Skills.** Learn which special skills an applicant can bring to a job.
- **Personal characteristics.** The job specifications should indicate personal characteristics necessary for doing a job. During an interview, try to identify, in addition to these characteristics, other personality factors that may affect the person's compatibility with you and your team members.

Leadership Lead

You can get much more (and more useful) information by asking open-ended questions. Rather than ask, "Do you know how to use WordPerfect?" ask, "Tell me about your experience in using WordPerfect."

The following list of interview questions can guide you in preparing the questions you want to ask a job candidate. Questions similar to these, tailored to the job involved, can provide a great deal of meaningful information.

Interview Questions

Work experience

(Add specific questions to determine job knowledge and experience in various aspects of the job for which you are interviewing.)

Describe your current responsibilities and duties.

How do you spend an average day?

How did you change the content of your job from when you started it until now?

Discuss some of the problems you encountered on the job.

What do you consider to be your primary accomplishment in your current job (or previous jobs)?

Qualifications other than work experience (helpful questions for applicants with no direct work experience)

How do you view the job for which you are applying?

What in your background particularly qualifies you to do this job?

If you were to be hired, in which areas could you contribute immediately?

In which areas would you need additional training?

In what way has your education and training prepared you for this job?

Weaknesses

Which aspects of your previous job did you do best?

In which areas did you need help or guidance from your boss?

In which areas have your supervisors complimented you?

Motivation

Why did you choose this career area?

What do you seek in a job?

What's your long-term career objective?

How do you plan to reach this goal?

Of all the aspects of your last job (or jobs), what did you like most? Least?

What kind of position do you see yourself in five years from now?

What are you looking for in this job that you're not getting from your current job?

Stability

What were your reasons for leaving each previous job?

Why are you seeking a job now?

What were your original career goals?

How have these goals changed over the years?

Resourcefulness

Describe some of the more difficult problems you have encountered in your work.

How did you solve those problems?

To whom did you go for counsel when you couldn't handle a problem yourself?

What's your greatest disappointment so far in your life?

In what way did this disappointment change your life?

Working with others

On what teams or committees have you served?

What was your function on this team (or committee)?

What did you contribute to the team's activities?

How much of your work did you do on your own? As part of a team?

Which aspect did you enjoy more? Why?

What did you like best about working on a team? Least?

Conducting an Interview

Suppose that an interviewer greets an applicant with a curt "What makes you think you can handle this job?" If you're looking for a tough, no-nonsense person who will be exposed to constant harassment and pressure, this approach might work.

But most jobs aren't like that. Even if applicants aren't intimidated by this approach, they're less likely to be forthright in their responses. It becomes a battle of wits rather than an elucidating discussion about qualifications.

Most job applicants are nervous or at least somewhat ill-at-ease in an interview. To make an interview go smoothly, put applicants at ease. Welcome them with a friendly greeting, a smile and a handshake, and offer a cup of coffee or tea. Introduce yourself and begin the discussion with a noncontroversial comment or question based on something from an applicant's background. For example, starting out with the comment, "I noticed that you graduated from Thomas Tech—two of our team members are Thomas grads" ensures an applicant that you're familiar with the school and are favorably inclined toward its alumni.

After you "break the ice," you're ready to move into the crux of an interview and ask the questions you have prepared.

> **Red Alert**
> When you use a list of questions, don't stick only to the questions on the list. Listen to the answers—not only to what an applicant says but also, more important, for what's *not* said. Follow up with probing questions to elicit more detailed information.

What to Do When an Applicant Isn't Telling You Everything

Have you ever had the feeling that an applicant is hiding something or is reluctant to talk about an aspect of his or her background? These three techniques may help open these closed doors:

- **Use silence.** Most people cannot tolerate silence. If you don't respond after someone has finished talking, he or she will usually fill in the gap by adding something more. ("I have experience in mass-mailing software." [Silence.] "I did it once.")
- **Make nondirective comments.** Ask open-ended questions, such as, "Tell me about your computer background." An applicant will tell you whatever he or she feels is an appropriate response. Rather than comment on the answer, respond with "Uh-huh" or "Yes" or just nod. This technique encourages applicants to continue talking without giving any hints about what you're seeking to learn. This approach often results in obtaining information about problems, personality factors, attitudes, or weaknesses that might not have been uncovered by direct questions. On the other hand, it can also bring out additional positive factors and strengths.
- **Probing questions.** Sometimes applicants can be vague or evasive in answering questions. Probe for more detail, as in this example:

  INTERVIEWER: For what type of purchases did you have authority to make final decisions?

  APPLICANT: I know a great deal about valves.

  INTERVIEWER: Did you buy the valves?

> **Leadership Lead**
> After an applicant has answered your question, *wait five seconds before asking your next question.* You'll be amazed at how many people add new information—positive or negative—to their original response.

Applicant: I recommended which valves to buy.

Interviewer: Who actually negotiated the deal?

Applicant: My boss.

Remembering an Interview

One of my most embarrassing moments occurred in my first job as a personnel manager. I interviewed several candidates for a sales position. Two of the candidates had similar backgrounds but quite different personalities. You guessed it—I mixed them up and made the job offer over the telephone to the wrong person. Was I shocked when he walked in the following Monday morning!

It's difficult to remember every person you interview. It's advantageous to record the highlights of an interview and, of course, the decision you made. Taking detailed notes during an interview is neither possible nor desirable; doing so often makes an applicant "freeze up," and, if you're busy writing, you can't fully listen.

Take brief notes during an interview. Write down enough information that you'll be able to remember who each applicant is, what makes one applicant different from another, and how each applicant measures up to the job specs for which she or he has been interviewed.

When you're evaluating several candidates for the same job, keep good records to help in comparing them. By using a standard interview report form, you can make a comparison more effectively. Often, more than one person interviews an applicant, and if each one reports comments on a standard form, evaluations are easier to interpret.

Leadership Lead

Elicit from applicants what they have done in previous jobs (or other areas of their lives) that they're particularly proud of. Past successes are good indicators of future achievements.

In the case of investigations by federal or state EEO agencies, good records of an interview can be your most important defense tool. When records are available or inadequate records have been kept, the opinion of the hearing officer is based on the company's word against the word of an applicant. Complete and consistent records give your company solid evidence.

As mentioned in chapter 4, in the section "Five Tricks to Make You a Better Listener," take brief notes during an interview and write your report immediately afterward. If it helps, use the sample interview summary sheet on the following pages.

Interview Summary Sheet

Applicant: ________________________ Date: ________________

Position applied for: ______________ Interviewer: ________________

Job factors: [1] ____

Applicant's background[2]: ____________ Qualification rating[3]: ____________

Duties: ____

____

____

Responsibilities: ____

____

____

Skills required: ____

____

____

Education required[4] (level): ____

Specific types: ____

____

____

Educational achievement: ____

____

____

Other job factors: ____

____

[1]*Job factors should be listed from job specifications for position applicant applies for.*

[2] *Interviewer should note aspects of applicant's background that apply to each factor in this column.*

[3] *Rate applicant on a scale of 1 to 5 for how closely background fits specifications.*

[4]*Level of education means how much schooling completed; type represents subjects related to job taken; achievement represents grades or standing.*

continues

Personal factors	Comments	Qualification rating
Growth in career		
Accomplishments		
Intangibles		
Appearance		
Motivation		
Resourcefulness		
Stability		
Leadership		
Creativity		
Mental alertness		
Energy level		
Communications skills		
Self-confidence		

Comments

Applicant's strengths: ____________________

Applicant's limitations: ____________________

[ ] Applicant should be hired.

Recommendations for additional training: ____________________

[ ] Applicant should NOT be hired.

Reasons: ____________________

Additional comments: ____________________

Providing Information

An important part of the interviewing process occurs when you tell applicants about your company and the job. An interviewer is too often so ill at ease about asking questions that he or she spends most of an interview describing the duties of the job, the advantages of working in the company, and the benefits the company offers.

There's a place in interviews for these issues, but not until you have obtained enough information about an applicant to determine whether he or she is a viable candidate.

At the beginning of an interview, briefly indicate the type of job you're seeking to fill. If you divulge too many details about a job, a shrewd applicant will tailor the answers to your questions to fit what you have described.

The best way to give information about job duties is to ask questions about an applicant's qualifications in that area before you give information:

> INTERVIEWER: How much of your previous job involved copy writing?
>
> APPLICANT: Most of it. I spent at least two-thirds of my time writing copy.
>
> INTERVIEWER: Writing copy is a major part of this job.

Red Alert
If you give applicants a copy of the job description before an interview, their responses to your questions will be influenced by what they have read.

Listening to an Applicant's Questions

Applicants usually have questions about your company and the job. Give them a chance to ask those questions. You should not only answer them but also listen for the type of questions they ask.

Questions about job content, opportunities to use their own initiative, how your team operates, and what types of training and development are offered show positive qualities in an applicant. But if the questions concern primarily vacations, pay raises, or personal benefits, an applicant may not be as job-oriented as you want.

The Least You Need to Know

- A good source for filling vacancies on your team are people employed in other parts of your company.
- Have all applicants complete an application form even if they have a résumé.

- Prepare interview questions before you see candidates. Be sure to include questions that will give you enough meaningful information so that you can make a hiring decision.
- By putting applicants at ease at the beginning of an interview, you get more and better information than you do when they're tense or uncomfortable.
- Follow up responses to your questions with additional questions to expand on, verify, or elucidate those responses.
- Keep good records of each interview.

Chapter 13

Making the Hiring Decision

In This Chapter

- Conducting team interviews
- Giving tests and making reference checks
- Overcoming roadblocks to making good hiring decisions
- Comparing applicants
- Making a job offer

An interview is one of the primary tools for choosing new employees, but it's not the only one. An interview is subjective, after all.

To supplement your reaction to applicants, have other managers or team members interview them. Because each person tends to look for different facets of an applicant's background, have several people do the interviewing to uncover much more about a candidate than any one interviewer can find. It's particularly helpful for team members to interview people who may join their team, because their reactions can help you make a better choice. Other techniques for obtaining information about prospective employees are to check their references and, in some cases, have them undergo testing.

This chapter discusses these and other approaches to learning as much as possible about applicants before making your hiring decision.

Conducting Multiple Interviews

Hiring an employee can be the most important decision you make as a manager. The people who comprise your team can make or break your endeavors. No matter how good you may be as an interviewer, it's a good idea to seek the reaction of others before making a final decision.

In larger companies, a member of the human-resources (HR) department has preliminary interviews with applicants. Only people who meet basic job requirements are referred to you.

If you're the only person who has interviewed an applicant, it's a good idea to have the applicant interviewed by at least one other person. You may have missed important facts or been overly influenced by one factor or another.

Leadership Lead
Before making a hiring decision, have an applicant interviewed by other people who will work closely with that person.

The person (or persons) asked to be the other interviewer depends on his or her type of job and level of responsibility. For jobs of a technical or specialized nature, a person with expertise in that area is the best choice. If a new employee will work closely with another department, the opinion of the manager of that department will be meaningful. Many companies require finalists to be interviewed by the manager at the next higher level (your boss).

Having Team Members Conduct Interviews

Because the team concept involves every member of a team, the process of choosing members for your team should be a team activity. The danger is that interviewing takes time: If every team member interviews every applicant, no other work gets done.

It's not necessary for every team member to conduct a full interview. Each team member should concentrate on the part of an applicant's background in which she or he has the greatest knowledge. All team members will have the opportunity to size up an applicant and to share their evaluations with the rest of the team.

As mentioned in chapter 12, by having each interviewer fill out an interview summary sheet, evaluations can be compared more easily.

Testing Applicants

Do tests help in choosing employees? Some companies swear by testing; others swear *at* them. In companies in which tests are used extensively as part of the screening process, the HR department or an independent testing organization does the testing. Except for performance tests (discussed later in this chapter), it's unlikely that you will have to administer tests.

The most frequently used tests in hiring are shown in this list:

- **Intelligence tests:** Like the IQ tests used in schools, measure the ability to learn. They vary from brief, simple exercises (such as Wunderlich tests) that can be administered by people with little training to highly sophisticated tests that must be administered by someone who has a Ph.D. in psychology.
- **Aptitude tests:** Are designed to determine the potential of candidates in specific areas, such as mechanical ability, clerical skills, and sales potential. These tests are helpful in screening inexperienced people to determine whether they have the aptitude in the type of work for which you plan to train them. Most aptitude tests can be administered and scored by following a simple instruction sheet.
- **Performance tests:** Measure how well candidates can do the job for which they apply. Examples include operating a lathe, entering data into a computer, writing advertising copy, and proofreading manuscripts. When job performance cannot be tested directly, written or oral tests on job knowledge may be used.

  Just asking an applicant to perform a portion of a job isn't a valid test. You must give the same test in the same manner to all applicants. In a word-processing test, for example, you must always use the same material, the same type of computer, and the same timeframe.
- **Personality tests:** Are designed to identify personality characteristics. They vary from the *Readers Digest* quickie questionnaires to highly sophisticated psychological evaluations. A great deal of controversy exists over the value of these types of tests. Supervisors and team leaders are cautioned not to make decisions based on the results of personality tests unless the full implications are made clear to them by experts. A large number of organizations offer personality tests. You can obtain information about tests that have been approved by the American Psychological Association.

Red Alert

Sometimes you can't win. If you hire someone whose test score is low and that person fails, management may blame you for not considering the test results. If the person succeeds, management often credits the test instead of complimenting you for using good judgment.

Checking References

Applicants can tell you anything about their experiences—but how do you know whether they're telling the truth? A reference check is one of the oldest approaches to verifying a background, but is it reliable? Former employers unfortunately don't always tell the whole truth about candidates. They may be reluctant to make negative statements, either because they don't want to prevent the person from working—as long it's not for them—or they fear that they might be sued. Still, a reference check is virtually your only source of verification.

Unless your company policy requires that reference checks be made by the human-resources department, it's better for you, the team leader, to do it. You have more insight into your team's needs and can react to the responses to your questions with follow-up questions that will help you determine whether the applicant's background fits your needs. Be careful to follow the same guidelines in asking questions of the reference as you do in interviewing applicants. Just as you can't ask an applicant whether she has young children, for example, you can't attempt to get this type of information from the reference.

Getting Useful Information

Most reference checks are made by telephone. To make the best of a difficult situation, you must carefully plan the reference check and use diplomacy in conducting it.

Leadership Lead

To make reference checks more successful, talk to an applicant's supervisor, not to a member of the HR staff. Prepare good questions. Begin with verification questions. Advance to detailed questions about job duties, and comment on responses. Then ask for opinions about performance, attitudes, and so on.

The following list provides some tips for making a reference check:

- **Call an applicant's immediate supervisor.** Try to avoid speaking to the company's HR staff members. The only information they usually have is what's on file. An immediate supervisor can give you details about exactly how that person worked in addition to his or her personality factors and other significant traits.
- **Begin your conversation with a friendly greeting.** Then ask whether the employer can *verify* some information about the applicant. Most people don't mind verifying data. Ask a few verification questions about date of employment, job title, and other items from the application.

- **Diplomatically shift to a question that requires a substantive answer, but not one that calls for opinion.** Respond with a comment about the answer, as in this example:

  YOU: Tell me about her duties in dealing with customers.

  SUPERVISOR: [Gives details of the applicant's work.]

  YOU: That's very important in the job she is seeking because she'll be on the phone with customers much of the time.

By commenting about what you have learned, you make the interchange a conversation—not an interrogation. You're making telephone friends with the former supervisor. You're building up a relationship that will make him or her more likely to give opinions about an applicant's work performance, attitudes, and other valuable information.

Overcoming a Former Employer's Reluctance

If a former employer refuses outright to answer a question, don't push. Point out that you understand any reluctance. Make the comment, "I'm sure that you would want to have as much information as possible about a candidate if you were considering someone." Then ask another question (but don't repeat the same one). After the responses begin coming more freely, you can return to the original question, preferably using different words.

What happens if you believe that the person you're speaking to is holding something back? What if you sense from the person's voice that he or she is hesitating in providing answers or you detect a vagueness which says that you're not getting the full story? Here's one way to handle this situation:

> "Mr. Controller, I appreciate your taking the time to talk to me about Alice Accountant. The job we have is very important to our firm, and we cannot afford to make a mistake. Are there any special problems we might face if we hire Alice?"

Here's another approach:

> "Ivan will need some special training for this job. Can you point out any areas to which we should give particular attention?"

From the answer you receive, you may pick up some information about Ivan's weaknesses.

Dealing with Poor References

Suppose that everything about Carlos seems fine, and in your judgment he's just right for the job. When you call his previous employer, however, you get a bad reference. What do you do?

If you have received good reports from Carlos' other references, it's likely that the poor reference was based on a personality conflict or some other factor unrelated to his work. Contact other people in the company who are familiar with his work and get their input.

Anna's previous boss tells you that she was a sloppy worker. Check it out some more. Anna's ex-boss may have been a perfectionist who isn't satisfied with anyone.

When you contact Pierre's former supervisor, you hear a diatribe about how awful he was. But you notice that he had held that job for eight years. If he had been that bad, how come he worked there for such a long time? Maybe his ex-boss resents his leaving and is taking revenge.

Bet You Didn't Know

One of the great paradoxes in reference checking is that companies want full information about prospective employees from former employers, but because of their fear of being sued for defamation, when asked for information about their former employees, they give little more than basic information—dates of employment and job title.

Knowing When to Check References

Check references after you believe that an applicant has a reasonable chance of being hired. If you have more than one finalist, check each one before making a final decision. A reference check may turn up information that suggests a need for additional inquiry: Arrange another interview to explore it.

Red Alert

Never tell an applicant that he or she is hired "subject to a reference check." If the references are good but you choose another candidate, an applicant will assume that you received a poor reference. Also, never tell a person that the reason for rejection is a poor reference. Reference information should be treated as confidential.

Making a Hiring Decision

The interviewing is over, and references have been checked. You now have to decide which candidate to hire. Before you make a decision, review the evaluations of all the people who interviewed applicants. Discuss the finalists with your team members and others who may have interviewed them.

One way you can help make a fair comparison of candidates is by making a comparison chart similar to the final selection worksheet on the following page.

Final Selection Worksheet

Job specifications

	Education	Experience	Intangibles	Other
Applicant 1 Name:				
Applicant 2 Name:				
Applicant 3 Name:				
Applicant 4 Name:				

Avoiding Decision-Making Boo-Boos

In making a hiring decision, make every effort to avoid letting irrelevant or insignificant factors influence you. These factors include the ones in this list:

- **Overemphasizing appearance.** Although neatness and grooming are good indicators of personal work habits, good looks are too often overemphasized in employment. This bias has resulted in companies rejecting well-qualified men and women in favor or their more physically attractive competitors.
- **Giving preference to people like you.** You may subconsciously favor people who attended the same school you did, who come from similar ethnic backgrounds, or who travel in the same circles as you.
- **Succumbing to the "halo effect."** Because one quality of an applicant is outstanding, you overlook that person's faults or attribute unwarranted assets to him or her. Because Sheila's test score in computer know-how is the highest you've ever seen,

for example, you're so impressed that you offer her a job. Only later do you learn that she doesn't qualify in several other key aspects of the job.

In making a final decision, carefully compare each candidate's background against the job specs and against each other. Look at the whole person (you have to live with your choice for a long time).

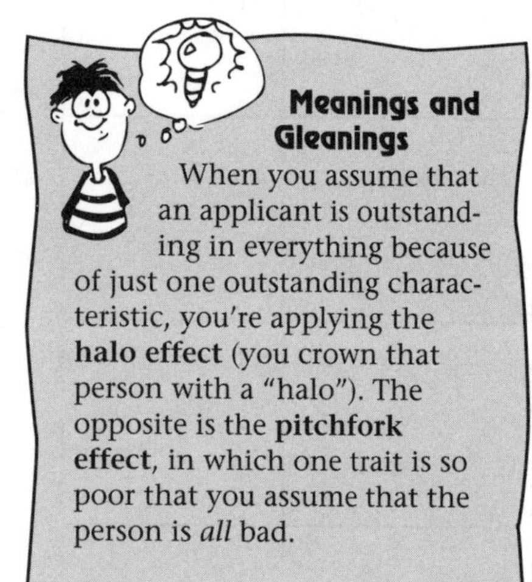

Meanings and Gleanings

When you assume that an applicant is outstanding in everything because of just one outstanding characteristic, you're applying the **halo effect** (you crown that person with a "halo"). The opposite is the **pitchfork effect**, in which one trait is so poor that you assume that the person is *all* bad.

Making a Job Offer

You've made your decision, and now you're ready to offer the job to the lucky candidate. A few problems remain, however: negotiating salary, getting an applicant's acceptance, and arranging a starting date. In addition, you must notify the people you interviewed who were not hired.

In most companies the final offer, including salary, is handled by the HR department. Usually the HR representative discusses directly with the applicant the starting salary, benefits, and other facets of employment. If you're responsible for making the offer in your company, however, it's a good idea to check all the arrangements with your boss and the HR department to avoid misunderstandings.

Finalizing the Salary Range

Most companies set starting salaries for a job category. You may have a narrow range of flexibility, depending on an applicant's background. But when jobs are difficult to fill and in many higher-level positions, starting salaries are negotiable.

In these types of jobs, an applicant is usually interviewed by several people, and you may have several interviews with finalists before making a decision. You should obtain a general idea of their salary demands early in this process so that you don't waste time in even considering people whose salary requirements are way out of line.

Companies traditionally have used an applicant's salary history as the basis for their offer. Ten or 15 percent higher than a person's current salary is considered a reasonable offer. Because women usually have been paid less than men, however, basing the salary you offer on current earnings isn't always equitable. If the job had been offered to a man and you would have paid a higher rate based on his salary history, you should offer a woman the same rate, even though her earnings record has been lower.

In negotiating salary, keep in mind what you pay currently employed people for doing similar work. Offering a new person considerably more than that amount can cause serious morale problems.

There are exceptions to this rule, of course. Some applicants have capabilities that you believe would be of great value to your company, and to attract these people, you may have to pay considerably more than your current top rate. Some companies create special job categories to accommodate this situation. Others pay only what they must and hope that it won't lead to lower morale.

Some companies believe that they can avoid these types of problems by prohibiting their employees from discussing salary. This "code of silence" is virtually impossible to enforce. People talk—and who makes how much makes for great gossip. One of my clients gave an employee a significant raise to keep him from leaving. He and the others in the company who were aware of the raise were sworn to secrecy. His boss told me, "That very afternoon our manager in Los Angeles called to ask whether the rumor about this raise was true. Asked where he picked up this information, he said that it was on his e-mail when he got back from lunch." The grapevine in action again!

> **Red Alert**
> Don't let your anxiety over losing a desirable candidate tempt you to make an informal offer—promising a higher salary or other condition of employment that hasn't been approved—with the hope that you can persuade management to agree to it. Failure to get this agreement will not only cause the applicant to reject the offer but can also lead to legal action against your company.

Salary alone isn't a total compensation package. It includes vacations, benefits, frequency of salary reviews, and incentive programs. All these items should be clearly explained.

Even when the salary you offer is less than an applicant wants, you may persuade that person to take your offer by pointing out how the job will enable him or her to use creativity, engage in work of special interest, and help reach career goals.

Arranging for Medical Exams

Many companies require applicants to take a medical exam before they can be put on the payroll. You cannot reject an applicant on the basis of a medical exam, however, unless you can show that the reason for the rejection is job-related. If a job calls for heavy lifting, for example, and the candidate has a heart condition that could be aggravated by that task, it's a legitimate reason for rejection. On the other hand, rejecting an applicant, not because of the work, but because it will increase your insurance premiums isn't acceptable.

> **Red Alert**
> The Americans with Disabilities Act (ADA) requires that a medical exam be given only after the decision to hire is made. The exam cannot be used as a reason for rejection unless a person's physical condition is job-related and your company cannot make accommodations for it.

Most companies arrange for a medical exam close to a person's starting date. They tell applicants that they are hired subject to passing a physical exam. If this is your policy, caution applicants not to give notice to a current employer until after examination results have been received.

Congratulations—You Got an Offer!

Although most companies make a job offer orally (no letter and no written agreement), an oral offer is just as binding as a written one. Some companies supplement an oral offer with a letter of confirmation so that there are no misunderstandings about the terms.

Red Alert

When you make a job offer, the salary should be stated by pay period—not on an annual basis. Rather than specify $30,000 per year, specify $1,250 per half-month. Why? Because some courts have ruled that if you quote a salary on an annual basis, you're guaranteeing the job for one year.

A job-offer letter should contain these elements:

- Title of job (a copy of the job description should be attached).
- Starting date.
- Salary, including an explanation of incentive programs.
- Benefits (may be in the form of a brochure given to all new employees).
- Working hours, location of job, and other working conditions.
- If pertinent, deadline for acceptance of offer.

Signing Employment Contracts

In some situations, the employer and employee sign a formal contract. These contracts are often used with senior management people and key professional, sales, or technical personnel. Although it's rare, some organizations require all salaried employees to sign a contract, which is often little more than a formalized letter of agreement concerning conditions of employment. In many cases, they're designed for the benefit of the company, and the employee has little room for negotiation.

One of the most controversial areas covered in many contracts is the so-called "restrictive covenant," which prohibits employees who leave the company from working for a competitor for a specified period of time. Although these types of contracts have been challenged, they usually are enforceable if they're limited in scope. Prohibiting a person from working for a competitor for a limited period of time, for example, is more likely to be upheld than prohibiting that type of employment forever.

Senior managers and other employees who hold critical positions in a company and applicants who have skills that are in great demand have the clout to negotiate personal contracts with the company. Any contract, whether it's generic or a negotiated special agreement, should be drawn up by a qualified attorney, not by HR or other managers.

Dealing with Applicants Who Can't Make Up Their Minds

You've narrowed the field, and your first choice is Hillary. Early in the interview process, you explored her salary requirements, and your offer is in line. At least that's what you thought. Now Hillary demurs. "If I stay where I am, I'll get a raise in a few months that will bring me above that salary. You have to do better."

Having received approval of the hire at the salary offered, you have to either reject it, persuade her to take the job by selling her on other advantages, or go back to your boss for approval of the higher rate. What you do depends on many factors. Do you have other viable candidates for the job? If, not, how urgent is it to fill the job? Determine whether you can legitimately offer other benefits, such as a salary review in six months, opportunity for special training in an area in which she is particularly interested, or other perks. Think over the situation carefully, and discuss it with your manager. ***Caution:*** Don't make commitments you don't have the authority to follow up.

If you and your boss agree that Hillary should still be considered for the position, determine how much above your original offer you're willing to pay and what else you can offer. The meeting with Hillary should take place as soon as possible after you and your manager have determined the maximum deal you can offer. With this in mind, you can negotiate with her and try to reach an acceptable arrangement. Usually, if this new negotiation doesn't lead to agreement, discontinue the discussion and seek another candidate. Continuing to haggle over terms of employment is frustrating and keeps you from concentrating on your other duties. You're better off using your time and energy to find another candidate.

Countering a Counteroffer

You've knocked yourself out reading résumés, interviewing applicants, and comparing candidates. You make the decision that you'll hire Tom, and he accepts your offer. A week later he calls to tell you that he has changed his mind: When he told his boss that he was leaving, his boss made him a counteroffer.

Frustrating? You bet. To minimize the possibility of a counteroffer, assume that any currently employed candidate will get one. At the time you make your offer, bring it up and make these points:

- You know that he has done a great job in his present company. You also realize that when he notifies his company that he's planning to leave, it will undoubtedly make him a counteroffer. Why? Because they need him *now*.

Leadership Lead
Don't notify unsuccessful applicants until shortly after your new employee starts work. If for some reason the chosen candidate changes his or her mind and doesn't start, you can go back to some of the others without having them feel that they were a second choice.

- If his company truly appreciated his work, it wouldn't have waited until he got another job offer to give him a raise. *You* would have given it to him long ago.
- Many people who have accepted counteroffers from a current employer find out that, after the pressure is off the company, it will train or hire someone else and let him go.
- He will always be looked on as a disloyal person who threatened to leave just to get more money.
- When the time for a raise comes around again, guess whose salary has already been "adjusted"?

When these arguments are used, the number of people who accept counteroffers decreases significantly.

Rejecting the Also-Rans

Some companies just assume that if applicants don't get an offer, they will realize that they were rejected. It's not only courteous but also good business practice to notify the men and women you have interviewed that a job has been filled.

You don't have to tell applicants why they didn't get the job. Explanations can lead to misunderstandings and even litigation. The most diplomatic approach is just to state that the background of another candidate was closer to your needs.

The Least You Need to Know

- When you interview a candidate to join your team, have other team members talk to the candidate.
- Tests can be a helpful screening tool, but use them as an aid, not as the chief source, for making your decision.
- Whenever possible, check the references of a prospective employee by speaking to the person to whom he or she reported, not to the HR department.
- When you compare candidates, consider the whole person, not just one aspect of his or her background.
- In making a job offer, make sure that the candidate fully understands the nature of the job, the salary and benefits, and other conditions of employment.

Part 5
Motivating Your Team for Peak Performance

Look at the word motivation. *Two other words that begin with the same three letters are* motion *and* motor. *We call the motors in our cars "internal combustion engines," and each of us has inside us a combusting engine that keeps us in motion.*

As a team leader, your job is to provide to each of your team members the fuel that will start their "motors" and keep them going. But not all motors take the same kind of fuel to keep them running; and so it is with people. What motivates one person may not work for another. To be able to help your team move forward, you have to know what kind of fuel to feed to each of your members, how and when to use it, and what reaction you can expect. Tough job? Sure, but it's worth the effort.

As you read the five chapters in this part of the book, you'll pick up some ideas to help you fuel those motors. Remember to keep an open mind*—some of the things you think are great motivators may not motivate anyone at all.*

Chapter 14

Motivating Your Team

In This Chapter

- Getting to know your team members
- Recognizing your team as a motivational force
- Making the transition from boss to team leader
- Learning how to lead when you don't work in teams

To make your team more than just a group of people who work together, you have to meld your team members into a cohesive group and work with them to develop within themselves that inner motivation that will propel them toward accomplishing the team's goals.

This chapter examines how successful team leaders start the process of developing this team spirit by taking the time to get to know the members of their team as individuals. Team members are humans, not robots, each with his or her own strengths and weaknesses, personal agenda, and style of working. Learning and understanding each team member's individualities is the first step in building a team.

In addition, the chapter explores how functioning as a team leader differs from being a boss and looks at some techniqúes that can help you become a more effective team leader.

Because many companies aren't organized on a team basis, the chapter provides suggestions for several principles of team management that can be applied in a nonteam environment.

Different Strokes for Different Folks

Remember the rocket ship analogy in chapter 1? You learned that, to get a rocket ship off the ground, each of its components must be in A-1 shape and then coordinated so that they work interactively. Your team is the rocket ship; its members are the components; you are the rocket engineer.

Your first job as a team leader is to develop the skills and abilities of each of your associates so that they can perform at top capacity. The best way to begin is to learn about each person as an individual.

You may believe that all you really have to know about your associates is how well they do their work. Wrong! Knowing the members of your team requires more than just knowing their job skills—that's an important part, but it's *only* a part of their total makeup. Learn about the things that are important to your team members—their ambitions and goals, their families, their special concerns—in other words, what makes them tick.

Learning Each Team Member's M.O.

If you've ever watched crime shows or read detective stories, you know about the term *M.O.* (*modus operandi,* or method of operation). Detectives often can tell who has committed a crime by his or her M.O., or the manner in which it was committed, because criminals tend to repeat the same M.O.s in their crimes.

M.O.s aren't limited to criminals. We all have M.O.s in the way we do our work and the way we live our lives. Notice the way each of your team members operates, and you'll discover his or her M.O. For example, one team member may always ponder a subject before he comments, and another may reread everything she works on several times before starting new work.

> **Meanings and Gleanings**
>
> A person's M.O. is his or her method, or mode, of operation (the patterns of behavior that person habitually follows in performing work).

Psychologists don't call them M.O.s; they call them "patterns of behavior." Whatever you call M.O.s, being aware of them helps you understand people and enables you to work with them more effectively.

You don't want to be nosy? Okay, you don't have to *ask* personal questions directly. By observing and listening, you can learn a great deal about your colleagues. Listen when they speak to you: Listen to what they say, and listen to what they *don't* say. Listen when they speak to others. Eavesdropping may not be polite, but you can learn a great deal. Observe how your team members do their work and how they act and react. It doesn't take long to identify their likes and dislikes, their quirks and eccentricities. By listening, you can learn about the things that are important to each of them and the "hot buttons" that can turn them on or off.

Leadership Lead
Encourage your associates to express their ideas, especially when they differ from yours. Their disagreements not only provide you with new ideas but also give you insight into the way they approach problems that will help you to work more effectively with them.

Getting to Know Your Team Members

How is listening important in developing productive team members? By observing and listening, you realize that Claudia is a creative person. If you want to excite her about her role in an assignment, you can do so by appealing to her creativity. You notice that Mike is slow when he's learning new things but that, after he learns them, he works quickly and accurately. To enable Mike to do his best, you know that you'll need patience.

It's easy to remember these individual characteristics when you supervise a small number of people, but if you're involved with larger groups or have high turnover in your department, it's not so easy. You need help. The Know-Your-Team worksheet on the following page can help you keep an informal reminder of each of your team members' traits.

Making Your Team Self-Motivating

After team members understand their new roles, you, as their team leader, must ensure that they begin to apply the team system on the job.

Let's look at how Denise did this. As sales manager, her primary role had been training, motivating, and leading her sales force. Denise discovered that, as in most companies, without the support of the office staff to obtain and maintain sales production, sales were lost and customers became dissatisfied.

Meanings and Gleanings
One thing in a person's make-up that really gets him or her excited—positively or negatively—is a **hot button**. Find someone's hot button, and you can really get through to them.

The salespeople in Denise's company were paid on a commission basis. They worked hard and long hours to get and keep accounts. They were often frustrated, however, when the order department stalled deliveries by finding petty problems or when customer-service representatives antagonized customers by showing indifference to their inquiries.

Know-Your-Team Worksheet

Member's name: ______________________________

Position: ____________________ Date employed: ______________

Spouse's name: ______________________________

Children's names and ages: ______________________________

____

Hobbies: ______________________________

____

Other interests: ______________________________

____

Schools and colleges: ______________________________

____

Other pertinent information: ______________________________

____

____

Behavioral traits: ______________________________

____

____

Hot buttons: ______________________________

Leadership Lead

To turn a team into a self-motivated unit, create "team spirit" among members by getting everyone on your team involved in every aspect of a job. Team members will then work together to ensure that goals are met.

Denise reorganized the department into five teams, each covering a different sales region. Each team was made up of salespeople, order clerks, and customer-service personnel.

Denise followed the TEAM acrostic for successful team development:

Train: All sales and support people were brought in for a weekend training program in which the new system was explained. By using group discussions, case studies, and role-plays, team members were trained to work together.

Enthusiasm: To make any team activity work, team members must not only accept an idea but also greet it enthusiastically. Denise borrowed some techniques used by sports teams, and her teams chose names and colors. She announced contests between teams and awards ranging from group dinners to cash bonuses.

Assurance: The teams were assured that they would not be left entirely on their own. Denise and other company executives would give them as much informational and financial support as necessary in addition to other resources, but the team members' ideas and concepts were the key to success.

Measurement: Specific goals were set for each team for the first period. After that, they were to set their own goals. Each team would be measured by how close it came to achieving their goals as a group and as individuals—they would be evaluated not only by their own performance but also by how they worked as a team.

The compensation system was changed so that rather than a salesperson alone being rewarded for making a sale, bonuses and raises for all team members would be based on the team's productivity.

At the end of the first year, sales had increased significantly. Rather than stall orders because of minor errors in an order form, order clerks went to the source and corrected the errors immediately. Secretaries and customer-service reps went out of their way to help customers, and morale in the department grew immensely.

Making the Transition from Boss to Team Leader

Many traditional supervisors find it difficult to make the transition to team leader. "If I'm going to be held accountable when anything goes wrong, how can I give up control?"

Yes, it's still the team leader's job to ensure that the goals of the team are met, but you can still accomplish this task in a team environment. The key to team control is self-control.

You, the team leader, must be sure that every member of your team is aware of what is expected from the team and of his or her part in meeting these expectations. Team members should be kept aware at all times of how the team is doing. In this way, they monitor their own activities (chapter 19 discusses this subject in detail).

Being Aware of Dangers to Avoid

So all you have to do is convert from traditional methods to team concepts and all your troubles are over, right? Of course not. Teams aren't a cure-all for management problems. They have their share of problems.

One common problem is that team members sometimes don't carry their weight and other members have to work harder to maintain their team's productivity. Team members can often overcome this situation themselves, by working with the weaker person to help build up necessary skills. If the reason for poor performance isn't a lack of skill but instead a lack of motivation, the others may encourage—or in some cases, shame—the slacker into better production. Peer pressure is a powerful tool. If all else fails, the person will have to be removed from the team.

Teams in the workplace have many advantages, but they're not a panacea. People who learn to work together in teams produce more, enjoy their work more, and are less likely to quit for superficial reasons. Teams create a motivational environment in the workplace and help to build the esprit de corps that is important to success in meeting goals.

Knowing What to Do When a Company Doesn't Use Teams

Many companies aren't ready to change from the traditional organizational structure to teams. You have to work within an established framework.

Your company may not be organized in teams. No matter what the organizational structure, you can use any and all of the techniques in this chapter and in this book to improve your effectiveness as a manager. Just glean the suggested techniques and begin applying them today!

After José returned from an intensive management-development weekend at the university, he bubbled with enthusiasm about all the ideas he had learned about. He wanted to take immediate action in restructuring his department into teams.

"Whoa," José's boss said. "Take it easy. We're not making any radical changes now." Rather than give up in frustration, José asked himself, "What can I do within the current structure to adapt what I've learned?"

Within the first few weeks, José made the following changes in his management style:

- He became more available to the people who reported to him. Rather than brush off their questions and suggestions, he took time to listen, evaluate, and respond to them.
- He overcame the temptation to make every decision. When asked for a decision, he threw the decision back to the person requesting it. "What do *you* think should be done?"
- Rather than plan the work himself when new assignments were received, he enlisted the participation of his entire team.
- He encouraged team members to acquire skills outside their usual work duties. He used cross training and assigned them work that required interaction with others in the group whose work was somewhat different from theirs.
- He conferred with all team members to ensure that they understood what was expected of them on the job and how their performance would be evaluated, and, most important, learned more about their individual goals and aspirations.
- He periodically held exciting and productive department meetings.
- He visited suppliers and subcontractors and invited them to visit the company and attend meetings.

The payoff didn't take long. Within a few months productivity increased, quality improved, and cooperation and collaboration among the group became a way of life. All this—without changing the structure.

The Least You Need to Know

- Learn and remember what's important in the lives of each member of your team.
- By identifying your associates' M.O.s and hot buttons, you'll understand them and work more effectively with each one.
- Develop a team spirit to make your team self-motivated.
- The key to team control is self-control. If all team members are aware of what's expected and are informed of what has been accomplished, they'll monitor their own activities.
- Peer pressure is a powerful tool for motivating weaker team members.
- If your organization isn't team-structured, use your initiative to create an atmosphere of collaboration and participation to motivate the people you supervise.

Chapter 15

Money Talks, but Does It Talk Loud Enough?

In This Chapter

- Understanding when money does and doesn't motivate
- Knowing when money is the scorecard
- Determining whether benefits are motivators or satisfiers
- Tying in money with performance

Here's a mini-lesson in logic:

A: The more money you earn, the happier you are.

B: The more work you produce, the more money you earn.

Therefore:

C: If compensation is based on productivity, people will stretch to produce more so that they can earn more and become happier.

Sounds logical, but is it true? The answer is "sometimes but not always."

Motivators versus Satisfiers

Remember that the word *motivate* begins with the same three letters as *motion*. Motivation is getting into motion, or making things move.

A team of behavioral scientists led by Frederick Herzberg studied what people want from their jobs and classified the results into two categories:

- **Satisfiers (also called maintenance factors):** Factors people must get from a job in order to expend even minimum effort in that job.

  These factors include working conditions, money, and benefits. After employees are satisfied, however, just giving them more of the same factor doesn't motivate them to work harder. Many of what most people consider motivators are really satisfiers.

- **Motivators:** Factors that stimulate people to put out more energy, effort, and enthusiasm in their job.

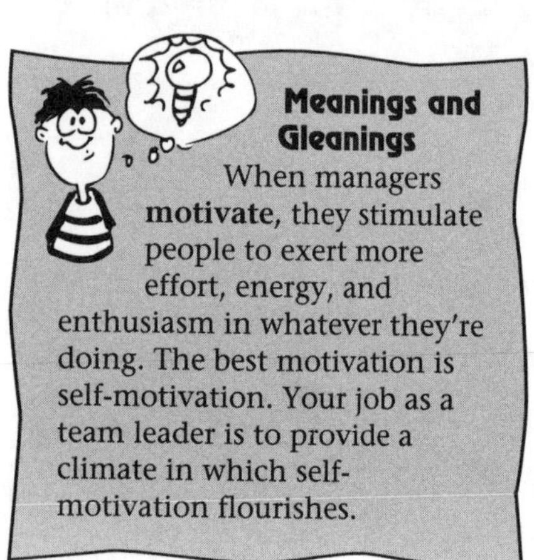

To see how this concept works on the job, suppose that you work in a less-than-adequate facility, in which lighting is poor, ventilation is inadequate, and space is tight. Productivity, of course, is low.

In a few months your company moves to new quarters, with excellent lighting and air conditioning and lots of space, and productivity shoots up.

The company CEO is elated. He says to the board of directors, "I've found the solution to high productivity: If you give people better working conditions, they'll produce more, so I'm going to make the working conditions even better." He hires an interior designer, has new carpet installed, hangs paintings on the walls, and places plants around the office. The employees are delighted. It's a pleasure to work in these surroundings—but productivity doesn't increase at all.

Why not? People seek a level of satisfaction in their job—in this case, reasonably good working conditions. When the working environment was made acceptable, employees were satisfied, and it showed up in their productivity. After the conditions met their level of satisfaction, however, adding enhancements didn't motivate them.

So What Does This Have to Do with Money?

Money, like working conditions, is a satisfier. You might assume that offering more money generates higher productivity. And you're probably right—for most people, but not for everyone. Incentive programs, in which people are given an opportunity to earn more money by producing more, are part of many company compensation plans. They work for some people, but not for others.

The sales department is a good example. Because salespeople usually work on a commission, or incentive, basis, they're in the enviable position of rarely having to ask for a raise. If salespeople want to earn more money, all they have to do is work harder or smarter and make as much money as they want. Therefore, all salespeople are very rich. Right? Wrong!

How come this logic doesn't work? Sales managers have complained about this problem from the beginning of time. They say, "We have an excellent incentive program, and the money is there for our sales staff. All they have to do is reach out—and they don't. Why not?"

Leadership Lead

Team leaders rarely have control over the basic satisfiers: working conditions, salary scale, employee benefits, and the like. These factors are set by company policy, but managers do have the opportunity to use the real motivators: job satisfaction, recognition, and the opportunity for team members to achieve successes.

To understand this problem, you have to delve deep into the human psyche. All of us set a personal salary level, consciously or subconsciously, at which we are satisfied. Until we reach that point, money does motivate us, but after that—no more. *This level varies significantly from person to person.*

Some people set this point very high, and money is a major motivator to them; others are content at lower levels. It doesn't mean that they don't want their annual raise or bonus, but if obtaining the extra money requires special effort or inconvenience, you can forget it.

Suppose that Derek is in your production group and that his salary is 60 percent of yours. His wife works, but you know by the nature of her job that it doesn't pay much. Derek drives a 12-year-old car and buys his clothes from a thrift shop. The only vacations his family has ever taken are occasional camping trips. You feel sorry for him. But now you can help Derek: You need several workers for a special project to be done over the next six Saturdays at double-time pay. When you ask Derek whether he wants the assignment, he says "No," and you can't understand why. It seems to you that he should be eager to make more money, but he has already reached his level of satisfaction. Taking the Saturday off is more important to him than the opportunity to earn more money.

Leadership Lead
A happy team is not necessarily a productive team. Permissiveness and indulgence lead to carelessness and poor work. A team leader's challenge is to develop, with team members, high performance standards that challenge them and motivate them to stretch to meet those standards.

This example doesn't mean that money doesn't motivate at all. The opportunity to earn money motivates everyone to the point that they are satisfied. Some people, like Derek, are content at lower levels. As long as they can meet their basic needs, other things are more important to them than money. To other people, this point is very high, and they "knock themselves out" to keep making more money.

By learning as much as you can about your associates, you learn about their interests, goals, and lifestyles and the level of income at which they're satisfied. To offer the opportunity to make more money as an incentive to people who don't care about it is futile. You have to find some other way to motivate them.

Money as a Scorecard

Barney was unhappy. As vice president of marketing in his company, he earned $250,000 per year in combined salary and bonus but believed that he was underpaid. "Our company had its best year in a decade," he said, "and it was chiefly due to my marketing efforts. I should be paid more."

When Barney was asked about his current quarter-of-a-million-dollar salary, he said, "I don't need the money. But my salary is the score that measures my success."

You don't have to be in the six-figure income bracket to consider your pay a scorecard. A merit raise given to a trainee or a production bonus paid to a factory worker is as much of a boost to that person's ego as is the money.

Leadership Lead
Money is a motivator for some people all of the time; for others, some of the time; and for everyone if it's combined with other motivators.

As discussed in the remainder of this part of the book, intangible motivators are extremely effective, and supplementing them with a reward in the form of a raise or bonus adds to their value. It's not only the money itself but also the tangible acknowledgment of success.

When a person is promoted to a higher-level position, the increase in pay that goes with the promotion is a recognition of the person's new status. Being in a higher salary classification adds prestige both within and outside a company.

Benefits: Motivators or Satisfiers?

Benefits are important in today's companies. Most companies provide some form of health insurance, life insurance, pensions, and other benefits to their employees. In fact, the benefits package is one of the factors that potential employees seek when they evaluate a job offer—but it isn't a motivator. (Have you ever known anyone who worked harder because the company introduced a dental-insurance program?)

Benefits are satisfiers. Good benefits attract people to work for a company, and it also keeps people from quitting. (Often the people you wish would quit don't.)

Bet You Didn't Know

According to the U.S. Chamber of Commerce, the fastest growing areas of benefits over the past five years have been day care for working mothers and flexible hours.

Adjusting Salaries

In most companies pay raises are now given as part of the performance review system (see chapter 19). It's only under unusual circumstances that an employee is given a raise at other times. Unless specified in a union or personal contract, there's no legal obligation to give employees raises. The amount of an increase and how and when it's given depends on each company's policy.

As discussed in chapter 11, companies have usually given all employees who met minimum performance standards an annual raise based on increases in the cost of living. In the 1990s, as business became more competitive and inflation was relatively low, even this expected annual raise was discontinued in many companies.

When people don't get as high a raise as they expect—or no raise at all—it leads to low morale. Team leaders are challenged to keep members motivated when they don't get the reward they expect. It's not easy. You can't ignore the situation and hope that it will go away. Encourage the team member to express disappointment. If the reason for not getting the raise is poor performance, discuss it and point out that you will help him or her improve performance so that the next review will warrant a raise. If the reason is a company freeze on pay increases, explain it and point out that it's a temporary situation that it should be alleviated soon. (Chapter 18 shows an example of how to handle this situation.)

Old and New Incentive-Pay Programs

From the earliest part of the Industrial Era, companies used financial incentives as part or all of their compensation programs. It was assumed that people would work harder and faster if they received a direct reward for production. This system was carried forward into the period of "scientific management." Frederic Taylor, the founder of this new movement, and his followers believed that people could be motivated by wages based on productivity and developed variations on piecework to achieve their goals.

In an economy that is moving rapidly away from mass production and manufacturing-based businesses to custom-engineered production and service-type industries, pay per piece has little value. New types of incentive programs have had to be developed. This section looks at some old and new incentive-pay plans.

Piecework

Wages based solely on the number of units produced was the primary pay plan in some industries. The harder you worked, the more money you received. In the early days of scientific management, speed of production was the primary factor in determining wages, and this method worked well. Abuse in the piecework system, however, was rampant. Often, when workers mastered their work and produced more than quotas required, companies reduced the price paid per piece to keep their overall costs down. This practice led to demotivation, in which workers set their own top limits, which defeated the purpose of the incentive program.

As work became more complex, paying by the piece was no longer practical. Because of pressure from unions and, later, minimum-wage laws, hourly rates replaced piecework rates in most industries.

Bet You Didn't Know

The straight piecework system has returned. In 1995 government agents raided illegal garment factories in which undocumented aliens worked in sweatshops for 12 or more hours a day at piece rates that netted them earnings well below minimum wage.

Quota Pay Plans

Industrial engineers in the age of scientific management (the 1920s and '30s) introduced a variation of piecework. Quotas were established based on time and motion studies, and people who exceeded quotas received extra pay. These types of programs still exist and, properly designed and administered, succeed in motivating some people. Even the best of these programs, however, have problems.

I saw how this system worked during the summers of my college years, when I worked in a factory that used this type of program. Because I was young and energetic and wanted to make money to pay my college expenses, I quickly mastered the work and soon exceeded my quota. One of my coworkers pulled me aside and said, "Hey, you're working too fast. You're making it bad for the rest of us." His implication was that if I didn't slow down, he would break my arm.

Sales-Incentive Programs

Most sales jobs are paid on an incentive basis. Salespeople earn a commission or bonus based on their personal sales. This system should motivate people to knock themselves out to make more sales, but, as mentioned, it doesn't always happen. Many salespeople set limits for themselves, and, when they reach that limit, they "take it easy."

Another result of sales incentives is that it encourages salespeople to concentrate on getting new business, often at the expense of neglecting established customers.

Incentive Plans That Work

In our tough, competitive economy, businesses need incentive plans. Even if money isn't the only, or even the best, way to motivate people, it can play an important role. Money combined with other types of motivation enhances the value of that approach. These programs may be based on exceeding predetermined expectations, special achievements, or sharing in the company's profits.

Management by Objective (MBO)

Management by objective is used in many companies as both a management tool and an incentive program. Although there are many variations, the basic idea is that managers and associates determine together the objectives and results expected for that period. After a time period is agreed on, associates work with minimum supervision to achieve the specified goals. At the end of the period, the manager and the associates compare what has been accomplished with the objectives that had been set. In some organizations, bonuses are awarded for meeting or exceeding expectations.

When a company is organized on a team basis, MBO is extended to the team. Rather than individual objectives, team objectives are set by the team leader and the entire team, and the team works collaboratively to meet these objectives. Results are measured against expectations at the end of the period, and, if rewards or bonuses are part of the plan, the entire team shares them.

Special Awards for Special Achievements

The Footloose Shoe Store chain has instituted periodic campaigns to emphasize various aspects of its work. One campaign, for example, centered around increasing sales of "add-ons" (accessories for customers who have already bought shoes from the company). The campaign, which lasted four weeks, began with rallies at a banquet hall in each region in which the chain operates. Staff members from all the stores in the region assembled in a party atmosphere, where food, balloons, door prizes, and music set the mood as the program was kicked off.

Footloose announced that prizes would be awarded, including $2,000 to be divided among all the staff members (both sales- and support people) from the contest-winning store. The salesclerk who made the most personal add-on sales in the region would receive $500, and the salesclerk who made the most add-on sales in each store would receive $100. The campaign was reinforced by weekly reports on the standings of each store and each salesclerk.

The result was not only a significant increase in accessory sales for that period but also an increase in regular sales, attributed to the excitement and enthusiasm generated by the campaign. Another party was held to present awards and recognize winners. Footloose runs three or four campaigns every year (more parties would lessen the novelty).

Xerox is another company that adds financial reward to recognition. To encourage team participation, special bonuses are given to teams that contribute ideas which lead to gains in production, quality, cost savings, or profits.

A company that has instituted a total-quality management (TQM) program, in which it puts special emphasis on providing high-quality products or services to customers, often augments the program by offering financial rewards based on reducing the number of product rejects, gaining measurable improvements in quality, and increasing customer satisfaction.

Profit-Sharing

Companies use many variations of plans in which a portion of the profits the company earns is distributed to its employees. Many of these plans are informal. The executive committee or board of directors sets aside at the end of the fiscal year a certain portion of profits to be distributed among employees. Other, more formal, plans follow a formula established for that purpose.

In many organizations, only managerial employees are included in a profit-sharing plan; in others, all employees who have been with a company for at least a set number of years; in still others, the entire workforce. Some profit-sharing plans are mandated by union contracts.

A number of profit-sharing programs are based on employee stock ownership. Various types of stock-ownership plans are used, including giving stock as a bonus, giving employees the option to buy company stock at below-market rates, and employee stock-ownership programs (ESOPs), in which employees own their company.

Another financial-incentive approach is *open-book management,* which is revolutionizing the entire traditional compensation system. Its goal is to get *everyone* in a company to focus on helping to make money.

In the old approach, bosses ran a company and employees did what they were told (or what they could get away with). This system has been replaced by empowered teams that are given all the facts and figures necessary to make decisions; they're rewarded for their successes and accept the risks of failure.

In a June 1995 article in *INC.* magazine, John Case presents these essential differences between an open-book company and a traditional business:

> **Red Alert**
> The benefits and incentive-pay area is complex and regulated by federal and state laws. Few companies have the expertise to institute effective programs without professional help. Some of the top consultants in this field are Towers Perrin, 245 Park Avenue, New York, NY 10167; Hay Group, 229 S. 18th Street, Philadelphia, PA 19103; and Hewitt Associates, 40 Highland Avenue, Rowayton, CT 06853.

- Every employee has access to numbers that are critical to tracking the company's performance and is given the training and tools to understand them.
- Employees learn that, whatever else they do, they must never lose sight of the goal to move those numbers in the right direction.
- Employees have a direct stake in their company's success. If the business is profitable, they share in the profits; if it isn't, there are no profits to share.
- There are many variations of open-book management. In some companies employees are given (or can purchase) shares in their company; in others, employees *do* own their company, through employee stock-option plans (ESOPs). In still other plans, ownership remains with stockholders, but the books are open and profits shared.

The resulting employee commitment is palpable. Rather than complain and gripe, employees pitch in to solve problems. Rather than evade assignments with the plaintive excuse "It's not my job," employees seek out areas in which they can contribute. They understand the reason that raises are frozen, that some of their actions have curtailed productivity rather than enhanced it, and what steps they can take to save their company and their jobs.

Bet You Didn't Know

The first management consultant in recorded history was Jethro, the father-in-law of Moses. When Jethro saw how overworked Moses was, he advised him to establish a management hierarchy: to choose leaders "to be rulers of thousands, and rulers of hundreds, rulers of fifties and rulers of tens." (Exodus: Chapter 18.)

The Least You Need to Know

- Motivation means getting into motion—getting moving in whatever endeavor you undertake.
- Money, benefits, and working conditions are satisfiers. Employees must be satisfied with these aspects of their jobs or else they don't work effectively. After people are satisfied, however, giving them more of the same factor doesn't necessarily motivate them.
- Everyone sets a level of income at which he or she is satisfied. Money motivates people up to that point, but, after it's reached—no more.
- A program of bonuses for productivity combined with other motivational factors is more effective than the bonus by itself.
- Profit-sharing plans give team members a vested interest in keeping their company profitable.
- Open-book management is a new variation on employee participation in profits. By sharing total information about how a company fares, everyone becomes an integral part of an organizational team.

Chapter 16

Recognition and Praise: Motivators That Work

In This Chapter

- Understanding that people are *people,* not cogs in a machine
- Recognizing achievement and making praise effective
- Putting your praise in writing
- Honoring team accomplishments

As pointed out in chapter 16, many things formerly considered motivators by conventional wisdom are now seen as *satisfiers*. Money, benefits, and working conditions are important in keeping employees satisfied, but they don't motivate people beyond a certain point. Some of the things that do motivate people are shown in this list:

- Recognition of each team member's individuality.
- Praise for achievements to stimulate continued achievements.
- Opportunity for growth.
- Challenge (remotivating when motivation has been lost).
- Job satisfaction—an ideal motivator.

This chapter discusses the first two items; chapter 17 discusses the other three.

Recognition

Human beings crave recognition. People like to know that others know who they are, what they want, and what they believe. Recognition begins when you learn and use people's names. Of course you know the names of the men and women on your team, but you will be coordinating work with other teams, with internal and external suppliers, subcontractors, and customers. Everyone has a name. Learn it. Use it. It's your first step in recognizing each person's individuality.

In Woody's exit interview after quitting his job with the Building Maintenance Company, he was asked what he liked most and least about the company. Woody responded that, although the salary and benefits were good, he never felt that he was part of the organization. "I always felt that I was looked at as nothing more than a cog in the machine," he said. "During the nine months I worked in the department, I made several suggestions, offered to take on extra projects, and tried to apply creative approaches to some of the work assigned to me. My boss didn't recognize what talents I could contribute."

Providing Positive Reinforcement

An autocratic boss continually criticizes, condemns, and complains and never forgets negative performance. He or she always takes good performance for granted, however. Team leaders today are more aware of the value of reinforcing the good things their associates do instead of harping on their mistakes and inefficiencies.

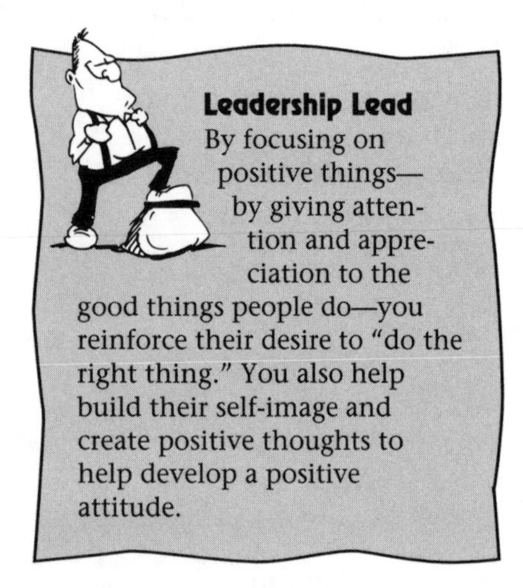

When people hear continual criticism, they begin to feel stupid, inferior, and resentful. Although someone may have done something that wasn't satisfactory, your objective is to correct the behavior, not to make the person feel bad.

The famous psychologist B.F. Skinner noted that criticism often reinforces poor behavior (the only time an offender gets attention is when he or she is criticized). He recommended that we minimize our reaction to poor behavior and maximize our appreciation of good behavior.

Rather than bawl out an associate for doing something wrong, quietly tell the person, "You're making some progress in the work, but we still have a long way to go. Let me show you some ways to do it more rapidly." When the work does improve, make a big fuss over it.

Showing That You Care

Just as you have a life outside the company, so does every member of your team. A job is an important part of our lives, but there are many phases of life that may be of greater importance: health, family, and outside interests, for example. Show sincere interest in a team member's total person.

Virginia, the head teller of a savings-and-loan association in Wichita, Kansas, makes a point of welcoming back associates who have been on vacation or out for several days because of illness. She asks them about their vacation or the state of their health and brings them up-to-date on company news. She makes them feel that she missed them—and it comes across sincerely because she really does miss them.

Jacob, a grandfather, realizes that children are the center of most families. He takes a genuine interest in the activities of his coworkers' children and has even accompanied associates to school events in which their children participate. Some people may consider this situation paternalistic or intrusive, but Jake's true concern comes across as positive interest and has helped meld his team members into a "working family."

Everyone Needs Praise, But What if They Don't Deserve It?

Human beings thrive on praise. Although all of us require praise to feed our egos and help make us feel good about ourselves, you can't praise people indiscriminately: Praise should be reserved for accomplishments that are worthy of special acknowledgment.

If all people need praise, though, how can you sincerely praise them when they don't do anything particularly praiseworthy?

Maria faced this situation in her team of word processors. Several marginal operators had the attitude that, as long as they met their quotas, they were doing okay. Praising them for meeting quotas only reinforced their belief that nothing more was expected of them. Criticism of their failure to do more than the quota required was greeted with the response "I'm doing my job."

Maria decided to try positive reinforcement. She gave one of the operators a special assignment for which no production quota had been set. When the job was completed, Maria praised the employee's fine work. She followed this practice with all new assignments and eventually had the opportunity to sincerely praise each of the word processors.

Leadership Lead
People need praise. If employees do nothing that merits praise, assign them projects in which they can demonstrate success and then praise their accomplishments.

Looking for Praiseworthy Situations

Sometimes you may tend to look for things to criticize rather than things to compliment. Because you expect your team to perform well, you concentrate on strengthening areas of weakness. Douglas, a regional supervisor for a California supermarket chain, made regular visits to the eight stores under his jurisdiction. He reported that when he went into a store he looked for *problems*. He criticized store managers for the way products were displayed, for slow-moving checkout lines, and anything else he noticed. "That's my job," he said, "to make sure that everything is being done correctly."

As you can guess, everyone working in the store dreaded his visits. When Douglas' boss discussed this problem with him, she acknowledged the importance of improving what was wrong but also pointed out that, because the stores exceeded sales-volume forecasts and kept costs down, the managers needed to hear compliments on their success. She suggested that Douglas seek out good things and express his approbation. She encouraged him to make suggestions for improvements to be made, but not to make them the focus of his visits.

Although it wasn't easy, Douglas followed her advice. Within a few months, store managers looked forward to his visits. They began to share new ideas and seek his counsel about store issues. Clerks and other store staffers soon overcame their fear of the "big boss" and welcomed his comments and suggestions.

Bet You Didn't Know

Some supervisors fear that giving praise indicates softness on their part. "We don't want to coddle our subordinates." Praise is *not* softness—it's a positive approach that reinforces good performance. When you stop thinking of your team members as subordinates and instead as partners working to reach team goals, appropriate praise will become a natural part of your behavior.

Five Tips for Effective Praise

As important as praise is in motivating people, it doesn't always work. Some supervisors praise every minor activity so that praise for real accomplishment loses its real value. In some instances, the manner in which the praise is given makes it seem to be phony. To make your praise more meaningful, follow these suggestions:

- **Don't overdo it.** Praise is sweet. Candy is sweet too, but the more you eat, the less sweet each piece becomes—and you may get a stomachache. Too much praise reduces the benefit that's derived from each bit of praise; if it's overdone, it loses its value altogether.
- **Be sincere.** You can't fake sincerity. You must truly believe that what you are praising your associate for is praiseworthy. If you don't believe it, you come across as phony.
- **Be specific about the reason for your praise.** Rather than say, "Great job!" it's much better to say, "The report you submitted on the XYZ matter enabled me to understand more clearly the complexities of the issue."
- **Ask for your team members' advice.** Nothing is more flattering than to be asked for advice about how to handle a situation. This approach can backfire, though, if you don't *take* the advice. If you have to reject advice, remember the Socratic approach—ask people questions about questionable issues until *they* see the negative aspects and reject their own poor advice (refer to chapter 5).
- **Publicize praise.** Just as a reprimand should always be given in private, praising should be done (wherever possible) in public. Sometimes the matter for which praise is given is a private issue, but it's more often appropriate to let your entire team in on the praise. If other team members are aware of the praise you give a colleague, it acts as a spur to them to work for similar recognition.

  In some cases, praise for significant accomplishments is extremely public, such as when it's given at meetings or company events.

  The Mary Kay cosmetics company is known for its policy of giving recognition to associates who have accomplished outstanding performance. In addition to receiving awards and plaques, award winners are feted at company conventions and publicized in the company magazine. Attending a Mary Kay convention is similar to attending a victory celebration: Winners are called to the stage and presented with their awards to the cheers and applause of an audience. Award winners report that recognition from senior executives and acclaim from peers is as rewarding as the award itself.

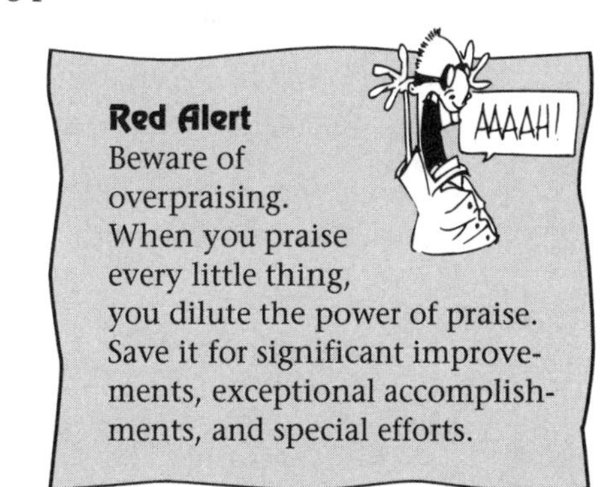

Red Alert
Beware of overpraising. When you praise every little thing, you dilute the power of praise. Save it for significant improvements, exceptional accomplishments, and special efforts.

Putting It in Writing

Telling people that you appreciate what they've done is a great idea, but *writing* it is even more effective. The aura of oral praise fades away; a letter or even a brief note endures.

You don't have to spend much money. It doesn't take much time. This section looks at how writing the praise has worked for some team leaders.

Writing Thank-You Cards

At the A&G Merchandising Company in Wilmington, Delaware, team leaders are given packets of "thank you" cards on which the words *Thank You* are printed in beautiful script on the front flap and the inside of the card is left blank. Whenever someone does something worthy of special recognition, that person's team leader writes a note on one of the cards detailing the special accomplishment and congratulating the employee for achieving it. The recipients cherish the cards and show them to friends and family.

Awarding Certificates and Plaques

No matter what type of award you give to employees—large or small (cash, merchandise, tickets to a show or sports event, or a trip to a resort, for example)—it's worth spending a few more dollars to include a certificate or plaque. Employees love to hang these mementos in their cubicles or offices, over their workbenches, or in their home. The cash gets spent, the merchandise wears out, the trip becomes a long-past memory, but a certificate or plaque is a permanent reminder of the recognition.

Maintaining Success Files

Hillary, the sales manager of a large real-estate office in Florida, makes a practice of sending letters of appreciation to sales staffers who do something special—selling a property that has been difficult to move, obtaining sales rights to a profitable building, or taking creative steps to make a sale.

With the first of these letters Hillary sends to a salesperson, she encloses a file folder labeled "Success File" with this suggestion: "File the enclosed letter in this folder. Add to it any other commendatory letters you receive from me, from other managers, from clients, or from anyone else. As time goes on, you may experience failures or disappointments. There may be times when you don't feel good about yourself. When this happens, reread these letters. They're the proof that you're a success, that you have capability, that you are a special person. You did it before; you can do it again!"

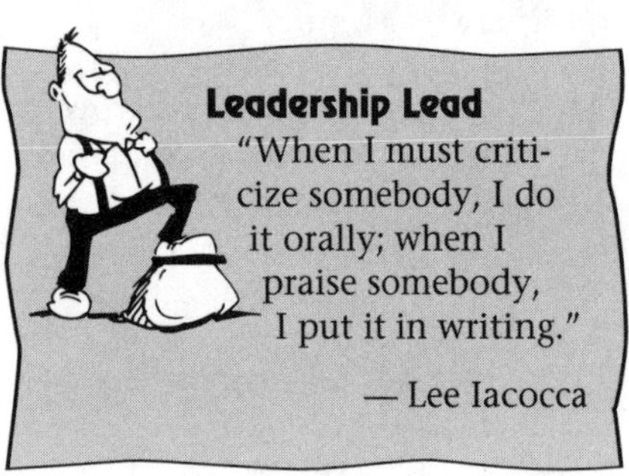

Leadership Lead

"When I must criticize somebody, I do it orally; when I praise somebody, I put it in writing."

— Lee Iacocca

The recipients of Hillary's letters repeatedly tell her how rereading the letters helps them to overcome sales slumps, periods of depression, and general disenchantment when things aren't going well. It "reprograms" their psyche by reinforcing their self-esteem and enabling them to face problems with new strength and confidence.

Creating Recognition Programs That Work

Any form of sincere recognition can be effective—some, for short periods of time; others, much longer. Recognition programs that affect the entire organization are usually developed and administered by the human-resources department. You participate in implementing the programs in your team. But even if there's no company-wide program, with a little imagination and initiative, you can create a variation just for your own team. This section discusses a few of these techniques.

Employee of the Month

Choosing an associate every month for special recognition is probably the most popular form of formal recognition program. The method of choosing employees and deciding which rewards and recognition to offer vary from company to company. This list shows look at some of the methods used and problems that have been faced in running an employee-of-the-month program:

- **Selection.** In most companies each team leader or department head nominates candidates for an award. A committee weighs the contributions of each candidate and chooses the winner. In some organizations, peers make nominations in each department, and, increasingly, any employee can make a nomination by writing a note or filling out a form. The committee makes its choice by comparing the nominees against a list of criteria and against each other.
- **Award.** Awards vary from company to company. The most frequently awarded prizes are cash, a day off with pay, or merchandise.
- **Recognition.** Almost all companies with employee-of-the-month programs have a permanent plaque prominently displayed on which the winners' names are engraved. In some companies a photo of the winner is also displayed during the month. In addition, individual certificates or plaques are given to monthly winners.

  Awards often are presented at luncheons to which all nominees for that month are invited. The winner is interviewed for an article in the company newsletter, and press releases are sent to local newspapers, radio, and TV stations.
- **Drawbacks.** Some people may believe that they are more suited for the award than the winner and resent not being chosen. Envy, a human trait, is difficult to overcome—there are always unhappy losers.

- **Overexposure.** After a while any monthly program can become overdone—it's difficult to maintain excitement and enthusiasm month after month.
- **Teams.** When people work in teams, individual efforts are subordinate to team efforts. When recognition belongs to a team, no single member of that team should be singled out for recognition.

Team Recognition

To overcome the drawback that employee-of-the-month programs recognize only one person at a time, companies have instituted team-recognition programs. In Xerox's successful program, individuals receive awards for special achievement, but, to encourage teamwork, teams also receive them. These awards include honoring teams that perform outstanding work and presenting special team awards for "Excellence in Customer Satisfaction."

Another way in which Xerox recognizes teams is by holding its annual Teamwork Day. In the first Teamwork Day, held in 1983 in a company cafeteria in Webster, New York, the objective was to teach managers the results of planning quality-circle activities and fostering a truly competitive team spirit. Thirty teams showed off projects that year and received *no rewards or cash,* just thank-yous. A combination of word-of-mouth and a company newspaper article helped ensure the participation of 60 teams the following year and an audience of 500 visitors.

In the third year of Teamwork Day, hundreds of teams wanted to participate, but there was room for only 200 (1,000 people attended the exhibits). In the fourth year the company rented the convention center in Rochester, New York, and 5,000 people attended. In its fifth year the program expanded internationally; teamwork fairs were held in Rochester, Dallas, London, Amsterdam, and elsewhere. Teamwork Day is now a highly anticipated annual event.

Peer Recognition

In the total-quality management movement (TQM), the commitment to work toward continuing improvement of quality has made every member of a team more aware of the importance of customer satisfaction. One way companies increase this awareness is by considering other employees with whom they interrelate as "internal customers" or "internal suppliers."

Encourage your associates to recognize the special achievements of their internal suppliers and any special assistance an internal customer receives that enabled him or her to serve more effectively.

Supervisors, managers, and team leaders aren't the only people who see special efforts their associates make. All team members and coworkers are exposed daily to each other's efforts. Enabling them to recognize the work of peers not only brings to the forefront any accomplishments that may not have been recognized by managers but also makes both the nominator and the nominee feel that they are part of an integrated, interrelated, and caring organization.

Minicircuit Labs, which has plants in Brooklyn, New York, and Hialeah, Florida, encourages this concept by providing all its members with "You Made My Day" forms (see the following figure).

Meanings and Gleanings

An **internal customer** is a member of your team or another team to whom you provide materials, information, or services. An **internal supplier** is another person in your organization who provides you with materials, information, or services. You may be a "customer" in some aspects of your work and a "supplier" in others.

You Made My Day!

Date: ____________

To: ____________ Dept.: ____________

From: ____________ Dept.: ____________

What you did: ____________

____

What it meant to me: ____________

____

Signed: ____________

Copy to Human Resources

Copy to team leader

Special Awards for Special Achievements

To win one of Mary Kay's highest and most coveted awards—those famous pink Cadillacs—at its award celebrations, its salespeople must meet a series of challenges and criteria (see the section "Five Tips for Effective Praise," earlier in this chapter). It's not easy to win the award, but every year more Mary Kay associates "make the grade."

Mary Kay doesn't *give* the cars away, however—it *lends* them for one year. Anyone who wants to keep a car or upgrade to the next year's model must continue to meet the standards. What an incentive to keep up the good work! As a result, relatively few winners have to give up their car.

In some organizations special awards are given not as part of a formal program, but on a manager's initiative. During the pre-Thanksgiving rush at Stew Leonard's food market in Norwalk, Connecticut, several office personnel noticed the long, creeping lines at checkout counters and—with no prompting from management—left their regular work duties to help cashiers bag the groceries, which helped speed up the lines.

Stew, the owner of the market, resolved to do something special for the employees who helped out. After the holiday rush was over, he bought for each of the employees a beautifully knitted shirt with the embroidered inscription "Stew Leonard ABCD Award." The inscription stands for "*a*bove and *b*eyond the *c*all of *d*uty." By giving special recognition to associates who do more than their jobs require, he not only gave credit where credit was due but also let everyone—the associates and their coworkers and supervisors, in addition to customers—know that he appreciated the extra effort.

The Least You Need to Know

- By showing sincere interest in each of your associates, you establish a climate that's conducive to cooperation and team spirit.
- Provide positive reinforcement by seeking out and praising accomplishments instead of concentrating on faults that need correction.
- Encourage team members to show appreciation for their coworkers through peer-recognition programs.
- To make praise truly sincere, specify the reason for the praise in the praise itself.
- Put your appreciation in writing. Brief notes, letters of commendation, and certificates of achievement give long-term value to the act of praising.
- Create ongoing programs to recognize the achievements of both individuals and teams. Find original ways to keep these programs exciting and rewarding.

Chapter 17

Keep 'Em Moving

In This Chapter

- When opportunity motivates—and when it doesn't
- The challenge of renewing lost motivation
- Do it or else—the pros and cons of negative motivation
- Motivation under adverse conditions

Almost everyone reacts positively to recognition and praise. But these are not the only ways to motivate people. When you work with a team, it's essential that you, as the team leader, identify how each person on the team reacts to various types of motivation. It's easy to fall into the trap of assuming that what motivates you or what has been successful in motivating other people in the past will work for everyone.

This chapter looks at some other motivators that work for some people, but not for all. It also explores problems that develop in motivating a team when companies downsize, freeze wages, or change policies.

Opportunity—For What?

You're ambitious. You knock yourself out to get ahead, so you assume that everyone is ambitious. Not so!

When I was an officer in the U.S. Army, I told one of the privates in my unit that I was recommending him for promotion to corporal. Instead of the elation I expected, he objected: "No, sir, I don't want all that responsibility. All I want to be is one of the boys." I couldn't understand his reaction.

Leadership Lead

Help develop career opportunities for your team members by recognizing each member's talents; helping to develop these abilities by coaching and training; and giving them assignments in which they can utilize their special skills and gain recognition for their achievements.

During the years I've been in the business world, I've heard similar reactions from men and women who are perfectly content to just "have a job." They do what they have to do and no more. Their real interests lie somewhere outside their work. Before you decide to offer a promotion to a team member, learn that person's real goals. Discuss the ramifications of the promotion in terms of additional time and effort that may be required. Unless you're sure that he or she will welcome this type of opportunity, to offer advancement is a waste of breath.

Red Alert

Don't project your ambitions on others. Their desires may be much different from yours. To motivate an individual, you must know that person's goals and what he or she seeks from a job.

Alicia was desolate. When her boss was transferred, she expected to be promoted to his job, but the company promoted someone else. She complained, "I've been in the department longer than anyone else and have never missed a day's work. My performance reviews are always good. I should have gotten the promotion."

Why was Alicia passed over? Seniority, good attendance, and satisfactory work are important, but they're not the only or even the primary reasons for promotion. Alicia was perfectly happy to do her work, but not one bit more. To her, advancement was something to which she was entitled, not something toward which she had to work.

Encouraging People to Aim for Advancement

Suppose that your organization has excellent opportunities for advancement. You believe that some of your team members have the potential to move up to those jobs, but they're perfectly content to do what they have to do and have no desire to do more. You don't want all that talent to be wasted. Here are some guidelines for motivating these folks to change their attitude:

- Find out what really turns them on. They may be satisfying their needs outside of work.
- Show how working toward advancement might help them meet their outside goals. For example, Christine is a winter skier and summer surfer. To pursue these sports, she needs money, and higher-level jobs pay higher salaries. As another example, Ken's life centers around his children. Working toward a higher-level job will give him the income to provide the type of education he wants for them.
- Some people are status-conscious. Point out how advancement increases prestige not only in the company but also in the community.
- Creative people can be encouraged to work for advancement by showing how higher-level positions give them the chance to use their own initiative and institute some of their creative ideas.

Dealing with People Who Want to Advance When There's No Opportunity

When ambitious people are frustrated by lack of opportunity for career advancement, it's tough to keep them motivated. They often quit or request a transfer to a department that offers better opportunities. If the chances for promotion are blocked because of a temporary economic situation or short-term internal problems, make sure that these factors are clear to everyone and that opportunities become available in the future.

If it's unlikely that advancement will occur in a reasonable period, you have to expect that ambitious people won't be content. Do your best to motivate them in other ways:

- Make special assignments to enable them to stretch their minds.
- Get them deeply involved in team projects so that their satisfaction in seeing the team's achievements replaces their personal desires.
- If you can, set up a compensation system that rewards them financially.

Some companies use a two-track compensation program so that people can be given financial reward and status without being promoted. One track is in management (the traditional promotional ladder); employees on the other track receive the equivalent pay and rank, but are nonmanagerial. A technical company's tracks may look like this:

Managerial	Technical
Section leader	Engineering leader
Department chief	Principal engineer
Project manager	Project engineer
Engineering manager	Chief engineer

Motivating the "Unmotivatible"

Meanings and Gleanings

Long-term employees who have gone as far as they can and are not likely to be fired because of their tenure may become **coasters** until they retire.

Red Alert

Don't assume that just because an employee is close to retirement he or she is a coaster. Many older people remain committed to their jobs and continue to give it their best efforts as long as they're part of the team.

You have to accept that some people just can't be motivated (short of putting a stick of dynamite under their chairs). With the right approach, many men and women who seem to be complacent and unmovable might be spurred toward improved performance.

Some employees have been with their organization for many years. They've gone as far as they can go—and they know it. They also know that it's unlikely they'll ever be fired as long as they meet minimum performance standards, because most companies don't fire long-term employees except under dire circumstances. People with the attitude "I'll do as little as I can get away with" are called *coasters*.

Coasting isn't limited to "old-timers." People of all ages, unfortunately, fall into this category. They meet your minimum standards, but make no effort to do more.

It's difficult to motivate people who really don't want to be motivated, and many managers and team leaders don't even try. They look at these people as crosses they have to bear.

Learning Not to Give Up

One often-successful approach to motivating coasters is giving them challenges—assignments or projects they can really "sink their teeth into."

Realistically, not everyone gets excited by challenges. Some people, faced with a challenge, turn away from it—it's too much trouble. But for those who are challenged by an assignment, it can be a powerful motivator. Here are some guidelines:

- **Make the coaster a mentor to a new team member.** Many "old-timers" are flattered when asked to pass on their know-how and experience to the next generation. To ensure that they train newcomers properly, they hone their own skills and brush up on the latest developments in their field. Serious mentors do more than just train—they set good examples for their new associates.
- **Assign special projects.** Before the Associated Merchandise Company introduces a new product, it conducts a test market in key cities, a task it usually subcontracts to a market-research firm. In testing its latest product, Associated tried a new approach: Rather than subcontract the job, it chose six men and women who had good marketing backgrounds but were now coasting. The six employees were temporarily relieved from their regular duties for four weeks. After a week of special training, each was sent to a test site to run the project. The challenge of a special assignment, enhanced by the success of the test, gave the coasters new enthusiasm that carried over into their regular work.
- **Plan future projects.** Coasters often feel left out. "I'll be retiring in a few years, so why worry about what the company will do then?" Their attitude is exacerbated by the fact that their managers have already given up on them. By bringing coasters into the process of planning projects along with younger employees, you let them know that they are valued team members, that they can bring to the group the value of their experience, and, conversely, that they will benefit by learning from other members.

Red Alert

AAAAH!

The downside of challenge as a motivator is that, after a challenging assignment ends, the excitement it generates carries over for a while but gradually fades. After a task is no longer a challenge, it's no longer a motivator either. You have to keep presenting new challenges.

Using the Best Motivator of All

If you enjoy your work, if it provides job satisfaction, if you can't wait to go to work every morning and hate to leave each evening, there's no need for any other type of motivation, right?

Is this a pipe dream? Although many new jobs being created in growth industries have the ingredients that lead to enjoyment and satisfaction, a large number of people have jobs that are routine, dull, and sometimes tedious. It's difficult, if not impossible, to generate excitement about these jobs.

One way to make dull jobs more "worker friendly" is to redesign these jobs. Rather than look at a job as a series of tasks that must be performed, study it as a total process. Make the job less routine by enlarging the scope of the job. Focus on what has to be accomplished rather than on the steps leading to its accomplishment by redesigning the manner in which the job is performed. This section presents some examples.

Enriching the Job

When Jennifer was hired to head the claims-processing department at Liability Insurance Company, she inherited a department with low morale, high turnover, and disgruntled employees. The claims-processing operation was an "assembly line" in which each clerk checked a section of the form and sent it to other clerks, each of whom checked another section. If errors were found, the form was sent to a specialist for handling. Efficient? Maybe, but it made the work dull and not very challenging.

Jennifer reorganized the process. She eliminated the assembly line and retrained each clerk to check the entire form, correct any errors, and personally deal with problems. Although operations slowed down during the break-in period, it paid off in a highly motivated team of workers who found gratification in working through the entire process and seeing it completed satisfactorily.

When team members are trained to perform all aspects of the jobs their team handles, you not only can assign any part of the work to any member (which gives a team leader much more flexibility), but also, because members do different work at different times, break the boredom of routine.

Involving Everyone in Planning

There are many types of work for which production quotas are established. Word-processing operators are given the number of letters they must complete each day; production workers are given hourly quotas; salespeople must meet monthly standards. Management usually sets these quotas, but most workers don't like having quotas imposed on them; if management wants to raise quotas, employees are resentful and resistant.

Have your team members participate in setting quotas for their own jobs. You might think that they'll set low quotas that are easy to meet, and it may happen. That's why the process is *participative*—you haven't stepped out of the picture completely. You're one of the participants. Your role is to ensure that realistic goals are set. In most cases, however, team members do set reasonable quotas, and because it's *their* goal, they accept it and work to achieve it.

Another example of participation in planning is the experience of Ford Motor Company, in its development of the Taurus. Ford didn't follow the usual industry practice of having a group of specialists design the car. Workers representing every type of job that would be involved in building the car were brought in to work with designers in the planning stage. The suggestions culled from workers' experience on the production line brought forth ideas that might never have occurred to the specialists. When the Taurus was brought to the factory floor, workers looked on it as *their* car. The result: The Taurus became the most troublefree and profitable car Ford has introduced in recent years—because the company's workers were involved.

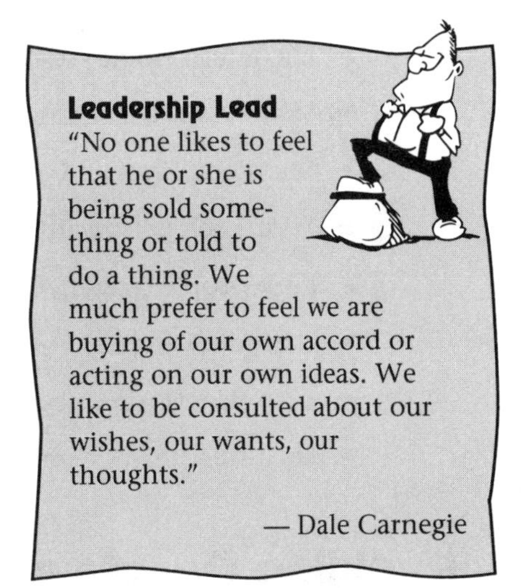

Leadership Lead
"No one likes to feel that he or she is being sold something or told to do a thing. We much prefer to feel we are buying of our own accord or acting on our own ideas. We like to be consulted about our wishes, our wants, our thoughts."

— Dale Carnegie

Some Motivators to Remember

This section lists some of the best techniques (in my experience) for motivating people to commit themselves to superior performance:

- Encourage participation by setting goals and determining how to reach them.
- Keep team members aware of how their job relates to others.
- Provide the tools and training necessary to succeed.
- Pay at least the going rate for jobs that are performed.
- Provide good, safe working conditions.
- Give clear directions that are understood and accepted.
- Know people's abilities and give them assignments based on their ability to handle those assignments.
- Allow team members to make decisions related to their jobs.
- Be accessible. Listen actively and empathetically.
- Give credit and praise for a job well done.
- Give prompt and direct answers to questions.
- Treat team members fairly and with respect and consideration.
- Help out with work problems.

- Encourage employees to acquire additional knowledge and skills.
- Show interest and concern for people as individuals.
- Learn employees' M.O.s and deal with them accordingly.
- Make each person an integral part of the team.
- Keep people challenged and excited by their work.
- Consider your team members' ideas and suggestions.
- Keep people informed about how they're doing on the job.
- Encourage team members to do their best and then support their efforts.

Avoiding Negative Motivation

Remember KITA? Chapter 2 debunked the myth that to get people to work you have to kick them in the you-know-what.

Threatening to fire people if they don't work is sometimes effective, at least temporarily. When jobs are scarce and people know that they won't have a job if they get fired, they *do* work. But how much work do they do? Some folks work just enough to keep from getting fired and not one bit more. This fear isn't real motivation; *real* motivation spurs people to produce more than just what's necessary to keep their job.

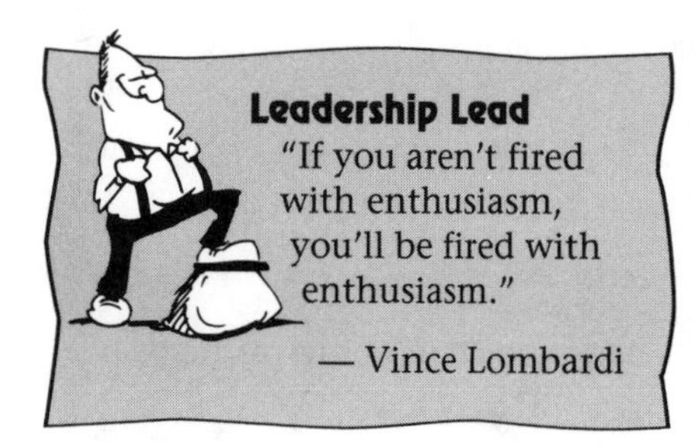

Leadership Lead
"If you aren't fired with enthusiasm, you'll be fired with enthusiasm."
— Vince Lombardi

Fear of being fired becomes less of a motivator as the job market again expands. If comparable jobs are available in more amenable environments, why work for a martinet?

Some people do respond to negative motivation. Maybe they've been raised by intimidating parents or have worked under tyrannical bosses for so long that it's the only way of life they understand. Good leaders must recognize each person's individualities and adapt to them.

Motivating People Under Unfavorable Circumstances

Things don't always go well. Businesses go into slumps. Companies downsize and eliminate jobs. Large companies swallow smaller ones. How can morale be maintained and staff members motivated when they see their economic world toppling down around them? It's not easy, but, as you'll learn in this section, there are ways to do it.

Downsizing

When business is slow, companies reduce costs by laying off employees. Layoffs have always been an element of the job world, particularly among blue-collar workers. When business picks up, workers are likely to be rehired.

Downsizing differs from traditional layoffs in that total job categories are eliminated: There's little chance that people who have held these jobs will ever be rehired. Downsized positions are increasingly white-collar and managerial jobs.

Elliot left his boss' office in shock. He had been told that the company was downsizing and that he would have to cut his team from 20 people to 15. He had worked hard to build a highly motivated team. Not only would he lose 5 good members but also the remaining employees would feel insecure, stressed, and demotivated.

After the trauma of the layoffs subsided, Elliot took these steps to begin the rebuilding process:

- Reassured team members that management had completed the downsizing process and that their jobs were secure.
- Set up a series of meetings to restructure the team so that all work would be covered.
- Assigned projects to subteams to implement the new structure with minimum loss of productivity in ongoing activities.
- Personally counseled team members who showed signs of unusual stress.

Within a short time Elliot's team again functioned at optimum capacity.

Meanings and Gleanings
Some companies, in their drive to cut costs or increase profits, eliminate total job categories. This process is usually called *downsizing*. Some companies prefer the terms "rightsizing" or "destaffing" or corrupt the term "reengineering" (see the definition in the glossary) to make it sound less threatening.

Leadership Lead
When you deal with survivors of downsizing, don't assume that things are the same as before. Take overt action to help your team members cope with their fears and stresses. Get your entire team involved in productive activities that not only keep them from brooding but also actively engage their minds and bodies.

Bet You Didn't Know

According to a survey made by the American Management Association of 1,000 companies in 1995, one-third of the companies surveyed who underwent major downsizing ended up with more employees because of the new workers they hired. On the downside, supervisors and managers were getting axed; on the upside, professional and technical workers were hired.

Knowing What to Do When Your Company Is Taken Over

It seems that every time you pick up a newspaper you read about another merger or acquisition. Chase Manhattan's acquisition of Chemical Bank is the largest bank merger ever, but it has resulted in the loss of thousands of jobs. Disney bought Capitol City-ABC, and more jobs were lost as its headquarters offices were consolidated. Your company could be next.

The people most likely to survive an acquisition are those who work for the acquiring company, but even that's not a sure thing. Federated Department Stores bought Macy's and closed several of its own stores.

Whenever a merger or acquisition occurs, employees of both groups are certain to be insecure and concerned. As a team leader, little ol' you can do nothing until the dust settles, which often takes months or even years.

The following suggestions can give your team a better chance of survival:

- **Work harder, work smarter.** When Associated Finance acquired Guardian Loan, all of Guardian's employees were concerned. They were sure that the larger company would eliminate their jobs. Alberta, Guardian's credit manager, thought differently. She told her team, "Our credit people are the best in the business. One reason they bought us was our excellent record in this area. They need us. It will take at least six months before Associated can make any changes here. Let's show them that we are essential to their success." And they did. When the reorganization finally took place, Associated merged several departments with its own, but the credit department was left intact.
- **Be prepared to do things differently.** Companies that acquire others install their own systems and procedures. Accept them without complaints. Neither you nor your associates should ever say, "We never used to do it that way." Work their way. If it requires you to learn new technology, learn it as soon as possible.

➤ **Be patient.** After you master the new company's methods and win the confidence of the new management team, they will listen to your ideas for improvements and innovations.

Realizing That Everyone Has to Work Harder

Regardless of whether a company has downsized or reorganized because of an acquisition or another reason, you usually wind up with fewer people having to accomplish more work.

Suppose that a team of six people has been reduced to four but that the amount of work hasn't decreased. Work previously done at a leisurely pace must now be rushed. People who went home at 5 P.M. now work regularly until 7 or 8. Everyone feels the pressure. Morale is at a low point.

How to motivate people who work longer hours and under constant pressure is the primary challenge managers face, and there are no easy answers. Some managers counter complaints by telling team members that they're lucky to have a job. This answer isn't a good one, though. As mentioned, negative motivation has limited value.

By encouraging your team to find shortcuts to better production, to eliminate unnecessary paperwork, and to come up with creative innovations, they can reduce some of the added burden.

Some companies have instituted stress-reduction programs to help people cope with downsizing and reorganization. Let team members know that, as business improves, temporary and eventually permanent staff members will be added to ease the workload.

Bet You Didn't Know

A 1995 survey of managerial and professional personnel by the U.S. Chamber of Commerce showed that the 40-hour work week is dead. Most respondents said that they work 9-hour days in addition to 1 or more hours at home in the evenings and at least 2 hours on weekends.

Motivating People When Wages Are Frozen

Suppose that your company hasn't raised anyone's wages for three years. Your team members are unhappy and resist all your efforts to get them to produce more. You repeatedly hear the complaint "Why should I knock myself out when they won't pay me more?"

Sanjay, a chief engineer at a chemical company, was tired of hearing this complaint. He had tried hard, but unsuccessfully, to get management to lift the freeze. At one of his team meetings he addressed the issue: "I know you haven't had a raise in three years. Neither have I, nor has my boss. You all know that business has been down during this time and that, after it improves, the freeze will end. Business is up this year, but not enough. So let's get to work so that we can do our part to make this a profitable company again."

This technique is one way to help team members understand the problem and that it's one which can and will be overcome. (It doesn't do any good, however, if people read in the newspaper that the company CEO has just taken a $1 million bonus.)

The Least You Need to Know

- Not everyone seeks advancement, but to those who do it's a great motivator.
- If opportunity for advancement is limited in your organization, you can motivate people by giving them assignments that enable them to stretch their minds, be creative, or take leadership roles in team activities.
- You can often "remotivate" coasters by giving them new challenges.
- The best motivator of all is to enrich the job so that people can obtain real satisfaction from their work.
- Survivors of downsizing are often worried and insecure. They need reassurance. Get them involved in productive projects that stimulate them and enable them to experience success.
- If your company is acquired by another, your chances of survival can be improved if you and your team make yourselves too valuable to drop.

Chapter 18

Empowerment: The Buzzword of the '90s

In This Chapter

- What empowerment is all about
- Empowerment and team development
- Why team members often resist empowerment
- How to make empowerment work for you

If you've been around management circles for any length of time, you've been exposed to buzzwords. *Everyone* uses these terms and phrases. You go to trade association meetings where these terms are the main topic of discussion. They pop up in casual conversations among businesspeople, and they're featured in every business publication.

Over the years, terms such as "scientific management," "industrial engineering," "sensitivity training," "management grid," and "management by objective" have come and gone.

The concepts these terms represented weren't fireworks that lit up the industrial sky for a short time and disappeared forever. We all learned something from each concept that, after the use of the buzzword faded, remained as part of the practice of management.

It's not easy to empower people: Some leaders don't want to give up their power, and some team members don't want to take the responsibility that goes with power. This chapter looks at how empowerment works in practice and how it can make you a more effective team leader.

Empowerment is the buzzword of the '90s. Whether the concept remains as a major force in management thinking or eventually fades away, it has already contributed a great deal to individual and team performance and productivity.

Calling the Shots

Who has the power in a company? Who makes the decisions that govern how a company, a department, or a team operates? In most companies, power is in the hands of management. In a typical hierarchy, the power flows downward from the CEO through the layers of management. Each layer has power over the one beneath it. For example, you have power over the people you supervise.

Here's how the traditional power structure works: Your boss gives you an assignment. You look it over, determine how it should be done, and assign various components of the job to your team members. Then you follow it through until it's completed.

Empowerment changes this process. You share with your team the power to make decisions about an assignment. Rather than tell team members what each of them will do, you work together to plan and execute the entire project.

The concept of empowerment isn't entirely new. For years companies have engaged in a variation called "participative management." Empowerment carries participation one step further. Team members not only participate in decision making but also are authorized to make decisions on their own without seeking approval from higher-level managers.

The installation of a new sprinkler system at the Woodbury Golf Club was the biggest job that All-Star Landscaping had ever received. Bill, the owner-manager, had just completed a management seminar on empowerment and thought that this project was a good chance to put into practice what he had learned in the course.

> **Meanings and Gleanings**
>
> **Empowerment** means sharing your power with the people over whom you have power. Team members are given the authority to make decisions that previously were reserved for managers.

A few weeks before the job was to begin, Bill invited his team members to his home for a breakfast meeting to discuss the job. He outlined the project and asked for ideas about how to proceed. One associate suggested that, in their regular landscaping work at the club, they could identify the best locations for the sprinkler heads and save the time and cost of a special survey. Another volunteered to examine the current system to determine which parts, if any, could be incorporated into the new system.

At their next meeting, the team planned the entire job and agreed on who would complete each part. When the work began, the team went to work full of enthusiasm, knowing that they were committed to successfully completing the job because they had been completely involved in the planning.

During the installation, as problems arose, the team members were empowered to make decisions to correct them without having to get Bill's approval every time.

Leadership Lead
To create enthusiasm and commitment on a job, get the people who will do the job involved in planning it.

Bill reported that if he had done all the preparatory work himself and had just assigned the work to his team members and required them to come to him to solve every problem, it would have taken longer and cost more and the workers involved would have looked at it as just another job.

The Three Pluses of Empowerment

As Bill learned from his first experience in empowerment, much can be gained from it. The three major benefits of empowerment are described in this section.

Ideas

You've heard the expression "Two heads are better than one." Perhaps ten heads are even better. People who work on a job know a great deal more about what's going on in their working environment than many managers realize. They see things that are done inefficiently, and they have ideas for improvement. By eliciting their input about new projects and assignments, you're likely to pick up ideas that may not have occurred to you.

Rachel, Baldwin Insurance Agency's office manager, empowered her staff to design and institute a new filing system. Some of the best suggestions came from a high-school student who worked part time. The young woman demonstrated that some of the practices they had followed for years and had assumed were the best methods could be made easier.

Synergism

As noted, when a team generates ideas, a suggestion one participant makes can trigger ideas from another person that he or she would never have come up with alone. This process leads to an abundance of ideas from an empowered team.

This process of *synergism* isn't limited to generating ideas, however. Synergism, defined as "two or more units (people, in this case) working together to achieve a greater effect than individuals can do by themselves," is exactly what happens in an empowered team.

If each of Bill's landscapers had worked alone to perform a specific phase of the sprinkler installation, the job would have been completed, but it would have taken longer and most likely errors would have occurred that had to be corrected later. By working as a team, each person knew what the others were doing and, if help was needed, could pitch in.

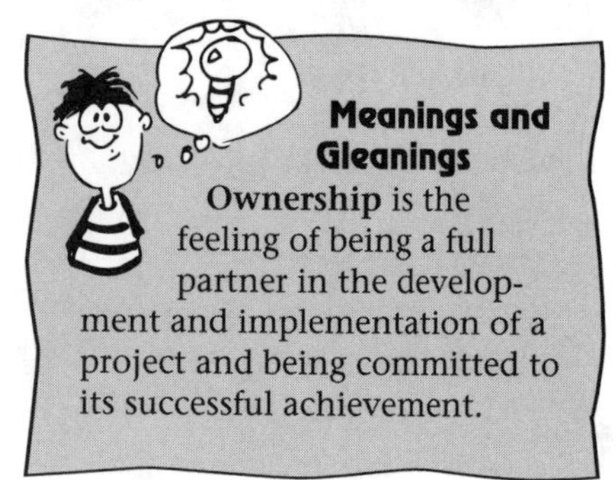

Meanings and Gleanings

Ownership is the feeling of being a full partner in the development and implementation of a project and being committed to its successful achievement.

When all members of an empowered team are engaged in the same type of work, each person should be trained to do all aspects of that work. As noted, some teams are multifunctional—they consist of people from different disciplines. Although each member of a team made up of marketing, engineering, and finance specialists cannot be expected to do the jobs of their colleagues in other areas of expertise, their total involvement in the planning process lets them know exactly what each team member is doing. The results are coordinated effort and goals that are easier to achieve.

Ownership

When people participate in planning a project, they identify with the project. Because *their* ideas are being implemented, they're committed to its success.

Leadership Lead

Empower people who deal with customer problems to deal with them without the usual delays and red tape that results from the need to seek approval from above. At Nordstroms' department stores, any sales clerk can make exchanges, give refunds, or provide special service. At ATT Universal Credit Company, requests for credit-limit increases are handled by the person receiving the call.

Gail looked at her job as routine and dull. She did what she had to do and no more. When her boss informed the department that the company was changing its structure to team empowerment, Gail was skeptical. "It's just another gimmick to get us to work harder," she thought.

When the first project under the new system was introduced, Gail sat quietly and listened. Instead of being told what had to be done, the group was asked how they thought the project should be approached. Gail was alert and interested. After awhile she timidly raised her hand and made a suggestion that everyone thought was a good idea. By the time the meeting ended, Gail and her associates were excited about the job and were eager to get to work and make it a success.

Three Problems of Empowerment

Empowerment can be a great way to motivate people to accomplish superior work, but it doesn't always work. This section looks at some of the major problem areas.

I've Earned the Right to Use My Power, and I Don't Want to Give It Up

Men and women who have worked hard to be promoted to managerial positions often believe that empowering their team members will lower their own positions. A couple of the reasons that they may feel this way are shown in this list:

- **Status.** Whether you work as a traditional manager or as the leader of an empowered team, you don't lose your status by sharing power with the team. It's a difference not in rank or position, but in methodology. Rather than "boss," you teach, inspire, and motivate your team. Being the leader of an empowered team is a high-status position.
- **Control.** Some managers ask the question, "I'm still responsible for this department—how can I give up my power without losing control?" You don't have to lose control when you share power. You're a member of a team. You're directly in the midst of every activity and know how each team project is progressing. You are aware of this, and so is *every member* of your team. Control becomes team control. As team leader, you guide your team to meet performance standards (see chapter 19).

Some People Don't Want to Be Empowered

Wendy was perplexed. She thought that her team members would be excited and enthusiastic about learning of their company's move to empowered teams. Instead, she realized that several people were upset. They had these reactions:

"I'm not paid to make decisions—that's your job."

"Just tell me what to do, and I'll do it."

"I work hard enough as it is. I don't want more responsibility."

Red Alert
Not everyone is thrilled to be empowered. Sometimes you have to sell them on the idea.

Your first job as team leader of a newly empowered team involves converting people who think this way into enthusiastic supporters of the new method of working. Here are some suggestions that may help you do this:

- **Many people don't want to stretch their brains.** Employees are often happy doing routine work in a routine way. Find the true reason that they feel this way. Perhaps they don't believe that they have the ability to do more than routine work. Sometimes you have to work with team members to build up their self-confidence.
- **Team members may not fully understand their new roles.** Take the time in the beginning to explain the true meaning of empowerment. Time spent in good orientation pays off in better team efforts.
- **Train your team members in methods for generating ideas, such as brainstorming.** Show videos about team participation. Have members of another team that has been successful in empowered activities describe how empowerment has worked for their team.
- **Get under way slowly.** Choose assignments or projects that easily lend themselves to participative effort in the beginning. Gradually progress to the point at which team members tackle all projects collaboratively.

Empowerment Makes Leaders Unnecessary

Some managers fear that their company will have no need for them after empowerment becomes the way of organizational life. If everyone is involved in what managers traditionally do, what role is left for managers?

In some companies the job of the team leader has been redesigned. Traditional teams are replaced by "self-directed" teams that have no permanent team leader (see chapter 22); the team chooses a project leader (or two or more leaders) for each project. Few companies now have totally self-directed teams, however. Because most teams work on multiple projects, a modified version may be used in which a permanent team leader serves the important purpose of coordinating all team activities and providing training and support.

Making Empowerment Work for You

Empowerment isn't a panacea for curing all management problems. Its primary benefit is that it enhances collaborative efforts to get a job accomplished by giving every member of a team the power to get things done.

In General Motor's Saturn division, any assembly-line worker can push the button that stops the line if he or she sees something that needs correction (a power most companies reserve for managers).

One GM employee reported on television that he "pushed that button once," after he realized that a part had not been inserted properly on a chassis. The correction took just a few seconds, but the employee said that it made him feel good that he had the power to stop the line and that he was able to help maintain the quality of GM's cars.

Jerry Junkins, the CEO of Texas Instruments, believes that the number-one strength of his organization is its 1,900 empowered teams.

Major companies such as General Electric, Kodak, and Federal Express have reported that instituting empowered teams has made them able to not only keep up but also move ahead in their tough, competitive industries. Thousands of smaller companies relate similar experiences.

Leadership Lead

Titles may change, and functions may be altered, but there will always be a role for people who can guide, counsel, and motivate their coworkers. Empowerment doesn't mean giving up power—it means *sharing* it. It doesn't mean that you abdicate responsibility either; instead, you create a climate in which all team members are as excited about the job as you are.

To help your empowerment program succeed, follow these guidelines:

- The program must have the full support of top management. Empowerment works most effectively when a company's CEO empowers its senior management group who in turn passes that empowerment down through the organization.
- Team members and team leaders should be trained in the techniques of empowerment. Because many companies assume that the transition to empowerment is more difficult for team members than for team leaders, they concentrate their training on team members. Because the program is collaborative, supervisors (now team leaders) and employees (now team members) should be trained together by consultants or others who are knowledgeable in this type of work.
- All team members should be given full information about team projects; support to acquire necessary skills and techniques; freedom to interact with the team leader and any team member to accomplish the team's goals; and encouragement to use their initiative in planning and implementing projects.
- Counseling should be available to assist people who have difficulty adjusting to the new techniques.
- Training should be ongoing. Many organizations have excellent training programs for orienting and starting up an empowered-team program; after the program is under way, however, assume that it will work smoothly. As teams mature, many initial problems are overcome, and new problems occur. Hold reinforcement training meetings periodically to discuss and resolve complexities that develop.

Leadership Lead

Many helpful training programs are available for training people in empowerment: The Covey Leadership Center, 3507 N. University Avenue, Provo, UT 84604 (1-800-331-7716); Dun & Bradstreet Business Education Services, 711 Third Avenue, New York, NY 10017 (1-800-999-1237); and Dale Carnegie Training, 1475 Franklin Avenue, Garden City, NY 11550 (1-516-248-5100).

- In self-directed teams, every team member may be required to coach and facilitate certain projects or parts of projects. These members should have the opportunity to take the same leadership-training programs that are given to permanent team leaders.
- In theory, everyone can be trained to be a leader, but in practice it doesn't always work. Some people aren't emotionally suited for leadership roles; they just aren't motivated to assume these types of duties. These people will not or cannot change their patterns of behavior from dogmatism to participation. Allowing them to remain in leadership positions is destructive—they must be removed. The team leader is the fulcrum on which a team revolves. Highly motivated, well-trained, committed team leaders are essential to the success of empowered teams.

The Least You Need to Know

- Empowerment is the sharing of power to make decisions in planning and implementing a job with the people who will perform that job.
- Empowerment fosters synergism. By interacting and collaborating, team members produce more and better work than they can as individuals.
- Empowerment fosters ownership. People involved in determining how a project will be accomplished are committed to its success.
- When you empower your team, you don't have to lose control. Empowered teams work with you to ensure that performance standards are met.
- Some team members may not want to be empowered. Win them over with a well-planned orientation, and, if necessary, augment it with individual counseling.
- Team leaders and members alike should be thoroughly trained in the way empowerment will change the way they work. This training should be conducted by experts in empowerment and should be reinforced with periodic refresher meetings.

Part 6
Dealing with Employee Problems on the Job

You have a good team in place, and all its members are carrying their weight—well, maybe not everyone. You know that some of your coworkers can do better. They're meeting their performance standards, but just barely. Performance-review time is approaching, so here's your chance to shape them up. There's Burt, who seems to be on the verge of burnout; Ellen, who is so sensitive you're afraid to correct her errors; Stacey, who's always finding something to gripe about; and then there's that new programmer, whom you suspect has a drinking problem. To keep your team functioning effectively, you feel that it's your job to counsel them and help them.

You've shaped up your team, but now some of your work is being done by telecommuters and subcontractors, and you're concerned about melding them into the total operation.

This part of the book provides tips and techniques to guide you through the continually challenging job of maintaining a top-performing team.

Chapter 19

Evaluating Team Members' Performance

In This Chapter

- Setting performance standards
- Completing a formal performance appraisal
- Deciding whether to measure by traits or by results
- Conducting an appraisal interview

"How am I doing?" you ask your boss. Just as you want to know what your bosses think of your work, your team members are concerned about your opinion of their work. Most companies have periodic (usually annual) employee appraisals. Team leaders shouldn't wait for this formal review, however: Between appraisal sessions, you should talk to your team members regularly about their performance and make it an ongoing part of your coaching.

This chapter discusses how to set performance standards that are meaningful to team members and describes some of the techniques for measuring performance. You'll also learn how to conduct a formal appraisal interview.

Setting Performance Standards

All employees should know just what's expected of them on the job. Many companies develop and incorporate performance standards at the time they create a job description. In other companies, a job evolves as standards are established.

In routine jobs, the key factors of performance standards involve quantity (how much should be produced per hour or per day) and quality (what level of quality is acceptable). As jobs become more complex, these standards aren't an adequate way to measure performance. Ideas and innovations that are conceived in creative jobs cannot be quantified, and quality may be difficult to measure. This situation doesn't mean that you can't have performance standards for these jobs, but it does require a different approach, such as the results-oriented evaluation system described later in this chapter.

Establishing Criteria for Performance Standards

Performance standards are usually based on the experiences of satisfactory workers who have done that type of work over a length of time. Whether the standards cover quality or quantity of the work or other aspects of the job, they should meet these criteria:

Meanings and Gleanings

Performance standards define the results that are expected from a person performing a job. For performance standards to be meaningful, all persons doing that job should know and accept these standards. Team participation in the establishment of performance standards is one way to ensure this understanding.

- **Specific.** Every person doing a job should know exactly what he or she is expected to do.
- **Measurable.** The company should have a touchstone against which performance can be measured. Measuring performance is easy when a standard is quantifiable; it's more difficult (but not impossible) when it isn't quantifiable. When a numerical measurement isn't feasible, some of the criteria may include timely completion of assignments, introduction of new concepts, or contribution to team activities.
- **Realistic.** Unless standards are attainable, people consider them unfair and resist working toward them.

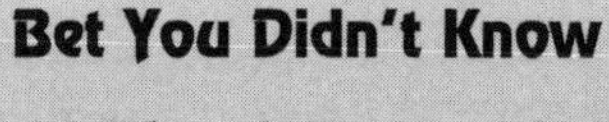

Bet You Didn't Know

W. Edwards Deming, the father of the quality movement, was strongly opposed to performance reviews. He believed that, in most companies, performance was equated with quantity at the sacrifice of quality. This was the case for a long time, but quality standards today are given equal or greater weight in evaluations.

Performing Self-Evaluation

When all team members know what's expected of them and against which standards they'll be measured, self-evaluation becomes almost automatic. Members don't have to wait for their team leader to tell them that they're below standard or behind schedule—they see that for themselves and can take corrective action immediately.

Self-evaluation makes a team leader's job easier. Like a good coach, he or she helps keep the team aware of the standards and provides support and encouragement to stay on target.

Conducting Formal Performance Appraisals

Even if team members know the performance standards and can measure their own performance, and if team leaders reinforce this process with ongoing discussions about performance, there's still a need for formal appraisals. Most formal appraisals are conducted annually. Many team leaders add an informal appraisal semi-annually or quarterly as a means of helping team members be aware of their progress.

This list describes some of the reasons that formal appraisals are important:

- They provide a framework for discussing a team member's overall work record. The team leader can use this meeting to recognize an employee for past successes and provide suggestions for even greater contributions.
- They become more objective and enable team leaders to compare all members of the team against the same criteria.
- They provide helpful data for determining what type of additional training team members need.
- In many companies, they're the primary factor in determining salary increases and bonuses.
- Their formality causes them to be taken more seriously than informal comments about performance.
- They can be used as a vehicle for goal setting, career planning, and personal growth.

Examining the Downside of Formal Appraisals

Formal appraisals have some inherent problems, some of which are listed in this section:

- They can be stressful for both leaders and team members.
- They make some team leaders so uncomfortable about making associates unhappy that the leaders overrate their performance.

- Many are inadequate, cumbersome, or poorly designed, which creates more problems than solutions.
- In some appraisals, good workers are underrated because their team leaders are afraid that team members might become competitors.

Bet You Didn't Know

In a survey conducted at Dun & Bradstreet seminars, supervisors were asked what they liked least about their jobs. The top reason was having to fire people; a close second was formal appraisal interviews.

A properly managed performance appraisal can be a highly stimulating experience for both team members and team leaders. To make it most effective, don't treat it as a confrontation. Treat it instead as a meaningful two-way interchange that leads to an employee's commitment to reach out for improvement and set and implement goals for the coming year that will lead to a more productive and satisfying work experience.

Choosing the Best System for You

Your company may have in place an appraisal system that you are obligated to use. It may be helpful, however, to use aspects of other appraisal methods in addition to the method formally requested by your company. In addition, many companies use an appraisal system that combines aspects of all the methods described here, so these aren't "pure" types.

Examining the Trait-Based Appraisal System

You've been rated by them. You've used them to rate others. The most common evaluation system is the "trait" format, in which a series of traits are listed in the left margin:

Quantity of work
Quality of work
Job knowledge
Dependability
Ability to take instruction
Initiative
Creativity
Cooperation

Across the top of the page you list these measurements:

Excellent (5 points)
Very Good (4 points)
Average (3 points)
Needs Improvement (2 points)
Unsatisfactory (1 point)

This system seems on the surface to be simple to administer and easy to understand, but it's loaded with problems:

- **A central tendency.** Rather than carefully evaluate each trait, it's much easier to rate a trait as average or close to average (the central rating).
- **The "halo effect."** Some managers believe that one trait is so impressive they rate all traits highly. Its opposite is the "pitchfork effect" (see chapter 13).
- **Personal biases.** Managers are human, and humans have personal biases for and against other people. These biases can influence any type of rating, but the trait system is particularly vulnerable.
- **Latest behavior.** It's easy to remember what employees have done during the past few months, but managers tend to forget what they did in the first part of a rating period.

Leadership Lead

When you rate your team members, don't be overly influenced by their most recent behavior. Employees know that it's rating time, and they'll be as good as a kid just before Christmas. Keep a running log of their behavior during the entire year.

Some companies encourage the use of the bell curve in rating employees. The bell-curve concept is based on the assumption that in a large population most people will fall in the average (middle) category, a smaller number in each of the poorer-than-average and better-than-average categories, and a still smaller number in the highest and lowest categories.

The trouble with the use of the bell curve in employee evaluations is that small groups are unlikely to have this type of distribution—and it may work unfairly against top- and bottom-level workers.

Suppose that Carla is a genius who works in a department in which everyone is a genius. Carla is the lowest-level genius in the group, however. In a bell curve for that group, she would be rated as "poor." In any other group, she probably would be rated "superior." Or suppose that Harold's work is barely satisfactory but that his entire group is performing below average. Compared with the other employees, he's the best. If you use a bell curve, you have to rate him "superior."

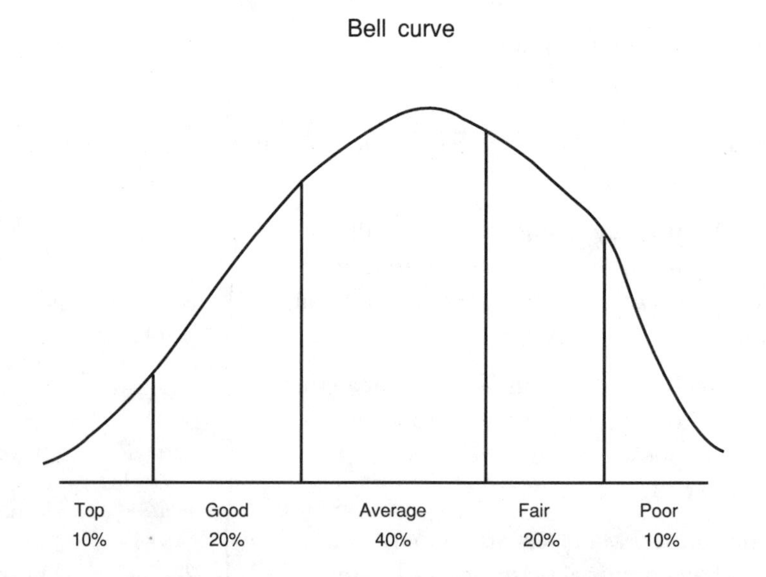

Overcoming Problems in Using Trait-Based Appraisals

The best way to overcome deficiencies in the trait system is to replace them with a results-oriented system (described later in this chapter). If your company does use the trait method, here are some suggestions to help make it more equitable:

- **Clarify standards.** Every manager and team leader should be carefully informed about the meaning of each category and the definition of each trait. Understanding quantity and quality is relatively easy. But what is dependability? How do you measure initiative, creativity, and other intangibles?

  By using discussions, role plays, and case studies, you can develop standards that everyone understands and uses.

- **Establish criteria for ratings.** It's easy to identify superior and unsatisfactory employees, but it's tougher to differentiate among people in the middle three categories.

- **Keep a running log of member performance throughout the year.** You don't have to record average performance, but do note anything special that each member has accomplished or failed to accomplish. Some notes on the positive side may say, for example, "Exceeded quota by 20 percent," "Completed project two days before deadline," or "Made a suggestion that cut by a third the time required for a job." Notes on the negative side may say, "Had to redo report because of major errors" or "Was reprimanded for extending lunch hour three days this month."

- ➤ Make an effort to be aware of your personal biases and to overcome them.
- ➤ Have specific examples of exceptional and unsatisfactory performance and behavior to back up your evaluation.

Introducing the Results-Oriented Appraisal

Rather than rate team members on the basis of an opinion about their various traits, in this appraisal system the people who do the rating focus on the attainment of specific results. Results-based ratings can be used in any situation in which results are measurable. This system is obviously easier to use when quantifiable factors are involved (such as sales volume or production units), but it's also useful in such intangible areas as attaining specific goals in management development, reaching personal goals, and making collaborative efforts.

In a results-oriented evaluation system, the people who do the evaluating don't have to rely on their judgment of abstract traits, but instead can focus on what was expected from team members and how closely they met these expectations. The expectations are agreed on at the beginning of a period and measured at the end of that period. At that time, new goals are developed to be measured at the end of the following period.

Here's how this system works:

- ➤ For every job, the team leader and the people doing the job agree on the KRAs (key results areas) for that job. Employees must accomplish results in these areas to meet the team's goals.
- ➤ The team leader and the team member establish the results that are expected from the team member in each of the KRAs.
- ➤ During a formal review, the results an employee attained in each of the KRAs is measured against what was expected.
- ➤ A numerical scale is used in some organizations to rate employees on how closely they come to reaching their goals. In others, no grades are given. Instead, a narrative report is compiled to summarize what has been accomplished and to comment on its significance.

Meanings and Gleanings

A **KRA (key results area)** is an aspect of a job on which employees must concentrate time and attention to ensure that they achieve the goals for that job.

➤ Some companies request that team members submit monthly progress reports compiled in the same format as the annual review. This technique enables both the team member and the leader to monitor progress. By studying the monthly reports, the annual review is more easily compiled and discussed.

The following figure is a sample form for a results-oriented evaluation.

Results-Oriented Evaluation

Team member: ______________________________

Job: Tax accountant　　**Date:** ____________

Results expected	**Results achieved**
Key Results Area 1	Prepare federal, state, and local tax returns on a timely basis.
______________	______________
______________	______________
______________	______________
______________	______________
Key Results Area 2	Advise management of changes in and administrative interpretations of tax laws.
______________	______________
______________	______________
______________	______________
______________	______________
Key Results Area 3	Study management policies and report on their tax ramifications.
______________	______________
______________	______________
______________	______________
______________	______________

Looking at the Downside of Results-Based Evaluations

Although results-oriented evaluations can be more meaningful than trait systems, they're not free of problems:

- **Unless you and the team member take an objective view of what he or she should accomplish, you may set unrealistic expectations.** The danger is that you may set standards so low that employees attain them with little effort or set them so high that employees have little chance of attaining them.
- **Not all goals are equal in importance.** You should consider the value of the expectation in comparison to the overall goals of the team and the company.
- **Intangible goals are more difficult to measure.** Even intangible factors, however, have tangible phases that can be identified. For example, rather than indicate that a goal is to "improve employee morale," specify it in terms that are measurable, such as "reduce turnover by X percent" or "decrease the number of grievances by Y percent." Rather than state a goal as "Develop a new health-insurance plan," break it into phases, such as "Complete study of proposed plans by October 31" or "Submit recommendations by December 15."

Introducing the Joint Leader/Associate Review

To make the results-oriented format even more meaningful, use the joint leader/associate model. If performance evaluations are based on the arbitrary opinion of a supervisor, they serve only part of the real value that reviews can provide. This model provides a formal evaluation for the purpose of raises or promotions and enables you to tell employees how to improve performance, but it doesn't involve team members in the process. A joint review can do this more effectively. The joint-associate review is particularly useful for evaluating creative jobs such as research and development or jobs in the arts. Team members and their leaders collaborate on the standards that are expected, build in the flexibility to accommodate the special circumstances under which they are working, and agree on the criteria that will be used in evaluating the work.

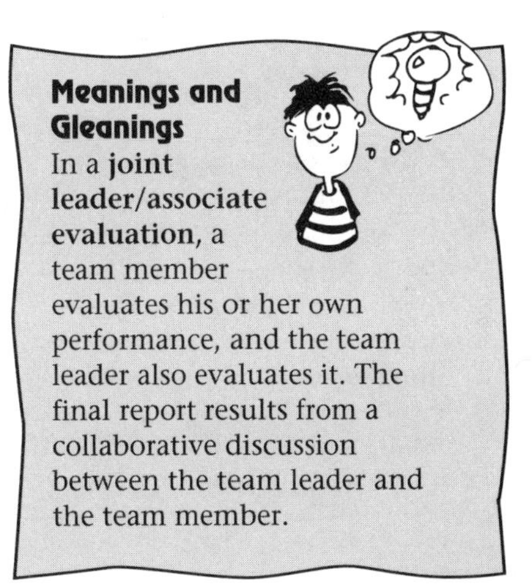

Meanings and Gleanings
In a **joint leader/associate evaluation,** a team member evaluates his or her own performance, and the team leader also evaluates it. The final report results from a collaborative discussion between the team leader and the team member.

The team member and team leader then complete the evaluation form. The KRAs and the "results expected" items are agreed on in advance (usually during the preceding review). The team member and the leader independently indicate the "results achieved."

Many companies that don't use joint evaluations ask employees to evaluate their own performance before meeting with their team leader. They complete a copy of the appraisal form. At the meeting, similarities and differences in the ratings are discussed, and adjustments in the ratings resulting from the discussions are reflected in the formal evaluation that's filed with the human-resources department. If the employee still disagrees with the evaluation after the discussion, in some companies a rebuttal may be written, which is filed along with the team leader's report.

At the appraisal interview (described later in this chapter), the team leader and the team member discuss the comments on the form. During this session, the appraisal begins to move from a report card to a plan of action for growth and teamwork.

Benefits of the Collaborative Review

A collaborative review of performance has the following advantages:

- Gives team members the opportunity to make a formal appraisal of their own work in a systematic manner.
- Allows for a thorough discussion between the team leader and the team member about differences in their perception of both expectations and results achieved.
- Enables a team leader to see areas in which he or she may have failed in developing a team member's potential.
- Helps the team member and the team leader identify problem areas that might easily be overlooked on a day-to-day basis.
- Pinpoints areas in which employees need improvement and in which they need additional training.
- Gives an opportunity to discuss areas in which a team member can become even more valuable to his or her team.
- Provides a base on which realistic goals for the next period can be discussed and mutually agreed on.
- Helps team members measure performance and progress against their own career goals and serves as a guide to determining the appropriate steps to move forward.

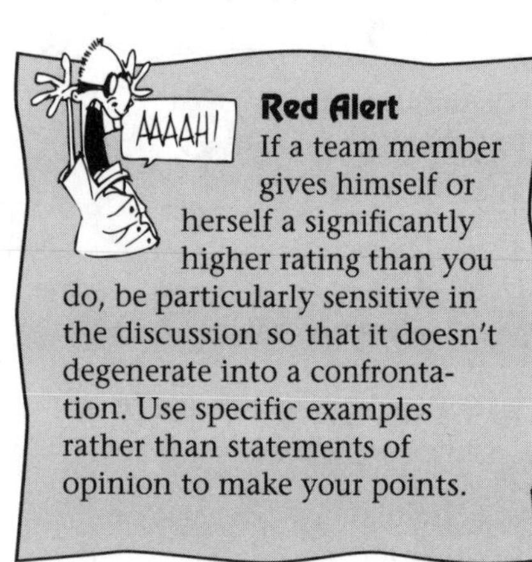

Red Alert

If a team member gives himself or herself a significantly higher rating than you do, be particularly sensitive in the discussion so that it doesn't degenerate into a confrontation. Use specific examples rather than statements of opinion to make your points.

Exploring the Appraisal Interview

Regardless of whether you have evaluated employees by the trait method or the results method and whether they have made a self-evaluation, the most important facet of the appraisal process is the face-to-face discussion of the evaluation.

To make this interview most valuable, you should carefully plan it and systematically carry it out.

Preparing for an Appraisal Interview

Before sitting down with a team member to discuss a performance appraisal, study the evaluation. Make a list of all aspects you want to discuss—not just those that need improvement but also those in which the employee did good work. Study previous appraisals, and note improvements that have been made since the preceding one. Prepare the questions you want to ask about past actions, steps to be taken for improvement, future goals, and how the team member plans to reach them.

Reflect on your experiences in dealing with this person. Have there been any special behavioral problems? Any problems that have affected her or his work? Any strong, positive assets you want to nurture? Any special points you want to discuss?

Meanings and Gleanings
The word **interview** is derived from *inter* (which means "between") and *view* (which means..."look"). An interview is a "look" at a situation "between" the parties involved. An appraisal interview isn't the leader telling the team member, "This is what you did well, and that is what you did poorly"—it's a two-way discussion about performance.

Discussing Team Members' Performance

After you have made a team member feel at ease, point out the reasons for the appraisal meeting. Say something like this: "As you know, each year we review what has been accomplished during the preceding year and discuss what we can do together in the following year."

Point out the areas of the job in which team members have met standards and particularly the areas in which they have excelled. By giving specific examples of these achievements, you let team members know that you're aware of their positive qualities.

Because salary adjustment is usually based on overall performance, team members should be made aware that your praise of one or a few accomplishments isn't a guarantee of a raise. You might say, "The way you handled the XYZ account shows that you're making great progress. Keep up the good work." By saying it this way, you show that you're aware

> **Leadership Lead**
> Most people are uneasy about appraisal interviews. Allay these fears by making some positive comments when you schedule an interview. You can say, "I've scheduled your appraisal interview for 2:30 on Wednesday. I want to talk about your accomplishments this year and discuss our plans for next year."

of the progress, but that there's still a way to go. Rather than interpret the praise as "Wow, I'm good—this means a big raise," the reaction is, "I'm doing fine, but I'm not there yet."

Encourage team members to comment. Listen attentively, and then discuss the aspects of performance or behavior that didn't meet standards. Be specific. It's much more effective to give a few examples where expectations haven't been met than to just say, "Your work isn't up to snuff." Ask what team members plan to do to meet standards and what help they want you to provide.

If employees' problems aren't related to performance, but rather to behavior, provide examples: "During the past year, I've spoken to you several times about your tardiness. You're a good worker, and your opportunities in this company would be much greater if you could only get here on time all the time." Try to obtain a commitment and a plan of action to overcome this fault.

Making Criticism Constructive

Many managers find it difficult to give criticism. Here are some guidelines to help deal with this sensitive area:

- Begin with a positive approach by asking the team member to assess the successes achieved and the steps taken to achieve those successes.
- Encourage him or her to talk about projects that didn't succeed and what caused the failure.
- Ask what might have been done to avoid the mistakes made.
- Contribute your suggestions about how the matter could have been done more effectively.
- Ask what training or help you can provide.
- Agree on the steps the associate will take to ensure better performance on future assignments.

> **Leadership Lead**
> In the evaluation interview, concentrate on the work, not on the person. Never say, "You were no good." Say instead, "Your work didn't meet standards."

Soliciting Team Members' Comments

Throughout interviews, encourage team members to comment on or make suggestions about every aspect of the review. Of course, they may have excuses or alibis. Listen empathetically—you may learn about some factors that have inhibited optimum performance. There may be factors within the company that keep an employee from performing adequately. For example, you may find out that someone has an older-model computer that has started "crashing" several times a day ever since the company upgraded software. You may not have been aware that this recurring problem was affecting the person's job performance. With this new information, you can take steps to correct the situation by budgeting for a computer upgrade. By giving the person the opportunity to express his or her reasons or arguments, you can take steps to correct the situation.

Even if a team member's excuses are superficial and self-serving, allowing them to be voiced clears the air. Then you both can be prepared to face real situations and come up with viable ideas.

Reviewing Last Year's Goals and Setting Next Year's

If the preceding year's goals were met, congratulate the team member. Talk about the steps that were taken to meet goals and what was learned from this experience. If not all the goals were met, discuss any problems and the steps that might now be taken to overcome them.

An appraisal interview isn't just a review of the past—it's also a plan for the future. Ask the question, "What do you want to accomplish during the next 12 months?" The answer might include production goals, quality improvement, behavioral changes, and plans for advancement.

In addition to goals directly related to work, team members' future plans may include personal career-development plans (such as obtaining additional training on the job or in school), participation in trade or professional societies; and other off-job activities that can enhance a career. Be supportive of these types of goals, and point out what your company can do to help, such as providing tuition reimbursement. Don't make promises, however, or give false hopes for advancement or career growth that may be more than you can deliver.

Have team members write down each of their goals, and indicate next to them what they plan to do to achieve them. Give one copy to the team member, and keep one with the performance-appraisal form. You can use it as part of the appraisal interview the following year.

Summarizing an Interview

At the end of an interview, ask the team member to summarize the discussion. Make sure that the person fully understands the positive and negative aspects of his or her performance and behavior, plans and goals for the next review period, and any other pertinent matters. Keep a written record of these points.

In many companies, team members who disagree with an evaluation are given the opportunity to write a rebuttal to be attached to the appraisal. When salary adjustments are based on ratings, some organizations provide a procedure for appealing a review.

End the interview on a positive note, by saying, "Overall, you've made good progress this year. I'm confident that you'll continue to do good work."

Recording the Review

In most companies the appraisal form is sent to the human-resources department to be placed in the employee's personnel file. Some companies require that a copy be sent to the next level of management—the person to whom the team leader reports.

Even if it's not a formal practice in your company, it's a good idea to give a copy of the appraisal to the team member. It serves as a reminder of what was discussed at the appraisal interview and can be referred to during the year. And, as mentioned, if it includes goals the employee and you have agreed on for the year, the employee can reread it from time to time to keep motivated.

The Least You Need to Know

- For every job, set performance standards that are clearly understood and accepted by those who will perform the job.
- When team members know what is expected of them, they can monitor their own performance on an ongoing basis.
- If you use the trait method to evaluate your staff members, be careful to avoid the dangers of central tendency, the halo and pitchfork effects, personal biases, and an emphasis on most recent behavior.
- Results-oriented evaluations measure actual performance against predetermined expectations.
- A joint leader/associate evaluation enables both parties to evaluate performance and agree on what can be done to reinforce strengths and build up weaknesses.
- An evaluation interview should be an interchange between you and your team member in which you openly discuss accomplishments, areas for improvement, and goals established for the next review period.

Chapter 20

Dealing with Problem Employees

In This Chapter

- Helping people who don't like themselves
- Dealing with sensitive, temperamental, and negative team members
- Avoiding stress and burnout
- Confronting alcohol- and drug-abuse problems

Your team is made up of people—human beings—who bring to their jobs skills, intelligence, and creativity. But people also have idiosyncrasies, attitudes, moods, and problems—and they also bring those things to the job. One of the great challenges of being a leader lies in recognizing and dealing with these types of problems so that your department will run smoothly.

Some of the more common problems that leaders must deal with are discussed in this chapter. Among them are helping build up team members' self-confidence so that they'll become better contributors to your team's efforts, overcoming negative thinking, and dealing with sensitive and temperamental people.

You'll also learn how to cope with members who are under stress and those who burn out. In addition, this chapter explores what can be done if team members have AIDS or are facing alcohol and drug use.

Building Up Low Self-Esteem

Most people recognize the importance of self-esteem. In a Gallup-Newsweek poll, 89 percent of respondents said that self-esteem is the primary factor that motivates them to work harder to succeed. Sixty-three percent said that the time and effort spent in developing self-esteem is a worthwhile endeavor.

Consider the phrase "developing self-esteem." Many people who have had a low opinion of themselves have been able to overcome it by making a commitment to make a change. Sometimes they seek professional help, but often they do it by self-determination, in which they rewrite the script on which they base their life. As a team leader, you're in a position to help these types of people develop self-esteem.

> **Meanings and Gleanings**
>
> **Self-esteem** refers to the way you feel about yourself—it's based on the perceptions you have about yourself. If you think of yourself as a success, you will be a success; if you think of yourself as second-rate, you will always be second-rate—unless you change your self-perception—and it *can* be done.

People with low self-esteem show it in the way they talk about themselves. They're more likely to complain about their failures than to brag about successes. They rarely express opinions that differ from those of other team members, and when they do, they preface it with an apology. When pressed to express their thoughts or ideas, they start their answers with, "I'm not sure about this" or "I'm probably wrong, but..." They never volunteer to lead a discussion, and they take charge of a project only when the leader assigns it and then express doubts about their ability to do it properly.

A person's low self-esteem (or worse, self-loathing) unfortunately may have deep psychological roots that stem from childhood. Parents may instill this trait in their children by being overdemanding (for example, if Jason gets a test score of 90 percent and his parents berate him for not getting 100 percent or if Sarah is a talented musician but her parents deride her playing because she's not a child prodigy).

Jason and Sarah are likely to write scripts for themselves as failures, doomed always to be inadequate. People whose scripts are based on parental belittlement need professional assistance to overcome it.

Focus on successes, not on failures. Most people don't loathe themselves, but they may have temporary self-esteem slumps that need bolstering. If they don't deal with those slumps, however, more serious consequences can occur. They don't need a shrink—they can do it themselves.

Focusing on Success, Not on Failure

Loss of self-esteem stems from failure. All of us have failures and successes in our jobs and in our lives. By focusing on failure, self-esteem deteriorates. Concentrate instead on the successes you have achieved.

One technique involves keeping a success log (see chapter 16). Enter in this log any accomplishments you're especially proud of—things for which you've been commended. These things prove that you've succeeded in the past and serve as your assurance that you can succeed again.

Additional Ways to Build Up Self-Esteem

In addition to suggesting that team members create a success log, you can help them build their self-esteem in other ways:

- Give them positive reinforcement for every achievement and praise for progress made in their work. Equally important, be positive when they come up with a good idea or make meaningful contributions to team discussions and activities. People with low self-esteem need to be continually reminded that you, the team leader, respect them and have confidence in them.
- Make assignments that you're sure they can succeed in performing and provide added training, coaching, and support to ensure that they'll succeed. The taste of success is a surefire way to build self-esteem.
- Suggest that they take courses designed to build self-confidence, such as the Dale Carnegie Course or assertiveness-training programs. Provide them with inspirational tapes or books.
- If, despite these efforts, a person doesn't become more self-confident, professional help may be necessary. Suggest that he or she see a counselor in your employee-assistance program (see chapter 21).

Leadership Lead
Keep a success log for your team. Enter in it the special achievements of each of your team members and of your team as a whole. Encourage each team member to keep a personal success log. When things don't go well or when you and your team members are feeling low, reread the log.

Dealing with Sensitive Sam, Temperamental Terry, Negative Nell, and Others

You undoubtedly have some of these people on your team. Every team leader does. They can make your life miserable or make it an ever-changing challenge. You can't ignore these folks—you have to deal with them, so this section gives you some suggestions.

Handling Overly Sensitive People

No one likes to be criticized, but most people accept constructive criticism. Some people resent any criticism, though. Whenever you make even the slightest criticism of their work, they pout and get defensive and accuse you of picking on them.

Be gentle with them. Be diplomatic. Begin by praising the parts of assignments that they have done well. Then make some suggestions about how they can do better in unsatisfactory areas.

Kathy's fear of being criticized has made her overly cautious in all areas of her work. Rather than risk a slight error, she checks, double-checks, and then rechecks everything she does. This process may minimize her exposure to criticism, but it's so time-consuming that it slows down her entire team. Worse, she stalls in making decisions, claiming that she needs more information. Even after she gets the information, she passes the buck to someone else.

Red Alert
Don't praise sensitive people *only* as a prelude to criticism. They may have low self-esteem and therefore need a great deal of positive reinforcement.

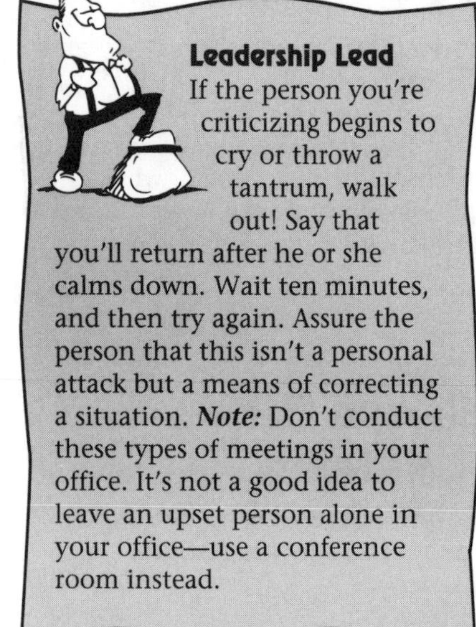

Leadership Lead
If the person you're criticizing begins to cry or throw a tantrum, walk out! Say that you'll return after he or she calms down. Wait ten minutes, and then try again. Assure the person that this isn't a personal attack but a means of correcting a situation. ***Note:*** Don't conduct these types of meetings in your office. It's not a good idea to leave an upset person alone in your office—use a conference room instead.

If members of your team behave the same as Kathy does, follow these guidelines to help them overcome their fears:

- Assure them that, because of their excellent knowledge in their field, their work is usually correct the first time and doesn't have to be checked repeatedly.
- Point out that occasional errors are normal and that they can be caught and corrected later without reflecting on the ability of the person who made the errors.
- If you agree that team members need more information before making a decision, guide them toward resources to help them obtain it. If you feel that they have adequate information, insist that they make prompt decisions.
- If team members ask you what to do, tell them that it's their decision and to make it quickly.
- In most cases, overly sensitive people have the expertise and do make good decisions. They may need your reassurance to help convert their thinking into action.

Tampering with Temper Tantrums

Terry is a good worker, but from time to time he loses his temper and hollers and screams at his coworkers and even at you. He calms down quickly, but his behavior affects the work of your entire team, and it takes a while to get back to normal performance. You've spoken to Terry about his temper several times, but it hasn't helped.

It isn't easy to work in an environment in which people holler and scream, particularly if you're the target. Because the poor victims of a tirade may be unable to work at full capacity for several hours afterward, this situation cannot be tolerated.

Here are some suggestions for dealing with someone who has temper tantrums:

- After the person calms down, have a heart-to-heart talk. Point out that you understand that it's not always easy for someone to control his or her temper but that that type of behavior isn't acceptable in the workplace.
- If another outburst occurs, send the person out of the room until he or she can calm down. Let the person know that the next offense will lead to disciplinary action.
- Recommend the old adage, "Count to ten before opening your mouth."
- If you have an employee-assistance program (see chapter 21), suggest that the team member see one of its counselors.

Negating Negativity

Almost every organization has a Negative Nell or Ned. Whenever you're for something, they're against it. They always have a reason that what you want to accomplish just can't be done. They can tear down your team with pessimism.

The reasons for a team member's negativity vary. It may stem from some real or perceived past mistreatment by your company. If that's the case, look into the matter. If the person has justifiable reasons for being negative, try to persuade him or her that the past is past and to look to the future. If misconceptions are involved, try to clear them up.

Negativity is often rooted in long-term personality factors that are beyond the ability of any team leader to overcome. In that case, professional help is necessary.

Let's look at some of the problems negative people cause:

- **Resistance to change.** Even people with a positive attitude are reluctant to change. It's comfortable to keep doing things the way they've always been done. Positive-thinking people can be persuaded to change by presenting logical arguments. Negative people resist change just for the sake of resisting. No argument ever helps. They often do everything they can to sabotage a situation so that the new methods won't work and they can say, "I told you so."

Leadership Lead
In dealing with negative people, acknowledge their arguments and persuade them to work with you to overcome their perceived problems so that the project can move along. Make the person part of the solution rather than an additional problem.

- **Impact on team morale.** Just as one rotten apple can spoil a barrel of applies, one negative person can destroy team morale. Because the negativism spreads from one person to another, it's tough to maintain team spirit under these circumstances.

When you present new ideas to negative people, get them to express their objections openly. Tell them, "You bring up some good points, and I appreciate it. As we move into this new program, let's carefully watch for those problems. We must give this new concept a try. Work with me on it, and together we'll iron out the kinks."

Negative Personalities

Opal exudes negativity. It's not what she says—it's how she acts. She takes any suggestion as a personal affront and takes on any new assignment with such reluctance and annoyance that she turns everyone off.

People such as Opal who behave in this way often don't realize how they come across to others. They probably act this way in their personal lives as well as on the job. They're the type of people who don't get along with their families, have few friends, and are the dissenters in any group to which they belong. Have a heart-to-heart talk with these people to let them know how their attitude affects your team's morale. Amazingly, many negative-thinking people have no idea that their behavior is disruptive to others. You might suggest that they enroll in a personal-improvement program.

Playing "Gotcha"

Have you ever worked with an associate whose greatest joy in life is to catch other people—especially you—making an error?

People who play this game are trying to show their superiority. Because they usually have no original ideas or constructive suggestions, they get their kicks from catching other people's errors, particularly their boss's. They try to embarrass you and make you uncomfortable, but don't give them that satisfaction. Make a joke about it ("What a blooper!"), or smile and say "Thanks for calling it to my attention before it caused real problems." If Gotchamongers see that you're not riled by their game, they'll stop and try to get their kicks elsewhere.

Working with Unhappy People

There's likely to be at any time at least one unhappy person on your team. We all experience periods when things go wrong at home or on the job—and it affects the way we do our work and how we interact with other team members. Team leaders should be alert to this likelihood and take the time to chat with the person. Giving a person the opportunity to talk about a problem often alleviates the tension. Even if the problem isn't solved, it clears the air and enables the team member to function normally.

Some people will always be unhappy about something, however. They often aren't satisfied with work assignments. Even when you comply with their requests and accommodate their complaints, they're not satisfied. They display their unhappiness by being negative. If someone's request for a change in scheduling a vacation is denied, for example, that person may get angry and let it show up both overtly and subtly in his or her attitude.

You can never make everyone happy. Rebuilding the morale of people who believe that they've been treated unfairly takes tact and patience. Team leaders can avoid some unfair situations by making sure—at the time a decision is made—to explain the reasons behind the decision. In the vacation example, you could explain that your company sets up the vacation schedule months in advance and that two other team members are taking their vacations at the same time. Then make it clear that your team can't spare more than one member on vacation at a time. You may even suggest that the unhappy person try to find another team member who will trade vacation time.

If this technique doesn't satisfy your team member, have a heart-to-heart talk with the person. Point out how constant griping and a negative attitude affect other team members. Make reassurances that the person is a valuable member of your team and that it's not always possible to get everything we want. As a mature person, encourage the person to accept disappointments and go on with life.

Addressing Stress and Burnout

All jobs have their share of stress. If they didn't, they would quickly become boring. It's when stress becomes *distress* that problems occur. The stress may show up in the way employees' behavior has changed. People who had always been patient become impatient. Calm people may become tense. Team members who have always been cooperative rebel. All these signs show up when people are under stress. Team members under stress may show physical symptoms or complain that they have trouble falling asleep or in sleeping through the night. They're often tired all the time—even if they do get a good rest. They may have stomach pains, a fast heartbeat, or frequent headaches.

"I'm So Tired I Can't Think Straight!"

Physical fatigue can be cured by rest, but most people are more likely to be mentally than physically fatigued on the job. If your team members work with computers or in other mentally strenuous jobs, remind them that physical exercise can alleviate fatigue and stress. Suggest that they take a lunchtime walk, go swimming or jogging, or participate in a sport after work. Some companies have exercise rooms in which employees can use a stationary bike or a weight machine during their lunch hour. People who have a regular regimen are less likely to become mentally fatigued.

Burnout

People are not lightbulbs. A lightbulb shines brightly and suddenly—Poof! It burns out. People burn out slowly and often imperceptibly. Although some burnouts result in physical breakdowns such as a heart attack or ulcers, most are psychological. Team members lose enthusiasm, energy, and motivation, and it shows up in many ways. They hate their job, can't stand coworkers, distrust the team leader, and dread coming to work each morning.

Meanings and Gleanings

Dr. Hans Selye defines **distress**, or **bad stress**, as the chronic state of anxiety caused by unremitting pressures of job, personal, or societal problems.

Red Alert

AAAAH!

If a team member is constantly fatigued from work, suggest that he or she see a physician for a thorough medical examination to rule out physical causes and for suggestions to relieve fatigue and stress.

Burnout can be caused by too much stress, but that's not the only cause. Some other reasons are frustration: Promises made weren't kept or an employee was passed over for an expected promotion or salary increase. Some leaders and managers burn out because of the pressures of having to make decisions in which a mistake can cause catastrophic problems. Others just burn out from having to work excessively long hours or do unrewarding work.

Often the only means of helping someone recover from burnout is to suggest professional help (see chapter 21). There are some things you can do, however, to help put a burned-out team member on the road to recovery:

- Be a supportive person. Demonstrate your sincere interest by encouraging the person to talk about and assess his or her concerns and put them into perspective.
- Consider changing job functions. Assigning different activities and responsibilities or transferring the person to another team changes the climate in which he or she works and provides new outlets that may stimulate motivation.

- Give the team member an opportunity to acquire new skills. This not only helps him or her focus on learning rather than on the matters that led to the burnout but also makes the person more valuable to your company.
- If, despite your efforts, he or she doesn't progress, strongly suggest professional counseling.

Plowing into Pressure

When pressure on a job becomes so great that you feel like you're going to break down, follow these suggestions:

- **Take a break.** If possible, get away from your workplace—get out of the building. If you work in a city, take a walk around the block. If you work in an industrial park, walk around the parking lot. If the weather is bad, walk around the building. In 10 or 15 minutes, you'll feel the stress dissolve and be able to face your job with renewed energy.
- **Exercise.** If you work in a crowded office, it's obviously not expedient to get up in the middle of the room and do jumping jacks or push-ups, but you can choose from several relaxation exercises without being obtrusive. Books and videotapes are available to show you how. If your company has an exercise room, get on the treadmill for five minutes (not enough to work up a sweat, but enough to relax your mind).
- **Change your pace.** Most people work on more than one project at a time. If the pressures are too great on your current project, stop for a while and work on another one. When you return to your original assignment, it will go much more smoothly.

Knowing What to Do When There's Too Much Work

Your team has survived downsizing and reorganization. You now have fewer members, and each of them is working longer and harder. Your boss is piling more and more work on you, and your team just can't handle it. Because there's a limit to any group's time and energy, you decide that you have to speak to your boss.

Before you approach your manager, thoroughly analyze the jobs your team is doing. Indicate how much time team members devote to each project, and determine each project's importance to the accomplishment of your team's goals. Reexamine your boss's priorities. Decide with your team what they can do to work smarter rather than harder.

If you still feel after this analysis that your team has more work than it can handle effectively, meet with your boss to review its results and try to reorder your team's

Leadership Lead
Learn to say No. When you're asked to take on a special assignment, if it won't help you meet your goals, decline diplomatically. Explain that you realize it's an important project but that you're already involved with several high-priority assignments and, as much as you want to help, you just can't.

priorities. Your boss may agree to defer certain time-consuming jobs because others are more important; reassign some jobs to other groups; or authorize additional personnel.

Don't let other teams push your team around. Sometimes pressure comes from other teams or departments with whom you're collaborating. You and the leader of the other team should try to work out a schedule that alleviates the pressure. If you can't agree, take it up with the manager who supervises both teams.

Sometimes the pressure results from you or members of the team volunteering for special projects. Learn to say No. Keep team members aware of your team's priorities, and point out that it's not an indicator of laziness or unwillingness to cooperate if they reject requests to volunteer for special projects outside the team's activities.

Managing Stress

Although some physicians treat stress with tranquilizers and other medication, unless you're under extreme pressure, you can take other steps to help manage your own stress:

- **Keep in tiptop shape.** Watch your diet, and engage in a regular exercise program.
- **Learn to relax.** Participate in deep meditation or programmed relaxation exercises. Be sure to reserve time to spend alone.
- **Learn to love yourself.** People with high self-esteem are less likely to be adversely affected by pressure from others.
- **Explore your spirituality.** Whatever your religion, spiritual experience can guide you toward peace of mind.
- **Keep learning.** The experience of ongoing learning keeps you alert, open-minded, and stimulated.
- **Develop a support team.** Avoid major stress by having friends and family members available to back you up when things don't go well.
- **Accept only commitments that are important to you.** Politely turn down other projects that drain your time and energy.
- **Seek new ways of using your creativity.** By rethinking the way you perform routine tasks, you make them less boring and stressful. By developing creative approaches to new assignments, you make them less stressful to handle.

- **Welcome changes.** Consider them new challenges rather than threats to the status quo.
- **Replace negative images in your mind with positive ones.**

Those Dreaded Boring Jobs

Some jobs are basically boring, but any job can become boring when you do it over and over again, day after day, year after year. In many companies, jobs are enriched to minimize boredom. By adding new functions and combining several simple tasks into a more challenging total activity, jobs can be made less boring.

To prevent jobs performed by your team members from becoming boring:

- Reexamine all routine work that your team performs. Encourage all people who perform the work to suggest ways of making it more interesting.
- People performing routine work often get into a rut. They start out every day performing aspect 1, and then go to aspect 2 and 3, and so on. Unless it's essential that work be done in a predetermined order, suggest that they change the pattern. Start one day with aspect 6, and then go to 3 or 7 or 1. Breaking the routine alleviates boredom.
- Cross train team members to do a variety of jobs so that they can move from one type of work to another and be less likely to become bored.

Dealing with Alcohol and Drug Problems

Suppose that one of your team members seems to have an alcohol problem. You've never seen the person drink or come to work drunk, but you often smell alcohol on the person's breath. He or she is frequently absent, especially on Mondays.

You can't ignore this situation. Speak to the team member about it, and prepare to hear all sorts of denials: "Me, drink? Only socially." Or, "Alcohol breath? It's cough medicine."

Rather than talk about a drinking problem, talk about job performance, absence from work, and other job-related matters. Inform the person that if the situation continues, you'll have to take disciplinary action.

If your team member continues this behavior pattern, bring up your concern about the drinking and suggest—or insist on—counseling.

Discussing Alcohol Problems

It isn't easy to discuss with a team member such a sensitive and personal matter as an alcohol problem. The U.S. Department of Health and Human Services suggests the following approach, in its pamphlet "Supervisor's Guide on Alcohol Abuse":

- **Don't apologize for discussing the matter.** Make it clear that job performance is involved.
- **Encourage your team member to explain why work performance, behavior, or attendance is deteriorating.** This approach may provide an opportunity to discuss the use of alcohol.
- **Don't discuss a person's right to drink or make a moral issue of it.** Alcoholism is a disease that, left untreated, can lead to many more serious illnesses.
- **Don't suggest that your team member use moderation or change drinking habits.** According to Alcoholics Anonymous, alcoholics cannot change their drinking habits without help. It's up to them to make the decision to stop drinking and take steps to get that help.
- **Don't be distracted by excuses for drinking.** The problem as far as you're concerned is the drinking itself—and how it affects work, behavior, and attendance on the job.
- **Remember that alcoholics, like any other sick people, should be given the opportunity for treatment and rehabilitation.**
- **Emphasize that your primary concern is the team member's work performance.** Point out that if the person's behavior doesn't improve, you'll have to take disciplinary action, including suspension or discharge.
- **Point out that the decision to seek assistance is the team member's responsibility.**

If your company has an employee-assistance program (see chapter 21), describe it and strongly recommend that it be used.

Leadership Lead

To prevent any misunderstandings or ambiguities, every company should have a formal policy prohibiting drinking on company premises or during working hours. This policy should be in writing and reviewed periodically with all employees. Restrictions should specifically include beer and wine in addition to "hard" liquor.

Preventing Drinking and Drug Use on the Job

In most companies, showing up at work drunk or drinking on the job is a punishable offense. But it's not always easy to prove that a person is drunk. Appearing to be drunk isn't enough. Even a police officer cannot arrest a suspect for driving while intoxicated, unless he or she substantiates the claim with a breath or blood test.

Red Alert
If you send drunk people home, don't let them drive. If they get into an accident, you or your company may share liability. Don't ask another employee to drive the person home. Call a taxi.

If one of your employees seems to be drunk, your safest course is to send the person to your medical department for testing. If that's not possible, don't allow the person to work—send him or her home. The next day, discuss the situation and point out that if it reoccurs, you'll take disciplinary action. Also make sure to suggest counseling.

Although drug use on the job has increased, it isn't nearly as common as drinking. Treat drug users in the same way as you deal with drinkers. Because drug use (and particularly the sale of drugs) is illegal, however, you should consult your attorney about the best ways to handle this situation.

Testing for the use of drugs is becoming an increasingly routine practice in many companies. A 1993 survey of more than 3,500 companies showed that 48 percent test job applicants and that 43 percent periodically test employees. Although some companies do conduct random drug tests, most of them test employees only when they suspect drug use.

The ADA (Americans with Disabilities Act) includes alcoholism and drug addiction as disabilities (see chapter 9).

AIDS in the Workplace

Despite all the articles and TV programs which make clear that AIDS is spread primarily through semen and blood, many people still have an unreasonable fear of even casual contact with a person with this disease.

Leadership Lead
You can obtain literature about AIDS and information about AIDS programs from your local health department or from the CDC National Aids Clearing House at 1-800-458-5231.

When it becomes known that an employee of a company has AIDS, many coworkers refuse to work with that person. If the person with AIDS (PWA) is on your team or works in conjunction with it, this attitude can disrupt your team's activities.

To avoid these situations, companies have instituted programs to inform employees of the true facts about the disease. AIDS-awareness programs include videos, pamphlets, articles in the company newspaper, and talks to employees by doctors.

The Least You Need to Know

- Build up team members' self-esteem by helping them to focus on their successes—not on their failures.
- When you discuss a team member's work and he or she is sensitive, be gentle, tactful, and positive.
- When you present new concepts to negative people, let them express their reservations and then get them to help develop solutions.
- Help your team (and yourself) alleviate mental fatigue by following a regimen of physical activity before, after, and even during working hours.
- When team members are overcome by the pressures of the job, suggest that they take a walk, do relaxation exercises, or shift to a different project. The tension will ease, their minds will clear, and they'll work more effectively.
- If an employee has an alcohol or drug abuse problem, don't ignore it. Discuss how it affects that person's work and the work of your entire team. Suggest counseling (and, if necessary, insist on it).

Chapter 21

The Manager as a Counselor

In This Chapter

- Knowing when counseling is appropriate
- Handling gripes, complaints, and grievances
- Resolving conflicts
- Understanding the counseling process
- Working with employee-assistance programs

It takes the coordinated effort of all team members to keep your team operating at optimum capacity. It takes only one member of the team who isn't functioning effectively to prevent your team from achieving its objectives. As coach of the team, you must identify problems in their early stages and correct the situation before it mushrooms into a major problem. Your tool: Counseling.

Counseling is a means of helping troubled associates overcome barriers to good performance. By careful listening, open discussion, and sound advice, a counselor helps identify problems, clarify misunderstandings, and plan solutions.

When a team leader "counsels" an associate, it's more analogous to that of a coach of an athletic team counseling a player than to a psychotherapist counseling a patient.

Professional counseling should be done by trained specialists, and, as you will learn in this chapter, sometimes referrals to these specialists are necessary.

Handling Gripes and Grievances

Sometimes you see a problem; sometimes you don't. You find out only when someone complains. A complaint may be your first hint of an impending problem, a reminder of an ongoing situation that hasn't been attended to, or it may just be one of your associates letting off steam. But you don't know until you check it out. This section addresses how you can best work through gripes and grievances with your team members.

Dealing with Chronic Complainers

You know your team members. Some of them are always complaining. They gripe about the temperature in the room. They gripe about the work they're assigned. They gripe about everything you tell them. You've heard these same complaints over and over again.

These types of people work in every company. They get their kicks from complaining. Sometimes they do have legitimate complaints, of course, so you can't just automatically ignore them. You have to listen—and that can be time-consuming and annoying.

One way to minimize this kind of griping is to pay more attention to the people who complain. The reason for the complaints is often their desire to be the center of attention. By talking to them, asking their opinions, and praising their good work, you satisfy their need for attention and give them less reason to gripe.

Checking Out Complaints

Most complaints are signals to you that shouldn't be ignored. Even if a complaint seems to have no validity, check it out anyway. You don't always have all the information, and you may discover facets of the situation you weren't aware of.

Follow these steps to find out what's going on:

1. **Listen.** Even if a complaint seems to be unfounded, in the mind of the complainant it's a serious matter.
2. **Investigate.** Take nothing for granted. Look at the record, and talk to others who know about the situation.
3. **Report back.** If the gripe is unfounded, explain your reasoning to the complainant. If it *is* substantiated, explain what you will do to correct it.
4. **Take action.** Do what must be done to correct the problem.

What Happens When You Don't Have the Authority to Correct a Problem

Suppose that a complainer is correct: Your investigation verifies that the complaint is justified, but you can't do anything about it. Find out who can. Bring the situation to the attention of your boss or whoever can adjust it.

Diana was frustrated. When she described to her boss, Charles, a problem her team members were having, he promised to rectify it but never did.

Diana's reminders were rebuffed. She was concerned about not only having to continue to work with this unsatisfactory situation but also losing the respect of her team members. She discussed the situation with Elizabeth, a manager who had been her mentor earlier in her career.

Elizabeth's advice: "Let Charles know how important it is to your team to have someone listen to their complaints and consider them seriously. Remind Charles that you deal with every problem over which you have authority, but that this one is out of your jurisdiction. Point out that you screen all complaints and don't pass on the ones that aren't justified. If there's a reason that action has not or cannot be taken, you want to know so that you can pass on the information to your team. Tell him that they're reasonable people who understand that they can't get everything they want, but that they expect that their complaints will be taken seriously. Then let your associates know what action you're taking and what results from it."

Meanings and Gleanings
A **gripe** is an informal complaint. A **grievance** is a formal complaint, usually based on the violation of a union contract or formal company policy.

Filing Formal Grievances

When a company has a union contract, the procedures for handling grievances are clearly outlined. Companies that don't have union agreements often set up their own procedures for dealing with employee grievances.

Here's a typical four-step approach:

1. The person making the complaint discusses it with his or her immediate supervisor or team leader. Every attempt to resolve the problem should be made at this level.
2. If no settlement is reached, the individual should be given an opportunity to bring the problem to the next level of management without fear of reprisal.
3. If the complaint is still unresolved, it may go to the general manager or a specially appointed manager (often the human-resources director). An agreement is usually reached in this stage.

4. Although arbitration is rare in a non-union environment, the management in some companies provide for a mutually agreed-on third party to be available if the company and the aggrieved person cannot work out their problem.

As the immediate supervisor or team leader, you play the key role in this process. You should make every effort to resolve grievances without having to go beyond step 1. Grievance procedures take time and energy that can be better used in doing your team's primary work. To help you deal with a grievance systematically, use the following sample grievance worksheet.

Grievance Worksheet

Complainant: ______________________________ **Date:** ______________

Team leader: ______________________________

Grievance: ____

____

____

____

Report of investigation: ____

____

____

____

If justified, action taken: ____

____

____

If not justified, reason: ____

____

____

Date reported to complainant: ______________________

Complainant's comments: ____

____

____

Team leader's comments: ____

____

____

Preventing Grievances

Dealing with grievances is time-consuming and takes you away from more productive work. This section provides some suggestions for preventing grievances from developing on your team:

- ➤ Let all team members know how they're doing regularly. People want feedback on not only their failures but also their successes.
- ➤ Encourage team members to participate in all aspects of planning and performing the team's work.
- ➤ Listen to team members' ideas.
- ➤ Make only promises that you know you can keep.
- ➤ Be alert to minor irritations and trivial problems so that you can correct them before they fester into serious dissatisfactions.
- ➤ Resolve problems as soon as possible after hearing about them.

Leadership Lead
If no complaints are called to management's attention, it doesn't necessarily mean that there are none. It may mean that communications are blocked. Grievances and gripes that aren't expressed so that they can be adjusted fester in the minds of the aggrieved and burst out sooner or later in low morale. Keep those channels open.

Resolving Conflicts Within Your Team

Two types of conflicts occur when people work together. One is tangible (a disagreement about a project, for example), and the other is intangible (two people just don't like each other, for example, and can't get along). In this section, you'll learn some techniques for managing both types of conflicts.

Mediating Disagreements About the Work

Suppose that you give an assignment to two of your team members, Ken and Barbie. They discuss the project and cannot agree about how it should be pursued. They both come back to you, their team leader, to resolve the problem.

You can use one of two approaches: Arbitrate or mediate.

Mediation is the preferred approach because it's more likely to result in a win-win compromise. The most negative effect of using mediation is that it's time-consuming (and you often don't have much time to solve a problem).

Suppose that you have chosen to mediate the disagreement between Ken and Barbie. To make a mediated conflict resolution work, all parties involved must be fully aware of the procedure to be followed. *Unless both parties have a clear understanding of the approach, it cannot succeed.*

First Barbie tells how she views the situation. You might think that the next step is for Ken to state his side—but it isn't. Instead, Ken is asked to state Barbie's view as he understands it.

The reason for this step is that when the first party explains his or her view to the other party, the other person typically only partly listens. That person may be thinking about what he or she plans to say and how to rebut the argument. By being aware of having to repeat the first person's views, that person becomes aware of having to listen carefully.

Leadership Lead

In explaining why you made a decision, treat your associates as adults. It's childish to say, "I'm the boss, and this is what I've decided." Let team members know the reason behind decisions, and clarify misunderstandings before implementing a decision.

Meanings and Gleanings

In **arbitration**, both parties present their side of a problem and an arbitrator decides what should be done. In **mediation**, both parties present their side of a problem and a mediator works with them to reach a mutually satisfactory solution.

Then the second person repeats the first person's side of the story, and any areas of misunderstanding are clarified before the second person presents his or her views. It's amazing how often disagreements are caused by these types of misunderstandings. The same process is then followed with the second person stating his or her views.

During this discussion, you (as the mediator) take notes. After each person presents his or her views, you review your notes with the participants. You might say, "As I view this, you both agree on 80 percent of the project. Now let's list the areas in which you disagree." Most disputes have many more areas of agreement than disagreement. By identifying these areas, you can focus on matters that must be resolved and tackle them one at a time.

Because you don't have an unlimited amount of time, you must set a time limit on these meetings. Suppose that you've set aside two hours for the first meeting. At the end of the specified time, you still have several more items to discuss. Set up another meeting for that purpose. Suggest that the participants meet in the interim without you to work on some of the problems. Often, after a climate of compromise is established, a large number of issues can be resolved without your presence.

Now the next meeting is scheduled for one hour, and more problems are resolved. If the project must get under way, this may be all the time you have. If some unresolved problems still exist, you have to change your role from mediator to arbitrator and make the decisions.

The following five steps can help you arbitrate a conflict, if you choose to deal with it in that way:

1. **Get the facts.** Listen carefully to both sides. Investigate on your own to get additional information. Don't limit yourself to "hard facts." Learn about underlying feelings and emotions.
2. **Evaluate the facts.**
3. **Study the alternatives.** Are the solutions suggested by the two parties the only possible choices? Can compromises be made? Is a different resolution possible?
4. **Make a decision.**
5. **Notify the two parties of your decision.** Make sure that they fully understand it. If necessary, "sell" it to them so that they will agree and be committed to implementing it.

Fighting Dissension in Your Ranks

If two people on your team dislike each other so much that it affects their work, you have to do something about it. First find out why the two people dislike each other. This type of animosity often stems from a past bitter conflict. In the rough and tumble of competition for advancement in many organizations, some people stab others in the back to gain an advantage. It's unlikely that you'll ever be able to get them to work together in harmony, however, because a deep-seated antagonism taints their every contact with each other.

If at all possible, transfer one or both parties to other departments in which they'll have little contact with each other. That option isn't always feasible, however. Because there may not be any other departments in which they can use their skills, you have to take steps to overcome this situation.

Speak to each person. If your attempts to persuade them to cooperate fail, lay down the law: "If this team is to succeed, all its members must work together. What happened in the past is past. Write it off. I'm not asking you to like each other. I don't care if you never associate with each other off the job. I'm demanding that you work together to meet our goals." If necessary, follow up this directive with disciplinary action.

Often the reason for the dislike isn't based on any specific factor. It happens to all of us: You meet a person and something about him or her turns you off and you immediately dislike that person.

Suppose that you introduce your new team member, Jack, to Rachel. Rachel's first reaction is, "I don't like him," and it carries over into their working relationship. Psychologists say that this reaction occurs because something about this person subconsciously reminds the other of some unpleasant past experience. Something about Jack (his haircut, the manner in which he speaks, a mole on his left cheek) reminds Rachel of a third-grade bully who made life miserable for her that year—and she hates him. These factors, called *minimal cues,* trigger long-forgotten subconscious memories that still influence our reactions to people.

Red Alert

As tempting as it may be to threaten to fire uncooperative team members, don't do it unless you really can carry it out. Most union contracts make the process for firing employees complex. Sometimes company policies, EEO implications, or other factors restrict these actions.

When you notice that team members have an unexplainable dislike for other members, tell them about minimal cues. Help them understand that their reactions are normal, but that it's important not to let these reactions influence their attitudes toward other people. Awareness of the psychology underlying this feeling will help overcome a person's irrational attitude.

Counseling About Personal Matters

Counseling about employee performance was discussed in chapter 19, and counseling about gripes and grievances was covered earlier in this chapter. Another area in which supervisors counsel their associates concerns outside matters that may affect employees' work.

Leadership Lead

When you have to work with someone you dislike, make an effort to find something you *can* like about the person: job skills, sense of humor, or a personality trait, for example. Focus on the good point. You'll soon forget the intangible factor that generated your dislike.

All of us have personal problems. We worry about our health, about our families, and about money. We always have something to worry about. People carry their worries with them into the workplace, and worries do affect their work.

You may be reluctant to pry into an associate's personal life—and many people resent prying. Sometimes it's necessary, however. It's much easier if you and your team member have a good personal relationship and if you've always shown interest in the person. Counseling is a natural follow-through on your usual interest.

If you have this type of relationship, begin the discussion by commenting about job-related matters. Ask a question about the project that's involved, for example. It may lead into a discussion of the problems the person is having with the project, which may be caused by personal matters.

Be an empathetic listener. Your role as counselor is to give team members an opportunity to unload their problems. Encourage them by asking questions. Don't criticize, argue a point, or make a judgment. Act as a sounding board to help release the pressures that are causing the problem. Help the person clarify the situation so that the solution will be easier to reach.

Red Alert
Don't give advice about serious personal matters. You're not a trained psychologist. Listen! Help put the problem into perspective. Provide or suggest sources for additional information. Help associates clarify a situation and come to their own conclusions.

Counseling isn't a cure-all. There are many areas in which you just can't help. When a problem is one you can help by just talking it out, your intervention can be useful. Don't lose patience or give up too easily. Often more than one session is necessary to build a sense of trust and to get a team member to open up.

Knowing What to Do When Talking Doesn't Help

When job problems are caused by alcoholism or drug addiction, there's little you can do other than encourage or even insist on appropriate programs (refer to chapter 20). When the real cause stems from deep-seated emotional factors, professional help is necessary.

You may be reluctant or even embarrassed to suggest that a team member see a professional counselor. Many people take umbrage at this suggestion: "Do you think I'm nuts?" Point out that going to a professional counselor is now as accepted as going to a medical doctor. Young people are exposed to counseling beginning in elementary school. The most frequently given advice offered by Ann Landers, Dear Abby, and other advice columnists is to seek counseling when faced with serious problems.

Not all problems that require professional assistance are psychological. They may be caused by a medical condition or serious financial troubles. Often they're marital or family situations.

If your company has an EAP (employee-assistance program), making a referral to it immediately relieves you of the burden of suggesting specific counseling (see the following section). If not, your human-resources department may help provide referrals. You may find it helpful to research the available sources of help in your community:

- **Medical:** If a company doesn't have its own medical department or an employee doesn't have a primary-care physician, local hospitals or medical societies can provide a list of qualified physicians.
- **Psychiatrists:** These M.D.s deal with serious psychological disorders.
- **Psychologists or psychotherapists:** These specialists usually have a degree in psychology or social work and handle most of the usual emotional problems people face.
- **Marriage counselors and family therapists:** These professionals deal with marital problems, difficulties with children, and related matters. Obtain from your local family-service association or mental-health association the names of qualified psychologists, psychiatrists, or marriage and family therapists in your area.
- **Financial counselors:** These people help others work out payment plans with creditors, develop budgets, and live within their income. Your bank or credit union can provide referrals.

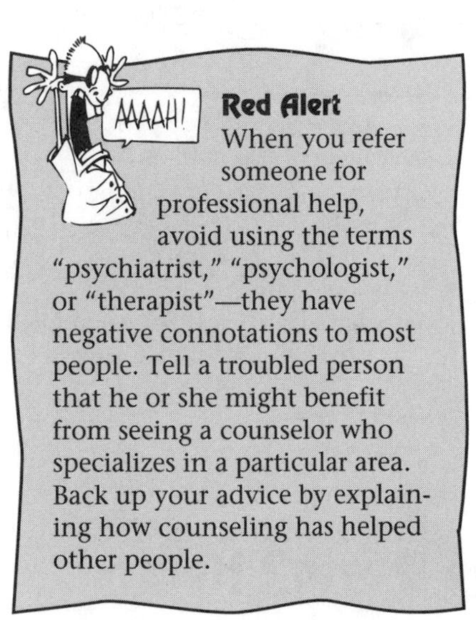

Red Alert

When you refer someone for professional help, avoid using the terms "psychiatrist," "psychologist," or "therapist"—they have negative connotations to most people. Tell a troubled person that he or she might benefit from seeing a counselor who specializes in a particular area. Back up your advice by explaining how counseling has helped other people.

Employee-Assistance Programs (EAPs)

An employee-assistance program, or EAP, is a company-sponsored counseling service. Many companies have instituted these programs to help employees deal with personal problems that interfere with productivity. The counselors aren't company employees, but instead are outside experts retained on an as-needed basis. Initiating the use of the EAP can be done in two ways, which are discussed in this section.

Sometimes an employee takes the initiative in contacting the company's EAP. The company informs its employees about the program through e-mail, bulletins, announcements in the company newspaper, meetings, and letters to their homes. Often a hot-line telephone number is provided.

Gerty believes that she needs help. Constant squabbling with her teenage daughter has made her tense, angry, and frustrated. In a brief telephone interview with her company's EAP, the screening counselor identifies Gerty's problem and refers her to a family counselor. Gerty makes her own appointment on her own time (not during working hours—EAPs are not an excuse for taking time off the job). Because the entire procedure is confidential, no report is made to the company about the counseling (in most cases, not even the names of people who undertake counseling are divulged).

Another way to start the process is by having a supervisor take the initiative to contact the EAP. Suppose that the work performance of one of your top performers has recently declined. You often see him sitting idly at his desk, his thoughts obviously far from his job. You ask him what's going on, but he shrugs off your question by saying, "I'm okay—just tired."

After several conversations, he finally tells you about a family problem, and you suggest that he contact your company's EAP.

Even though you've made the referral and the employee has followed through, don't expect progress reports. From now on, the matter is handled confidentially. Your feedback comes from seeing improvement in the employee's work as the counseling helps with the problem.

Employee-assistance programs are expensive to maintain, but organizations who have used them for several years report that they pay off. EAPs salvage skilled and experienced workers who, without help, may leave a company.

Bet You Didn't Know

EAPs aren't new. They began in the 1940s as alcohol rehabilitation programs. People who couldn't perform their job duties because of a drinking problem were usually fired. Companies that often had invested large amounts of money in developing employees' skills started these programs to protect their large investments.

The Least You Need to Know

- Chronic complainers may just be seeking attention. To ward off some of their complaints, speak to them, ask for their opinions, and listen to them regularly.
- Even if a complaint seems unfounded, you may not be familiar with certain facets of the situation. Investigate, report back, and, if justified, correct the situation.
- If you can't resolve a complaint, refer it to someone who can. Keep the complainant advised of what's going on.
- By resolving problems as soon as possible after hearing about them, you avoid having to file time-consuming formal grievances.
- In mediating conflicts among your team members, make sure that each party fully understands the other's viewpoint.

- When personal dislikes inhibit team harmony, make every effort to resolve differences. If you can't, take a firm stand. Insist that if they can't put aside their personal feelings and work together, you'll take disciplinary action.
- When you counsel a team member, be an empathetic listener. Let the other person do most of the talking. Help put the problem into focus, but don't give advice about serious personal matters.
- When your employees' work performance suffers because of personal problems, refer them to your company's employee-assistance program. If your company doesn't have one, refer them to an appropriate professional.

Chapter 22

Working in a Nontraditional Environment

In This Chapter

- The scattered workforce
- Outsourcing: The workplace of the future
- Self-directed teams

In the late 18th and early 19th centuries, as a result of the industrial revolution, the workplace moved from small, often home-based shops to large, centrally located factories and offices. Villages gave way to towns, and towns to cities.

As we move into the 21st century, centralization is giving way to smaller, decentralized units. It's no longer necessary in many types of work for all employees to be located in the same building—or even in the same city. Advanced technology has made this type of decentralization feasible and often more advantageous.

An increasing number of employees work in small branch offices that enable them to serve customers more effectively, and many work from their own homes, receiving assignments and returning finished work by way of computers, faxes, and express-delivery services.

In this chapter, you'll learn how to manage your way through the special challenges resulting from nontraditional working arrangements, where team members may be operating from a location across town or across an ocean. You'll also learn how a self-directed team functions and about its impact on the role of the team leader.

Understanding the Problems of Decentralization

Team leaders in a decentralized environment face many new challenges. You must know how to do the following:

- Manage people when they aren't close by.
- Get to know team members when personal contact is limited.
- Ensure that work gets done when your team members are scattered in several locations.
- Motivate your team, solve problems, resolve conflicts, and carry out all the functions of your job from a distance.

So What's New About This?

Working in a decentralized environment isn't a totally new type of problem. For years, sales managers have managed their sales staffs in locations far removed from the home office; dispatchers have managed truck drivers who are continually on the road; and chain-store operators have managed stores in hundreds of locations. Study the way these people manage their employees. You can learn from them.

Jacqueline, the sales manager for a large cosmetics company, manages 20 sales areas in the United States and Canada, each employing from 10 to 15 sales representatives and support crews. She attributes her success in keeping her sales staff motivated and productive to five principles:

> **Meanings and Gleanings**
>
> **Decentralization** shifts the focus of a business from one central facility in which all decisions are made by central management and most work is performed on the premises to localized facilities in which decisions are made and work is performed by local staff with minimum control from the central office.

- **All area managers and their staff members are treated as full members of the sales team—not as second-class citizens.** They're continually informed about all the same things that employees in the home office are told. The company shows them previews of advertising campaigns, sales brochures, and other materials before they're released and encourages their input.

  No matter where team members are located, they're kept informed of team and departmental goings-on. Jacqueline believes that a major factor in building team spirit is the day-to-day chitchat among team members about their interests and activities. Because employees miss out on this type of conversation when they work in different locations, the company sends to every salesperson a weekly chatty newsletter that includes tidbits about what's going on in its employees' lives.

- **The team leader takes a personal interest in each team member.** Jacqueline telephones each of her area managers at least once a week just to chat about how things are going. If a sales rep does something special, she personally makes a congratulatory call. On an employee's birthday, she sends a card or an e-mail message, and on special occasions, such as weddings, births, or special anniversaries, she sends flowers or a snack basket to the team member's home.
- **Meetings are held periodically so that members from various locations can regularly meet face to face.** To supplement the annual convention that all company salespeople attend, quarterly regional meetings are held. Sales reps at the meetings can meet reps from other regions in a more intimate environment than the convention provides. It gives them an opportunity to exchange ideas, get to know their colleagues as real people, and build up the team's esprit de corps.
- **Sharing of ideas among members in all facilities is expedited.** The exchange of ideas isn't limited to meetings. Sales reps and area managers are encouraged to communicate with each other by phone, fax, and e-mail. They share with each other their experiences, sales approaches, and advice about handling problems.
- **The team leader maintains personal contact with all members.** Jacqueline plans her regular office visits so that she can go out in the field with sales reps, hold motivational meetings, and discuss special problems. She makes occasional unannounced visits, just to say "hello" and let them know that she's personally interested in them.

These principles can be helpful with not only salespeople but also outside service technicians, branch-office staff members, and others who work in remote locations.

Leadership Lead

Employees in remote locations often feel left out of company business. Keep them informed of what's going on in the home office and in other regions. Let them share in celebrations and participate in successes.

Introducing Telecommuting

The computer and modem (a device that enables your computer to share information with other computers via phone lines) have enabled companies to communicate in real time with anyone at another location who also has a computer. Documents, drawings, and statistical tables can be transmitted electronically to one person or to dozens of people simultaneously. This process has not only enabled companies to improve their decentralized operations but also to create the entirely new concept of telecommuting.

Meanings and Gleanings

The process of **telecommuting** uses technology to enable people to perform their work at home or at a remote location from the central office by receiving assignments and submitting completed work through a computer equipped with a modem.

Many people prefer working at home over having to fight traffic to and from their office. Some parents have turned to telecommuting to enable them to spend more time with their children and reduce day-care expenses.

Companies have discovered that it's often advantageous to let employees telecommute: It frees up office space for other people and enables a company to use the services of experienced workers who may not be able to come to the office regularly. These workers include parents with young children, people who can't leave their homes because they care for elderly or ill relatives, and people with a temporary or permanent disability.

Not every type of job is suitable for telecommuting. Many jobs require constant interaction with others on the job or the use of expensive or complex equipment that cannot be provided for home use.

Many jobs *can* be done at home, however:

- Various types of clerical work
- Data entry
- Telemarketing
- Customer service
- Certain accounting functions
- Design and drafting
- Creative work such as writing advertising copy, writing technical manuals, artwork, and editing

With a little imagination, jobs that seem to be limited to the office often can be redesigned so that they can be done at home.

Making Telecommuters Part of Your Team

Dr. Frank Ashby, a consultant who has worked with many companies that use telecommuters, suggests that the key to success for both telecommuters and companies is a well-designed plan for orienting and training all people who are either hired as telecommuters or have transferred to that type of work. This plan should be followed by ongoing interaction between the leader and the telecommuter. This section presents some strategies to help you more effectively manage telecommuting employees.

Provide guidelines for dealing with the special problems of working at home. Many people who are accustomed to the routine of an office find that they flounder when they have to work without direct supervision.

Ashby recommends training in at least the areas of time management and priority setting. He recommends these guidelines for telecommuters:

- **Set specific hours that you plan to work—and stick to them.** Although some telecommuters are paid on an hourly basis and must keep time logs, most work in salaried jobs in which their work is measured not by hours worked but by their achievement of key results areas (see chapter 19).

  Some jobs require telecommuters to be available at the telephone or at the computer during normal business hours; in others, the specific hours worked aren't important as long as the work is done and the manager knows when the employee can be contacted.
- **Set up working hours when children are in school or napping.** If you have children who aren't in school, arrange working hours for times when you're less likely to be disturbed or when another adult is available to take care of them.
- **Set priorities so that you're always aware of deadlines and progress on each assignment.**

Managers should make telecommuters as much a part of the team as people who work side by side in the office and treat them accordingly:

- Keep them informed of all team activities, even those in which they're not directly involved.
- Have them come to the office for business meetings, training programs, and company or department social events.
- Invite them to participate in such extracurricular activities as bowling leagues, softball teams, and family picnics.
- Put them on the distribution list for all the same materials they would receive if they were in-house employees.

- Require that they visit the office regularly—not just for discussion of their own work but also for in-person discussions about team activities and to give them an opportunity to interact with other team members.
- Make yourself easily accessible by telephone, and return voice mail or other messages promptly. Many leaders call telecommuters periodically just to show a personal interest and to give them the opportunity to exchange ideas about overall activities—not just specific work assignments.

Prospective telecommuters should be made aware of the many potential problems of working at home. One home-based computer programmer complained that her friends and neighbors barged in for friendly chats or to ask her to accept deliveries, be available for service people, and even watch their children. She had to make clear to them that she was an at-home worker, not a lady of leisure. Being assertive cost her some "friends," but it was essential.

> **Leadership Lead**
> Make sure that prospective telecommuters are fully aware of the negative as well as the positive aspects of working at home. Have them try it for a trial period before agreeing to a permanent arrangement.

Another at-home worker soon found that the freedom of working at home, setting his own time schedule, and avoiding rush hour didn't make up for the socialization of the workplace. He missed the interaction of daily contact with colleagues, the gossip around the water cooler, and even the daily parrying with his boss. He chose to return to the office.

Working with Independent Contractors

It's expedient for some companies to subcontract major aspects of their operations to companies better suited to deal with them. Subcontracting enables them to concentrate on what they do best and not be hindered by facets of their work that others can do more effectively.

One frequently outsourced company function is payroll. By subcontracting this nonproductive activity to specialists, companies save time, money, and aggravation. ADP, one of the largest computing firms in the United States, computes payroll for more than 200,000 companies.

Navistar International, a manufacturer of heavy equipment and trucks, subcontracted the management of its tire warehouse to Goodyear, which has more expertise in managing a tire warehouse. Goodyear's expertise resulted in major savings in inventory and storage costs.

A major Midwestern university's attempt to enter the growing business-seminar field became bogged down because, although it had the faculty and the facilities to provide excellent programs, it didn't have the expertise to market them to the business community. By subcontracting this activity to an established seminar organization, the university was able to build the program into a much-needed profit center.

If your company is considering outsourcing a function over which you have jurisdiction, follow these suggestions to help ease the transition:

- **Help choose the contractor.** As a knowledgeable person in your field, you should be familiar with companies that specialize in the areas involved. Volunteer to research available companies, interview the owners, or become the primary contact with prospects. When the contract goes into effect, you and the contractor will have already established a working relationship.
- **Use the soon-to-be displaced manager (if there is one) as the contractor.** When Holly was told that her market-research section was to be eliminated and the function outsourced, she was devastated. She had worked long and hard to attain her position. Her manager called her aside and said, "Holly, I've looked into some of the firms that are possible sources for our work, and none of them is as good as you. You have the experience and know-how, and, moreover, you're familiar with our products and could get to work on them with minimum disruption. You should set up your own market-research firm. We'll be your first customer, and our work should give you a good start. You'll be free, of course, to seek other customers. It could be the break of a lifetime."

  For Holly, the situation was the beginning of a great new career. For the company, it eased the transition because the long working relationship between Holly and her manager eliminated the starts and stops incumbent to a new relationship.
- **When you begin a new working relationship with a contractor, take the time to get to know each other.** Visit the contractor's facility. Invite her to attend a staff meeting and discuss with your team how she operates and how they can work together to obtain the greatest benefit from the new system.
- **Clearly set up the manner in which you expect the contractor to interact with your team.** For example, rather than have a single end deadline for a large project, you may prefer

> **Meanings and Gleanings**
> Companies increasingly **outsource**, or subcontract to outside sources, work that previously had been done in-house. As companies become "leaner and meaner," they outsource activities that are peripheral to their main functions. Some examples are payroll, traffic, training, computer programming, advertising, and certain manufacturing activities.

to establish interim deadlines by which the contractor should complete particular portions of the job. If you want to receive weekly status reports or meet personally with the contractor on a predetermined schedule, spell that out up front.

- **Hold regular meetings.** Make it a regular practice to meet periodically with the members of the contractor's staff who work on your account. Your attention will make them feel that they're part of your team and solidify the relationship.
- **Handle problems quickly.** Deal immediately and diplomatically with any problems that develop between you so that your working relationship doesn't suffer.
- **Make the contractor's staff part of your team.** Invite the members of the contractor's staff who work on your account to company conventions, social functions, and in-house training sessions that relate to matters of mutual interest.
- **Review the contractor's work in the same way you evaluate an employee.** Cooperative contractors welcome honest performance evaluations so that they can meet their customers needs and maintain a high level of customer satisfaction.

Bet You Didn't Know

The "flattening" of companies—eliminating layers of middle managers—has increasingly led companies to contract work to outsiders. Some companies have become, in a sense, "general contractors," in which their management consists of a cadre of specialists who set goals, develop concepts, and then assign work to and coordinate the activities of contractors.

Working with Self-Directed Teams

Some management gurus predict that the role of supervisors and managers will eventually change completely from leader to advisor. They believe that all work will be accomplished by self-directed teams: no boss, no team leader—just a team of dedicated people working to service their internal or external customers.

Utopian? Idealistic? Maybe. It's unlikely that this system will take place soon or ever be the standard business structure, but self-directed teams are already in place in certain parts of some companies.

As noted in chapter 18, self-directed teams are part of the empowerment process. Self-management isn't the only way to empower people, but it is the end-all of true empowerment.

Making Self-Direction Work

Most people—leaders and members alike—need careful preparation for their new roles. Training in group dynamics is the first step. Managers and team leaders accustomed to making decisions and giving orders must be conditioned to look at their roles as that of advisor and counselor. Members accustomed to having decisions made for them must be trained in decision-making and be oriented to accepting responsibility.

As a manager, keep in mind that you can't rush into making a major change in the way people work. Change should be made by evolution, not revolution. You cannot just put out a bulletin that says, "Effective this date, we work in self-directed teams." It takes time and conditioning for such a radical change to work its way into the system.

The team leader still has an important place in the early stages of self-direction. It's that person's responsibility to ensure that the group dynamics work, to assist members in problem-solving techniques, and to stay available to do what is necessary in the transition.

The team leader gradually becomes the team coordinator, and leadership functions are shared with team members. He or she devotes more time to coordinating with other teams and projects outside the immediate team.

When a self-directed team is finally in place, members do the day-to-day planning, operations, and decision-making. They set goals, measure their own performance, and, if necessary and appropriate, discipline members. The former team leader becomes the team's advisor, providing technical support and acting as a consultant.

Meanings and Gleanings

A **self-directed team** has no permanent team leader. Team members are self-managed. Some teams have permanent administrative leaders to handle paperwork, but members rotate as project leaders. Team members schedule work, hire and train new members, budget funds, and monitor their own performance.

Red Alert

If your organization is moving toward self-directed teams, your role can change from leader to just another team member. There's nothing wrong with this situation if that's want you want, but it can also provide you with the opportunity to move up to an even higher position. If this is your goal, accept the change as a challenge.

The Downside of Self-Direction

Self-directed teams have been hailed by some managers as the wave of the future. But these types of teams are not a panacea, and they have their limitations:

- Except for some very progressive organizations, the concept of self-directed teams is too radical for many companies to seriously consider. It involves changes in their thinking for which they are not ready and may take them years to understand and accept.
- Many team members find it unpleasant or difficult to evaluate a peer's performance and to recommend disciplinary action against other team members.

Leadership Lead

As your role as team leader shifts from day-to-day managing to advice and counsel, it opens new challenges for you. It's your opportunity to use your creativity in planning long-term assignments, taking on assignments that broaden your background, and becoming even more valuable to your organization.

- As noted in the discussion of empowerment in chapter 18, many people don't want to be empowered.
- Self-directed teams call for a highly motivated group of people who strive for peak performance from themselves and their co-workers. A large percentage of people are satisfied being "average" workers and aren't committed to putting out the necessary extra effort and energy.
- Current team leaders are sometimes reluctant to give up the power and authority of being a leader—even in more traditional working teams. Many fear not only that they'll lose power but also that their jobs will become superfluous.

The Least You Need to Know

- The workplace is changing from a centralized facility to groups of people working in distant locations or even from their homes.
- When team members are scattered in different locations, keep them informed of what's going on via newsletters, e-mail, telephone calls, and personal visits.
- To ensure that telecommuters feel that they're part of your team, follow up careful initial orientation and training with ongoing interaction between you and the telecommuters.
- Treat telecommuters the same way as you treat other members of your team. Have them come to your office periodically for face-to-face discussions with you and other team members.
- Get to know your subcontractors' staff members. Make them a part of your team by keeping in close touch, visiting their facilities, and inviting them to yours.
- Self-directed teams, in which the team leader becomes a coordinator and advisor, is one way people can be empowered.

Part 7
Doling Out Discipline

When you hear or see the word discipline, *the first thing that usually pops into your mind is punishment. Look at that word again. Notice that by dropping two letters (in), it turns into* disciple, *which is a synonym for "student." Both words derive from the Latin word meaning "to learn." If you look at discipline not as punishment but as a means of learning, you get much more out of it. You are the* coach, *and your associates are the* learners.

People unfortunately do not always learn what is taught to them. Sometimes, despite your teaching, people on your team may not perform satisfactorily. Even though you clearly explain the rules, infractions still occur, and you must take steps to get things back on track.

Regardless of the cause, discipline *begins when you work to correct the problem. You make every effort to help them learn and only when all else fails does discipline take the form of punishment.*

This part of the book looks at the steps involved in progressive discipline and explores the dos and don'ts of punishment and termination.

Chapter 23

Spare the Rod and Spoil the Employee

In This Chapter

- The steps of progressive discipline
- How and when to reprimand
- Written warnings
- Probation and suspension
- Is there a better way to discipline?

Some companies have workers who have always met all the requirements of their jobs, followed all the company rules and regulations, and never had to be disciplined. They are robots, but even in technocrats' wildest dreams, robots will never totally replace humans. All except the most routine and highly structured work must be done by people, who from time to time don't meet expectations, are absent or come to work late, and violate company rules and must be corrected.

This chapter looks at the system of progressive discipline used by most organizations today and examines how it can be used effectively by team leaders. You'll learn when a reprimand is appropriate and how to reprimand a team member without causing resentment.

You'll also learn when and how to "write up" an employee and when he or she should be placed on probation or suspended. This chapter also explores some alternative approaches to progressive discipline.

Keep in mind that the contents of this chapter are based on general practices that are used in many organizations. Your company's policies may differ. You may get some good ideas from this chapter that you can't use now, but you can suggest them to your company's management. Until your company incorporates these ideas into its policies, however, follow your company's current practices.

Understanding Progressive Discipline

In most organizations, it's important for every member of a team to be at his or her workstation at starting time. If one person comes to work late, it can hold up an entire team.

Suppose that an employee was late three times in his first month on the job. You spoke to him about it, and for several months he kept his promise to be on time. He was late one day last week, and this morning he was late again. His reason for the tardiness is vague. Your informal chats with him about the matter haven't done any good, so now you're ready to apply progressive discipline, which is described in this section.

The Reprimand: An Informal Warning

The chats you've had with the team member weren't part of the progressive discipline system; instead, they were a friendly reminder of his responsibility to your team.

> **Meanings and Gleanings**
>
> **Progressive discipline** is a systematic approach to correcting rule infractions. A typical program has six steps, beginning with an informal warning. If the warning doesn't succeed, the following steps are taken, in order: disciplinary interview, written warning, probation, suspension, and termination (if necessary).

The first official step in the progressive discipline system is often called the "oral," or "verbal," warning: You take the team member aside and remind him that the two of you have discussed his lateness and that, because he continues to come to work late, you must put him on notice that tardiness cannot be accepted on your team. Inform him of the next steps you'll take if the behavior continues.

You may be exasperated about a team member's failure to keep a promise to be on time. It's normal to be annoyed if your team's work is delayed, but don't lose your cool. A typical conversation shows you what *not* to do:

You (angrily): How many times do I have to tell you that we need you here at 8 o'clock? You know that we

> have a deadline to meet today. Haven't you any sense of responsibility?
>
> EMPLOYEE (annoyed): I was only ten minutes late. It's not my fault—I ran into a traffic problem.
>
> YOU: If you had left home early enough, you wouldn't have had a traffic problem. The rest of us were here on time. You just don't have a sense of responsibility.
>
> EMPLOYEE: I have as much of a sense of responsibility as anyone.
>
> YOU: If you're late again, I'll write you up.

Red Alert
Never reprimand people when you're angry, when they're angry, or in the presence of other people. Reprimands should be a private matter between two calm people working together to solve a problem.

Did this conversation solve anything? The objective of an informal warning is to alert team members that a problem needs correction. By using an angry tone and antagonistic attitude, you only rile the person and avoid solving the problem.

Let's replay that reprimand in a better way:

> YOU: You know how important it is for you to be here when the workday begins. The entire team depends on all of us being on time.
>
> EMPLOYEE: I'm sorry. I ran into unusual traffic this morning.
>
> YOU: We all face traffic in the morning. What can you do to make sure that you'll be on time in the future?
>
> EMPLOYEE: I've tried alternative routes, but it doesn't help. I guess I'll have to leave earlier every day so that, if I do run into traffic, I'll at least have a head start.
>
> YOU: That sounds good to me. You're a valuable member of our team, and being on time will help all of us.

When you're preparing to reprimand someone, to ensure that you conduct the reprimand in the most effective manner, reread the guidelines for reprimanding on the following page.

Guidelines for Reprimanding

Time the reprimand properly. As soon as possible after the offense has been committed, call the employee aside and discuss the matter in private.

Never reprimand when you're angry. Wait until you have calmed down.

Emphasize the *what,* not the *who.* Base the reprimand on the action that was wrong, not on the person.

Begin by stating the problem and then ask a question. Don't begin with an accusation: "You're always late!" Say instead, "You know how important it is for all of us to be on the job promptly. What can you do to get here on time from now on?"

Listen! Attentive, open-minded listening is one of the most important factors of true leadership. Ask questions to elicit as much information about the situation as you can. Respond to the associate's comments, but don't convert the interview into a confrontation.

Encourage your team member to make suggestions for solving the problem. When a person participates in reaching a solution, there's a much greater chance that it will be accepted and accomplished.

Provide constructive criticism. Give your team member specific suggestions, when possible, about how to correct a situation.

Never use sarcasm. Sarcasm never corrects a situation; it only makes the other person feel inadequate and put upon.

End your reprimand on a positive note. Comment on some of the good things the person has accomplished so that he or she knows that you're not focusing only on the reason for this reprimand, but instead on total performance. Reassure the person that you look on him or her as a valuable member of your team.

They Always Have an Excuse

If you've been in management for any length of time, you've probably heard some wild excuses. No matter how silly, ridiculous, or improbable the excuse may be, listen—and listen carefully—for these reasons:

- Until you listen to the entire story, you cannot know whether it has validity. In most companies, there are acceptable reasons for not following a company rule or procedure. Under extenuating circumstances, it's sensible to be flexible when you enforce the rules.

- Even if an excuse is unacceptable, let your team member get it out of his or her system (a process called *catharsis*). When people have something on their mind, they won't listen to a word you say until they get their story out. Whether it's a team member's tardiness or a customer's complaint, let the person talk. Only after a person's mind is clear will he or she listen to you. Afterward, you can say, "I understand what you're saying, but the important thing is to be here on time."

Asking for a Plan of Action

When you deliver a verbal warning, throw the problem back to your team member. Rather than say, "This is what you should do," ask "What do you think you can do to correct this situation?" Get people to come up with their own plan of action.

In a simple situation such as tardiness, a plan of action is relatively easy to develop: "I'll leave my house 15 minutes earlier every day." In more complex situations, a plan may take longer to develop. You may suggest that the person think about the problem for a day or so and arrange a second meeting in which to present and discuss it.

Documenting a Reprimand

Even informal reprimands shouldn't be strictly oral. You should keep a record of it. Legal implications mandate that you document any action that could lead to serious disciplinary action.

Some team leaders document an informal warning by simply noting it on their calendars or entering it in a team log. Others write a detailed memo for their files. You should use the technique your company prefers.

Conducting a Disciplinary Interview

If an employee repeats an offense after receiving a verbal warning, the next step is the disciplinary interview.

This interview differs from a reprimand in that it is more formal. A verbal warning is usually a relatively brief session, often conducted in a quiet corner of the room. A disciplinary interview is longer and is conducted in an office or conference room.

A disciplinary interview should always be carefully prepared and result in a mutually agreed-on plan of action. Whereas a plan of action after a verbal warning is usually oral, the resulting plan in a disciplinary interview should be put in writing. It not only reminds both the leader and the team member of what has been agreed on but also serves as documentation.

To ensure that a disciplinary interview is carried out systematically, use the following discipline worksheet.

Discipline Worksheet

Part I (Complete before interview begins)

Team member: ______________________ Date: ______________

Offense: ____

____

____

Policy and Procedures provision: ________________________

Date of occurrence: ____________________________________

Previous similar offenses: ______________________________

____

What I want to accomplish: _____________________________

____

Special considerations: ________________________________

____

Questions to ask at beginning of interview: _______________

____

____

PART II (Keep in front of you during interview)

- Keep calm and collected.
- Get the whole story.
- Listen actively.
- Don't interrupt.
- Emphasize the *what,* not the *who.*
- Avoid sarcasm.
- Give *team member* an opportunity to solve the problem.

PART III (Fill out near end of interview)

Suggestions made by team member: _______________________

____

____

Agreed-on solution: ____________________________________

____

____

PART IV (Action taken: Fill in when interview is finished)

Documentation completed: _______________________________

____

Writing Up Warnings

The next step in progressive discipline is to give the offender a written warning—a letter or form that will be placed in his or her personnel file. Written warnings often are taken more seriously than the first two steps. Employees don't want negative reports in their personnel files, and even the possibility that they'll be "written up" serves as a deterrent to poor behavior.

If the written warning concerns poor performance, specify the performance standards and indicate in what way the employee's performance fell short of the standards. Also state what was done to help the employee meet the standards. This will protect you against potential claims that you made no effort to bring the performance up to standard.

If the warning concerns infraction of a company rule, specify the nature of the offense and what disciplinary steps were taken before writing the warning (see the following two sample letters).

Leadership Lead
An alert and observant team leader can anticipate problems before they develop. Be alert for any deviations from standards before they become problems. By dealing with team members' rule infractions early on, you can usually avoid disciplinary procedures.

Memo for Poor Conduct

From (team leader): ______________________ Date: __________

To: ____

On (date) ___________, we had a discussion concerning ______________

____

____

At that time, you agreed to ________________________________

____

Because you have not complied with this agreement, you are being formally notified that if the above matter is not corrected by (date)______, additional disciplinary steps will be taken as specified in Section ____ of the Policies and Procedures manual.

Signed (team leader): ______________________________

Team member's comments: ______________________________

____

____

Signed (team member): ______________________________

To protect your company from potential legal problems, check any form letters concerning discipline with your legal advisors before sending them to be printed.

Although it's always advantageous from a legal standpoint to have employees sign *all* disciplinary documents, it becomes imperative when the warning itself is in writing.

You can't force anyone to sign anything. If an employee refuses to sign a disciplinary document, call in a witness—
a person not directly involved in the situation—and repeat your request. If he or she still refuses, have the witness attest to that response on the document.

To avoid misunderstandings, give copies of all disciplinary documents to the employee. In addition, you should send
a copy to the human-resources department to include in the person's personnel file.

The two sample letters can help you prepare written warnings: one for poor performance and one for poor conduct. Refer to them for ideas about how to phrase a written warning.

Memo for Poor Performance

From (team leader): ______________________ **Date:** ____________

To (team member): ______________________________

The performance standard for (specify job) ______________ **is (specify standard in quantity, quality, or other terms)** ______________________

____

____

Your performance has not met these standards (give details): ______________

____

____

To help you, I gave you ____ hours of special coaching. The areas covered include:

____

____

Signed (team leader): ______________________________

Team member's comments: ______________________________

Signed (team member): ______________________________

Putting Employees on Probation

Until now all your attempts to correct a team member's performance or behavior have been positive, and you've provided advice and counsel. If that hasn't worked, your next step is to put the team member on probation. Set a deadline for adjusting the situation.

What you're doing is giving your associate one more chance to shape up before you invoke some form of punishment. Most people take probation seriously—they know that you mean business.

The two primary reasons for progressive discipline are poor performance and poor conduct. If performance is a problem, probation is the last step before termination. If all the retraining, counseling, and coaching you give a team member fails, you can give one last chance to overcome the problem over a probationary period. If that doesn't help, additional disciplinary steps won't help. If you can transfer the person to a more suitable job, do so; if not, you have no other choice than to terminate him or her.

Company practices for administering probation vary considerably. They're governed by union contracts, company-policy manuals, or sometimes unwritten (but previously followed) practices. Usually the notification of probation is in the form of a written statement, signed by the team leader or a higher-ranking manager and acknowledged by the employee. The employee keeps one copy; the team leader gets another copy; and the human-resources department keeps a copy in its files.

Meanings and Gleanings
One way of providing a team member with another chance to improve performance or correct unsatisfactory behavior is to give the member a specified period of time (30 days, for example) to accomplish the change. If the improvement is not made during this period of **probation**, the next step in the progressive discipline is taken.

Red Alert
It's not a good idea to extend a probationary period. If a team member makes some progress by the end of the probationary period but his or her behavior still isn't up to expectations, you can extend the time period—but only once. Continuous probation is bad for morale and rarely solves the problem.

Probationary periods vary from as few as 10 days to the more customary 30 days and sometimes even longer. If an employee makes significant progress, lift the probation. If he or she repeats the offense after the probation is lifted, you can either reinstate the probation or invoke the next step.

When an offense violates company rules (tardiness, absenteeism, or other misconduct), proceed to the next step, which is usually suspension.

Suspension: The First Real Punishment

You're severely limited in the ways you can punish employees. Ever since flogging was abolished, only a few types of punishment can be legally administered. The most commonly used method, short of termination, is suspension without pay.

Although team leaders often have some leeway in determining the length of a suspension, most companies set specific suspension times depending on the seriousness of the offense.

Leadership Lead
The downside of suspending a team member is that you lose that person's contribution to the team effort during the suspension period. Make every effort to keep the person employed by training and counseling so that suspension isn't necessary.

The mechanics of issuing a suspension are similar to that of probation. Because suspension is a much more serious step, union contracts often require consultation with a union representative before suspending an employee. Most companies aren't unionized and require approval for suspensions by both the manager to whom the team leader reports and the human-resources department. Appropriate documentation specifying the reason for the suspension and the exact period of time involved should be made, signed by the appropriate manager, and acknowledged by the suspended employee.

If an employee returns from a suspension and continues to break the rules, your next step may be a longer suspension or even termination.

Termination: The Final Step

The chief purpose of progressive discipline is to give the offending employee an opportunity to change his or her behavior and become a productive, cooperative team member. Take stricter steps only after less strict steps have failed to solve the problem. The objective is to help the person succeed so that termination isn't necessary. If the employee fails to improve, however, the termination should take place.

The practical and legal facets of terminating employees are discussed in detail in chapter 25.

Affirming Affirmative Discipline

Some companies have done away with punishment, based on this logic: Team members are adults, adults take responsibility for their own actions, and punishment is therefore childish.

Here's how affirmative discipline works:

1. When a person is hired, the team leader and the new team member thoroughly discuss company rules and policies. The new employee is asked to make a commitment to comply with the rules.
2. If a rule is violated, the team leader points out the infraction and reminds the person of the agreement to comply with the rules. Both parties sign a memo to document the meeting.
3. If a violation occurs again, a second conference is held. The team member is asked to sign a special affirmation statement to show that the company takes the rules seriously and expects all employees to do the same.
4. If a member violates a minor rule for the third time or a major rule even one time, the leader asks the team member whether he or she really wants to continue working for the company. If the answer is yes, the team member is asked to sign a document acknowledging the violation and indicating that he or she understands that additional violations will lead to termination.
5. In some organizations, the employee is then asked to take a day off—with pay—to consider seriously whether he or she can live up to the commitment. Why is it a paid day off? By paying an employee under these circumstances, the company is expressing confidence in the person and in the system: It puts its money where its mouth is, not by punishing them, but by treating them as adults.

Companies that use affirmative discipline report that although terminations do occur occasionally, discipline problems significantly decrease.

In most organizations, senior management makes the decision to convert to an affirmative discipline system and ensures that it's applied throughout the company. With the increasing autonomy some companies grant to teams, the team itself may have the authority to implement affirmative discipline within the team.

Letting Team Members Monitor Their Team

When you have a highly motivated team, the need for discipline becomes superfluous. Each member of the team becomes a support person and a motivator to other members.

If a team member is slow in some aspect of his or her work, other team members can share their working shortcuts; if someone arrives at work late or frequently takes extra time at lunch, his or her colleagues can explain that it affects their activities. The team leader often doesn't have to reprimand or engage in formal disciplinary measures.

If everyone on a team is committed to meeting its goals and is given the tools to measure their own and the team's progress, they become self-controllers. The need for formal discipline fades into the background and is used only rarely, when all other means have been exhausted.

The Least You Need to Know

- Progressive discipline gives employees several opportunities to correct their behavior before any form of punishment is applied.
- When you reprimand a team member, stay cool, be constructive, and focus on the problem—not on the person.
- Disciplinary interviews should result in a mutually accepted plan of action to correct the situation.
- All disciplinary actions should be documented ("If it ain't written down, it ain't never happened.")
- Probationary periods give team members another chance to improve performance or correct behavior.
- Affirmative discipline treats employees as adults: Counseling replaces threats, and commitment replaces punishment.
- Well-coordinated teams control their own performance and influence the behavior of every team member. Formal discipline usually becomes unnecessary.

Chapter 24

"You're Fired!"

In This Chapter

- Terminating someone after progressive discipline has failed
- Preparing for a termination meeting
- Terminating employees spontaneously
- Knowing what "employment at will" really means

It's never pleasant to fire someone. Even if you're glad to get rid of someone, firing is a disagreeable task that most people do reluctantly. Yet sometimes your only course of action is to terminate an employee. A series of disciplinary steps usually leads to this final act, but occasionally circumstances warrant an unplanned discharge.

Terminating employees is a serious matter that must never be done without careful consideration. In most companies, before a supervisor or team leader can terminate anyone, approval must be obtained from both the person to whom the leader reports and the human-resources department. This step is important to ensure that company policies and legal requirements are fully observed. This chapter examines the importance of this process.

Taking the Last Step in Progressive Discipline

Employees who have experienced the steps of progressive discipline (see chapter 23) should never be surprised when they get fired. Presumably, at every step along the way they were told what the next step would be. When you suspend an employee—the next-to-the-last stage in the disciplinary process—you must make clear that, if he or she doesn't improve in the areas that are suggested, the next step is termination.

Preparing for a Termination Meeting

Because the issue of firing employees is such a sensitive one, you must do it diplomatically and be fully aware any of legal implications. Ask your HR department for advice about dealing with this situation.

Some team leaders get more upset about having to fire someone than the person who is being fired. Here are some suggestions to help you prepare:

- Review all documents so that you're fully aware of all the reasons and implications involved in the decision to terminate the team member.
- Review all that you know about the team member's personality:

  What problems have you had with the person?

  How did he or she respond to the preceding disciplinary steps?

  How did you and the team member get along on the job?

  How did he or she relate to other team members?

  What personal problems does the person have that you're aware of?
- Review any problems you've had in firing other employees, and map out a plan to avoid those problems.
- Check your company's policy manual or discuss with the human-resources department any company rules that apply.
- Relax before the meeting. Do whatever helps you clear your mind and calm your emotions. If you've done your job correctly, you've made every effort to help the team member succeed. The progressive discipline system has given the person several chances to change, so you don't have to feel guilty about the firing.

> **Leadership Lead**
> Some people are likely to sue for any real or imagined reason. When you fire someone, you may have to defend your actions in court. Keep complete records and appropriate documentation for all steps that led to the termination. Make sure that what you do is in accordance with your company's policies. Or, if there's no written policy, study how similar situations were handled in the past.

It's Showtime!

You've stalled as long as you can. Now you're ready to sit down with the employee and make clear that this is the end of the line.

Find a private place to conduct the meeting. Your office is an obvious spot, but it may not be the best one. A conference room is better because, if the fired employees breaks down or becomes belligerent, you can walk out.

Most people who are fired expect it and don't cause problems. They may beg for another chance, but this isn't the time to change your mind. Progressive discipline gives people several "other chances" before they reach this point. Don't let the termination meeting degenerate into a confrontation.

> **Leadership Lead**
> If an employee raises his or her voice, lower yours. Most people respond to a raised voice by raising their own. By responding in a soft voice, you disarm the other person. It has a calming effect.

If the employee gives you a hard time, keep cool. Don't lose your temper or get into an argument.

It's a good idea to have another person in the room at a termination meeting. A person being fired may say or do inappropriate things. Also, you may become upset and say something that's best left unsaid. The presence of a third person keeps both you and the employee from losing your temper and from saying or doing something that can lead to additional complications.

The best "third person" in a termination meeting is a representative from the human-resources department. If this person isn't available, call in another manager or team leader. If the employee belongs to a union, the union contract usually stipulates the presence of a union delegate.

Having a third person in the room when you terminate an employee also provides a witness if an employee later sues your company. Suppose that a former employee files an age-discrimination suit several weeks after being fired for poor performance. He or she claims that during the termination meeting, you stated that the company needs younger people in order to meet production standards. Although the claim is false, you'll have to spend time, energy, and money to defend against it—and it's your word against the other person's.

If you request that a third person attend termination meetings, former employees will be less likely to file false claims because they know that they'll be refuted by a witness.

Bet You Didn't Know

Most people are fired at the end of the workday on Friday afternoon. Some companies prefer to terminate employees in the middle of the week, however, so that people have a chance to begin looking for a new job the next day and not brood about the firing over the weekend.

In most organizations, when a termination meeting ends, the employee is sent to the human-resources department for outprocessing, or handling the administrative details for completing the separation procedure. If your company has a team leader handle this chore, follow its procedures carefully.

Use the termination checklist on the following pages to ensure that you take the necessary steps in terminating an employee.

Spontaneous Termination

Are there times when you're so annoyed with people that you wish you could just be the old-school boss and tell them to get out? Of course, there are. That's why progressive discipline was instituted—so that supervisors don't let their emotions of the moment dictate their actions.

Leadership Lead

As angry as you may be about the trouble an employee has caused or how nasty he or she may be, don't use the termination meeting to tell the person off. A termination is a business decision, not a personal one.

Occasionally, termination without warning is permitted. These occasions are rare and usually limited to a few serious infractions that are clearly delineated in company policies. Serious offenses include drinking on the job, fighting, stealing, and insubordination. Because these charges aren't always easy to prove, be very careful before you make the decision to fire someone spontaneously. You must have solid evidence that can stand up in court. Law books are loaded with cases in which people who, because of a rash firing decision, have sued former employers for unlawful discharge, defamation of character, false imprisonment, and whatever else their lawyers can dream up.

Red Alert

To avoid legal problems, be sure to have all the facts before you fire someone. Investigate: Get witnesses, and get legal advice. Don't discuss the case with people who don't have a need to know.

Insubordination, which is one of the most frequent causes of spontaneous termination, isn't always easy to prove. If an employee simply fails to carry out an order, it's not enough grounds for termination. Unless a failure to obey instructions can lead to serious consequences, it's better to use progressive discipline.

Termination Checklist

Name of employee: ______________________ Date: ____________

Part I: If discharged for poor performance, steps taken to improve performance:

Date Action

____

____

____

Comments: ______________________________________

____

____

If discharged for poor conduct, list progressive disciplinary steps taken:

Date Action

____________ Informal warning

____________ Written warning

____________ Disciplinary interview

____________ Suspension

____________ Other (specify) ______________________

____

Comments: ______________________________________

____

____

Part II

Have you reviewed all pertinent documents? ______

Have you treated this case in the same way as similar cases in the past? ______

Has this action been reviewed by your immediate superior? ______

By human-resources department? ______

By legal department? ______

Does employee have any claim pending against company? ______

Any worker's compensation claims? ______

Other (specify): ______________________________________

continues

Part III: Termination interview

Conducted by: ______________________________

Date: ______________ **Place:** ______________________

Witness: ______________________________

Comments: ______________________________

____

____

Final actions: ______________________________

____

ID and keys returned? ______________

Company property returned? ______________

Final paycheck issued? ______________

Additional comments: ______________________________

____

____

On the other hand, if a team member becomes unruly in his or her refusal (if he or she hollers and screams or spits in your face, for example), spontaneous discharge may be appropriate.

Documenting a Spontaneous Discharge

When you fire someone after progressive-discipline procedures fail, you have an entire series of documents to back you up. In spontaneous termination, however, you have no documents.

Immediately after a termination, write a detailed report describing the circumstances that led up to it. Get written statements from witnesses. If you can, get the employee to sign a statement presenting his or her side of the story. In the event that this discharge is challenged, having the terminated employee's immediate comments will protect you in case he or she presents a different version of what happened.

You Can't Fire Me—I Quit!

Suppose that, after all your efforts to help someone improve his performance, you tell him that you have to let him go. You explain that if he quits voluntarily, it will look better when he applies for another job. This option may sound sensible, but what happens if Mark applies for unemployment insurance and is told that he's not eligible because he quit?

> **Meanings and Gleanings**
> When an employee quits because of intentional unfair treatment on the job, it is "constructed" by the courts to be equivalent to being fired and is referred to as **constructive discharge**.

If you give someone the option of resigning, be sure to inform the person about loss of unemployment insurance and any other negative factors.

Now suppose that you think you'll be shrewd in getting rid of the person: "If I fire him, he'll give me problems. I'll just make his life so miserable that he'll quit." Over the next few weeks, you give him as many unpleasant assignments as you can. You time his returns from breaks and even how long he spends in the restroom. You chastise him for every minor violation of company rules, and, after a few weeks, he quits.

Don't be shocked when the person sues your company for unlawful discharge! When you tell the court, "I didn't fire him—he quit," the judge will respond "Not so. This is a constructive discharge—your treatment forced him to quit." You must then pay the person back wages, rehire him, or make a satisfactory financial settlement.

Employment at Will

Unless you have a personal contract with your employer or are a member of a union, you and all your team members are "employees at will."

> **Meanings and Gleanings**
> **Employment at will** is a legal concept under which an employee is hired and can be fired at the will of the employer. The employer has the right, unless restricted by law or contract, to refuse to hire an applicant or to terminate an employee for any reason or no reason.

This concept has governed employment since colonial times. Bosses always had the right to fire employees, and, ever since slavery was abolished, employees could always quit. Only recently has this concept been challenged.

To understand employment at will, you first have to know a little about our legal system. Americans are subject to two kinds of law: legislated acts and common law. The former are the laws passed by

Congress, the states, and local governments. Common law is based on accepted practices as interpreted by court decisions over the years.

The primary difference between the two types of law is that common law can be superseded or modified by legislation and can be changed in individual cases by mutual agreement between the parties involved. A violation of common law is not a criminal offense and is handled in a lawsuit as a civil action. Legislated statutes can be changed only by amendment, repeal, or court interpretation.

Employment at will, a common-law principle, has been modified over the years by various statutes. For example, some laws prohibit a company from firing or refusing to hire someone for union activity, race, religion, national origin, gender, disability, and age. Your right under common law to hire or fire at will is therefore restricted in these circumstances.

Red Alert
You cannot waive a legislated right by signing a contract. An employee cannot agree to work for less than the minimum wage, for example.

This principle also means that you can agree to waive employment at will by mutual consent. You can sign a contract with your company in which you agree not to quit and it agrees not to fire you for the duration of the contract. Or your company and a union can agree that no union member will be fired except under the terms of the contract. In both cases, the company has given up its right to employment at will.

Employment Rights When No Contract Exists

During the past several years, a number of cases have extended employees' rights that are not covered by specific legislation. Courts in several states have ruled that, although a company's policies-and-procedures manual isn't a formal contract, it can be considered to have the same effect as a contract.

In one case, a supervisor at a New York publishing firm was fired without having the benefit of progressive-discipline measures. He sued on grounds that the policy manual called for progressive discipline before terminating an employee. In his supervisory capacity, he was required to follow the manual when he had to discharge one of his staff members. When he was fired, however, the company didn't follow the procedure. The company's contention was that the manual was intended only as a guide and not as a rigid procedure. The court ruled in favor of the employee. It said that, if a policy is published in a manual, employees can expect that it will be followed.

To avoid this type of problem, attorneys advise their clients to specify clearly in their company-policy manuals that they are "at-will" employers and to include a statement to that effect on their employment-application forms.

Oral Commitments

Suppose that during an interview, you told Stella that her job would be permanent after a six-month probationary period. A year later, your company downsizes, and Stella is laid off. She sues. She says, "I left my former job to take this one because the team leader assured me that it was a permanent job." You respond, "I made that comment in good faith. Our company had never had a layoff." Your reply won't be good enough—the court will award Stella a large settlement.

An Ounce of Prevention

To avoid these types of these complications, follow these guidelines:

- All managers and team leaders should be trained in procedures concerning termination and adhere to them.
- Team leaders or anyone who represents management should never make commitments concerning tenure or other employment conditions orally or in writing.
- Make written job offers only after consulting with legal specialists.
- Never use the term "permanent employee." *No one* is a permanent employee. If your company must differentiate between temporary and part-time staff members, refer to the full-time people as "regular employees."
- On all documents and records relating to employment conditions, state that the company has a policy of employment at will.

The Least You Need to Know

- Prepare for a termination meeting by studying all the pertinent documents, reviewing the team member's personal characteristics, and psyching yourself up for the meeting.
- Check with your human-resources department to ensure that all policies are followed and laws complied with.
- Invite a third party to participate in and witness termination meetings.
- Use spontaneous termination only for extreme infractions.
- Other than for reasons prohibited by law or waived by contract, an employer can fire any employee for any reason or for no reason ("employment at will").
- Oral commitments to an employee about tenure or conditions of employment are as binding as written agreements.

Chapter 25

Separations, Layoffs, and Downsizing

In This Chapter

- Uncovering the real reasons people quit
- Temporary reductions in the workforce
- Downsizing: Bye-bye, job!

The days when a person joined a company after graduating from high school or college and stayed until retirement have long since passed. Most people now have several jobs during their working years. Sometimes it's a personal decision to leave a company, and sometimes it's involuntary—a company reduces its workforce, or an individual is discharged.

Every time an employee leaves a company, whether it's voluntary or involuntary, it costs the company a great deal of money. The investment involved in hiring, training, and supervising that person in addition to the enormous administrative expenses that are incurred are lost forever. The company loses production output until a replacement is hired and trained, and the interaction among team members is disrupted every time there's a change in the makeup of the group. Team leaders must make every effort to keep turnover down. This chapter explores those issues.

Knowing What Happens When an Employee Says, "I Quit!"

Suppose that you've worked hard to build up a team member's skills and that, just when she has become effective, she quits. Then, another employee, who for several years has been one of your steadiest, most reliable workers, comes in one day and gives you his notice.

People may leave a job for any number of reasons. Sometimes it's personal: A spouse has to relocate for a job or someone decides to return to school to pursue a different career. There's not much a team leader can do to reduce turnover based on personal factors.

Leadership Lead
Employees often have deeper reasons for leaving than the one they give you. Probe to find the real reasons.

Often, the reason is job-related. Employees may feel that they aren't making the progress they had hoped for, that their salary is too low, that working conditions are unsatisfactory, or that the job has become boring. In these cases, it's sometimes possible to reduce turnover by identifying recurring problems and correcting them so that other team members don't leave for the same reasons.

Conducting a Separation Interview

A *separation interview,* sometimes called an *exit interview,* is designed to help team leaders or supervisors determine the real reasons people leave a job and to obtain information about the company or the job that may have caused discontent.

Leadership Lead
An unbiased, objective separation interview shouldn't be conducted by the team leader or supervisor of the employee who is leaving. The interview should be conducted by a member of the human-resources (HR) department, the leader of another team, or another management-level person.

One reason you may be able to get more information during a separation interview is that people often feel freer to open up when they have nothing to lose.

Usually separation interviews are conducted by the HR department. But when teams work in locations that have no HR representative, team leaders may be required to interview people who leave other teams in that facility.

Here are some guidelines for conducting an effective separation interview:

- To avoid getting superficial or even misleading reasons from a departing employee, don't ask, "Why are you leaving?" You can develop better information by asking good questions.

- Ask questions about the job itself:

  What did you like most about the job? Least?

  How do you feel about the progress you've made in this company?

  How do you feel about compensation, benefits, and working conditions?

  From the patterns of answers you get from people who are leaving your company, you can gain insight into facets of the job you hadn't realized. If you hear numerous reports of dissatisfaction in specific areas, take action to investigate them; if the reports are valid, correct the problem or else turnover will continue to climb.

- Ask questions about supervision, such as, "How would you describe your team leader's style of leading the team, and how did you react to it?" and "What do you feel were your team leader's strengths and weaknesses?"

  It's important to explore the area of employee-supervisor relations because it causes problems in many companies. Feedback from an exit interview makes team leaders aware of factors that may have caused problems so that they can take steps to correct them. They can also learn why they've been commended and be encouraged to reinforce those areas.

- Ask questions that might give you insight into other problem areas: "If you could discuss with top management exactly how you feel about this company, what would you tell them?"

  This open-ended question often elicits interesting responses. Let employees speak freely. Avoid leading questions, and encourage people to express their true feelings, attitudes, perceptions, fears, and hopes about your organization.

- If an employee has accepted a job with another company, ask, "What does your new job offer you that you're not getting here?" The answer may repeat some of the things you've already discussed, but it may also uncover some of the ways your company failed to meet this person's hopes, goals, or expectations.

Knowing What to Do When Employees Give Notice

Some supervisors and team leaders take an employee's resignation as a personal affront. "How could she do this to me?" Be aware that other team members are carefully monitoring the way you handle this situation, however. Take care to make the transition smooth.

The following suggestions help reduce the confusion that often results when a team member leaves your company:

- **Don't blow up.** I once worked for a manager who considered anyone who quit to be disloyal. If someone gave him the courtesy of two weeks' notice, he ordered the person to leave immediately. He then bad-mouthed the employee to everyone in the company. The result was that employees quit without giving notice, which caused serious production problems.

> **Leadership Lead**
> No law requires employees to give notice when they leave a company. The customary two-week notice is a courtesy that gives team leaders the opportunity to plan for a smooth transition. If you feel that the continued presence of this person may be disruptive to the team, you don't have to accept the notice, and you can then arrange for immediate separation.

- **Agree on a mutually satisfactory departure date.** You may need time to readjust your plans.
- **Request a status report on the team member's projects so that you can arrange for others to handle them.** Develop a list of vendors, customers, or other people outside your department that the member interacts with so that you can notify them of the change.
- **Contact your personnel department to arrange for either an internal transfer or hiring from outside.**
- **Let other team members know as soon as you're notified.** Tell them how it will affect their work until someone else is hired.

Dealing with Temporary Layoffs

If you work in an industry in which work is done seasonally (construction, certain clothing manufacturing, landscaping, and the automobile industry, for example), you're accustomed to temporary layoffs or furloughs. Workers in these fields expect to be laid off at certain times of the year and plan their lives accordingly. They're usually covered by unemployment insurance or, in some union contracts, additional payments. When the new season begins, most of them are rehired.

> **Leadership Lead**
> When a team member leaves, reexamine the job description and specifications. A person performing a job often molds it to conform to his or her special interests or talents. You may not have the same view of the job, however, and this is your chance to readjust the job description.

Some layoffs are unexpected, however, even though they're temporary. Business may slow down or a company may cut its payroll, for example. Laid-off workers have a reasonable chance of being rehired when business picks up, but they have no guarantee.

Although some people will wait for a recall, many choose to look for other jobs. This situation poses a problem for the company because many experienced workers won't be available when they're needed.

Understanding Alternatives to Layoffs

When team members know that a layoff is for a specified period and that the company has a history of calling back the entire team after a furlough, they're less likely to seek other jobs. If a layoff is indefinite but you know that you will be rehiring sooner or later, take steps to keep available as many people as you can so that, when the recall comes, your team will be intact and ready to function.

When you're part of a smooth-running, highly productive team, a layoff can be devastating. The loss of some workers means that the surviving members will have to do more work to pick up the slack. Team interaction that had been developed over time is lost and must be rebuilt. Morale suffers, and productivity is most likely reduced. The best way to rebuild morale is to find alternatives to a layoff.

> **Meanings and Gleanings**
> When companies don't have enough work to keep their workforce busy or when they want to reduce payroll to increase profits, workers are dismissed. These **layoffs** are sometimes temporary (until the workers are needed) and sometimes permanent.

This list describes some ways companies have avoided layoffs:

- **Pay cuts.** The main reason for most layoffs is to reduce payroll. When companies institute a general pay reduction for all employees (including management), the entire workforce shares the burden.

  It's easier to reduce the payroll in a unionized organization. Because a union speaks for its entire bargaining unit, it can negotiate this technique as a means of saving its members' jobs.

  Where no union exists, a company can arbitrarily cut its payroll. No one wants to take a pay cut, of course, but some people aren't willing to suffer a small personal loss to save even a close colleague's job. Unless management can "sell" it to employees by appealing to their nobler motives, a pay cut causes more problems than it solves.

- **Work sharing.** All team members share the work that remains after jobs are eliminated. The standard workweek is reduced by working fewer hours each day or fewer days each week; another alternative involves working full weeks, but fewer weeks each month. With this strategy, hourly pay remains the same, but reduced hours decrease the payroll.

  Work sharing enables companies to keep skilled employees during slow periods and enables teams to stay together. Employees earn less total pay but retain their benefits. Some states have amended their unemployment-insurance laws so that employees can collect some unemployment benefits during work-sharing periods.

Red Alert

As much as you may want to keep laid-off team members available for recall, don't mislead them with false hopes. It not only isn't fair to someone who may turn down another job but also can have legal repercussions. Former employees have sued companies because of implied promises to rehire that didn't materialize.

- **Early retirement.** One way to minimize the number of employees who are laid off during an indefinite layoff is by encouraging older workers to retire earlier than they had planned. Under the Age Discrimination in Employment Act (see chapter 9), companies cannot compel employees to retire. They can offer incentives, however, to make it worth their while. When higher-paid senior employees leave a company, the payroll is reduced significantly.

Usually, an entire team isn't laid off. Unless you have a union contract or rigid policy which mandates that layoffs happen on a seniority basis, keep your best team members—those who can form the cadre of a new team if some of the laid-off members don't return when they're recalled.

Keep in touch with laid-off team members. Phone them, and send them the company newsletter. Let them know that you still consider them part of your team and that you're looking forward to the recall so that you can work together again.

Rehiring Laid-Off Workers

Leadership Lead

Even if you know that a laid-off team member has accepted another job, offer the person the opportunity to return to your team. He or she may not be satisfied with the new job and may prefer to rejoin your team.

Seniority in most companies is the basis of both layoffs and recalls. The most senior employees are the last to be let go and the first to be rehired. This approach isn't always the most desirable one, however. If you have no contractual obligation to do so, it may be more advantageous to rehire people according to the skills you need as the work expands. Your immediate need might be for a specialist in one area, but the most senior furloughed member may have a different skill. In this way, you can rebuild your team most effectively.

Downsizing: The Permanent Layoff

As defined earlier, downsizing involves the elimination of a job. An entire facility may be closed, an entire unit or department eliminated, or an organization restructured by doing away with certain jobs or entire job categories.

The downsizing of major corporations over the past few years (see chapter 17) has eliminated tens of thousands of jobs, causing disruptions not only in the lives of laid-off workers but also often to entire communities. This section explains how to cope with the fallout from downsizing cuts.

WARN: The Law on Downsizing

To ease the burden on laid-off workers, Congress passed the Worker Adjustment and Retraining Notification Act (WARN). This law applies to companies that have 100 or more employees when they have mass layoffs or plant closings. The law exempts companies with fewer than 100 employees. Companies that are covered aren't required to comply with the law when they lay off small numbers of workers. It affects only mass layoffs.

A *mass layoff* is a layoff or reduction in hours at a single site that affects 500 or more full-time employees or 50 or more if they constitute at least 33 percent of an active, full-time workforce. A *reduction in hours* means to cut hours worked by 50 percent or more each month for a six-month period or longer. A company must give notice to employees who will be laid off at least 60 days before their final day of work. There are some exceptions to this rule, so check with your legal department to determine how it affects you.

> **Leadership Lead**
> When a company closes a facility or lays off a large number of people, you may need certain employees for continuing production. Offer them financial incentives so that they'll stay to the end after they've been given notice. At this point, you need them more than they need you.

Dealing with Downsizing and the EEO Laws

Until relatively recently, members of some minority groups and women weren't usually hired or promoted to certain positions because of past company policies or community practices. During the past few years, many companies have made significant strides in bringing minorities and women into the workforce.

If seniority is the policy followed during downsizing, minorities and women—who often have relatively low seniority—are often the first to have to leave. This practice can have an adverse effect on a company's affirmative-action endeavors.

The Civil Rights Act of 1964 specifically exempts companies that have established a seniority system for layoffs and rehiring from being charged with discrimination if seniority is the basis for their actions. There's an exception, however: If a member of a protected group can show that he or she personally experienced discrimination that resulted in lower seniority than if there had been no discrimination, that person may claim protection.

Suppose that a woman was rejected for a job as a traveling auditor in 1980 because that company didn't hire women in that category and that she applied again in 1985 and was hired. If she is laid off later because of her lack of seniority, she can sue, claiming that, if not for that discriminatory policy, she would have had higher seniority. Each case is decided on its own merits, however.

Providing Continuing Benefits

Under the federal law known as COBRA (Consolidated Omnibus Budget Reconciliation Act), employees of companies with 20 or more employees are entitled to maintain their health-insurance coverage for 18 months after they leave a company. (Disabled people can maintain it for 29 months.) The company isn't expected to pay their premiums, however. Former employees who enroll in COBRA must pay the full premium at the same rate the company had been paying (usually considerably less than if they had to purchase individual insurance) plus a small administrative charge.

COBRA also provides for continuing health-insurance coverage for survivors of employees who die.

Processing Out Laid-Off Employees

The administrative details of the separation processing in most companies is done by the human-resources department. In smaller companies or at branch facilities that have no HR department, a team leader usually handles the process.

Inform the people who are to be laid off at an appropriate time. If your company is covered by WARN, you must provide written notice 60 days in advance. If it's not covered by WARN, there's no required time, but it's only fair to give adequate notice about when they will be laid off. For temporary layoffs, two weeks is typical; for permanent layoffs, 30 days.

At the time of the separation, follow these guidelines. Using a checklist will ensure that everything is covered.

- Discuss the continuation of benefits under COBRA, as discussed earlier in this chapter.
- Discuss separation pay. No law requires severance pay, but some union contracts do mandate it. Many companies voluntarily give severance pay to laid-off workers. The amount varies from company to company and often within a company by job category. Check your company policy.
- If appropriate, discuss the callback procedure.

- If an employee isn't receiving a final paycheck at the same time he or she is leaving the company, specify when it's expected.
- If provisions have been made to help laid-off employees seek other jobs, refer the person to whomever is responsible for that function.
- Retrieve company property: keys, credit cards, ID cards, tools, company computers used at home, computer logon IDS, or computer passwords, for example.
- If an employee has incurred expenses for the company, such as travel and entertainment that have not yet been reimbursed, arrange for prompt attention to this matter.
- Answer any questions the employee has.
- Arrange for the employee to clean out his or her desk, office, or locker.
- Arrange for forwarding of any mail and messages that are received at the company after the employee leaves.
- Express your good wishes.

The Least You Need to Know

- By conducting good separation interviews, you can learn the real reasons that people leave a company and then take the appropriate preventive measures to reduce turnover.
- When a team member resigns, ease the transition by getting a status report about what he or she has been working on. Reassign that work until a successor is in place.
- Try to find alternatives to layoffs, such as work sharing, shorter hours, or general pay cuts.
- Keep in touch with temporarily laid-off team members to ensure the likelihood that they'll return when needed.
- If your company is covered by the WARN law, it must give 60 days notice when it closes a facility or lays off a large number of employees.
- COBRA mandates that laid-off employees be allowed to continue their medical-insurance coverage for a specified period if they pay their own premiums.

Appendix

Meanings and Gleanings Glossary

affirmative action A written plan to commit to hiring women and minorities in proportion to their representation in the community where the firm at which they work is located. Applies to companies that have government contracts in excess of $50,000 and more than 50 employees.

affirmative discipline A technique in which employees, instead of being punished, are counseled and asked to make commitments to comply with company rules.

Age Discrimination in Employment Act (ADEA) As amended, prohibits discrimination against individuals 40 years of age or older. Some state laws cover all persons over the age of 18.

Americans with Disabilities Act (ADA) Prohibits discrimination against people who are physically or mentally challenged.

aptitude test A test designed to determine the potential of candidates in specific areas, such as mechanical ability, clerical skills, or sales potential. The tests are helpful for screening inexperienced people to determine whether they have the aptitude in the type of work for which a company plans to train them. Most aptitude tests can be administered and scored by following a simple instruction sheet.

arbitration A process in which two parties present their sides of a problem and an arbitrator decides how the problem should be resolved.

behavioral science The study of how and why people behave the way they do.

benchmarking A process of seeking organizations that have achieved success in an area and learning about their techniques and methods.

body language A method people use to communicate—not only by what they say but also by their gestures, facial expressions, and movements.

bona fide occupational qualifications (BFOQ) Positions for which a company is permitted to specify only a man or only a woman for a job. There must be clear-cut reasons, however, for why a person of only that gender can perform the job.

brainstorming A technique for generating ideas in which participants are encouraged to voice any idea, no matter how "dumb" or useless it may be. By allowing participants to think freely and express ideas without fear of criticism, they can stretch their minds and make suggestions that may seem worthless but that may trigger in the mind of another participant an idea which has value.

buzzword A term or phrase everyone uses for a short time.

case study A description of a real or simulated situation presented to trainees for analysis, discussion, and solution; used in graduate schools, seminars, and training programs to enable trainees to work on the types of problems they're most likely to meet on the job. Case studies are often drawn from the experiences of real companies.

channel of communication The path information takes through the organization. If you want to give information to (or get it from) a person in another department, you first go to your boss, who goes to the supervisor of the other department, who in turn goes to the person with the information, who gets it and conveys it back through the same channels. By the time you get the information, it may have been distorted by a variety of interpretations.

charisma The special charm some people have that secures for them the support and allegiance of other people.

Civil Rights Act of 1964 Title VII, as amended, prohibits discrimination in employment on the basis of race, color, sex, religion, and national origin.

coasters Long-term employees (not likely to be fired, because of their tenure) who have gone as far as they can and "coast along" until their retirement.

COBRA An acronym for the Consolidated Omnibus Budget Reconciliation Act, in which employees of companies with 20 or more employees are entitled to maintain their health-insurance coverage for 18 months after they leave the company (29 months for people who are disabled at the time they leave). The company isn't expected to pay their premiums. Former employees must pay the full premium at the same rate the company had been paying (usually considerably less than if they had to purchase individual insurance) plus a small administrative charge.

communication The process by which information, ideas, and concepts are transmitted between persons and groups.

constructive discharge When an employee quits because of purposeful unfair treatment on the job, it is "constructed" by the courts to be an involuntary termination.

control point A point in a project at which you stop, examine what has been completed, and correct any errors that have been made (before they blow up into catastrophes).

counseling A means of helping troubled associates overcome barriers to good performance. With careful listening, open discussion, and sound advice, a counselor helps identify problems, clarify misunderstandings, and plan solutions.

cross training A method of training team members to perform the jobs of other people on the team so that every member is capable of doing all aspects of the team's work.

decentralization When the focus of a business is shifted from one central facility where all decisions are made and most of the work is done to localized facilities where, within guidelines, decisions are made and work is performed autonomously.

delegation A process that enables you to position the right work at the right responsibility level, helping both you and the team members you delegate to expand your skills and contributions, while ensuring that all work gets done in a timely manner by the right person with the right experience or interest in the right topic.

documentation A written description of all disciplinary actions taken by a company to protect it in case of legal actions. ("If it ain't written down, it ain't never happened.")

downsize To lay off employees, primarily when business is slow, so that a company can reduce costs. Downsizing differs from traditional layoffs in that total job categories are eliminated—people who held these jobs have little chance of being rehired (*see* layoff).

employee-assistance program (EAP) A company-sponsored counseling service. Many companies have instituted these types of programs to help their employees deal with personal problems that interfere with productivity. The counselors aren't company employees; they're outside experts who are retained on an as-needed basis.

employee stock-ownership program (ESOP) A program in which a major portion of a company's stock is given or sold to employees so that they actually own the company.

employment at will A legal concept under which an employee is hired and can be fired at the will of the employer. Unless restricted by law or contract, the employer has the right to refuse to hire an applicant or to terminate an employee for any reason or no reason at all.

empowerment Sharing your managerial power with the people over whom you have that power.

Equal Pay Act of 1963 An act which requires that the gender of an employee not be considered in determining salary (equal pay for equal work).

goals/objectives Interchangeable terms to describe an organization's or individual's desired long-run results.

going rate An amount paid to employees to keep them from leaving a company.

grievance A formal complaint, usually based on the violation of a union contract or formal company policy.

gripe An informal complaint about working conditions or other aspects of an employee-company relationship.

halo effect The assumption that, because of one outstanding characteristic, all of an applicant's characteristics are outstanding (that person then "wears a halo"). The opposite is the *pitchfork effect,* or the symbol of the devil: You assume that, because one trait is so poor, the person is entirely bad.

hot button The one thing in a person's makeup that really gets him or her excited—positively or negatively. (To really reach someone, find that person's hot button.)

"I"-meeting An idea-generating meeting at which each participant presents at least one idea for solving the problem being considered.

intelligence test Like the IQ test administered in schools, this test measures the ability to learn. It varies from brief, simple exercises that can be administered by people with little training to highly sophisticated tests that must be administered by a person with a Ph.D. in psychology.

job analysis The process of determining the duties, functions, and responsibilities of a job (the *job description)* and the requirements for the successful performance of a job (the *job specifications*).

job bank A computerized list of the capabilities of all employees in an organization.

job description A listing of the duties, responsibilities, and results a job requires.

job enrichment Redesigning jobs to provide diversity, challenge, and commitment (and to alleviate boredom).

job instruction training (JIT) A systematic approach to training that has four steps: preparation, presentation, performance, and follow-up.

job posting A listing on company bulletin boards of the specifications for an available position. Any employee who is interested can apply. After preliminary screening by the human-resources department, employees who meet the basic requirements are interviewed.

job specifications The requirements an applicant should possess to successfully perform a job.

joint leader/associate evaluations Using the same evaluation format, associates evaluate their own performance. The leader also evaluates the performance. The final report results from a collaborative discussion between leader and associate.

just-in-time delivery Rather than store large inventories of supplies, companies today arrange with suppliers to deliver supplies as needed. The project manager or team leader must interface with the suppliers to schedule and ensure that supplies are delivered at the exact time they're needed.

KITA *A k*ick *i*n *t*he you-know-what.

KRA (key-results area) An aspect of a job in which employees must concentrate time and attention to ensure that they achieve the goals for that job.

lateral thinking Looking at a problem from different angles that may give new insights into its solutions (instead of approaching it by logical thinking).

layoff Termination of employees permanently or for a specific period of time due to lack of work or restructuring of an organization.

leadership The art of guiding people in a manner that commands their respect, confidence, and wholehearted cooperation.

M.O. (method, or mode, of operation) The patterns of behavior a person habitually follows in performing work.

management The process of achieving specific results by effectively using an organization's available resources (money, materials, equipment, information, and employees).

mediation A process in which two parties present their sides and a mediator works with them to reach a mutually satisfactory solution.

mentor A team member assigned to act as counselor, trainer, and "big brother" or "big sister" to a new member.

motivators Factors that stimulate a person to expend more energy, effort, and enthusiasm in a job (*see* satisfiers).

negative personality A person's outlook in which any suggestion is taken as a personal affront, any new assignment is accepted with reluctance, and relations with coworkers and leaders are usually considered confrontational.

network To make contacts with managers in other companies to whom you can turn for suggestions and ideas.

objective *See* goals.

open-book management A management style in which employees are considered full partners in the operation of a business. One characteristic of this management style is that employees have a direct stake in their company's success (if the business is profitable, they share in the profits; if not, there are no profits to share). Another characteristic is that every employee has access to numbers that are critical to tracking the company's performance and are given the training and tools to understand them.

opportunity The combination of being in the right place at the right time and having the ability and desire to take advantage of it.

outsourcing Contracting to outside sources any work that previously had been done in-house. As companies become "leaner and meaner," they outsource activities that can be done more effectively by outside specialists. Some examples are payroll, traffic, training, computer programming, advertising, and certain manufacturing activities.

ownership A feeling that you're a full partner in the development and implementation of a project, committed to its successful achievement.

performance standards The results expected from persons performing a job. For performance standards to be meaningful, every person doing that job should know and accept these standards.

performance test A test that measures how well candidates can do the job for which they apply (for example, operating a lathe, entering data into a computer, writing advertising copy, or proofreading manuscripts). When job performance cannot be tested directly, a company may use written or oral tests about job knowledge.

personality test A test designed to identify personality characteristics that varies from the *Readers Digest* quickie questionnaires to highly sophisticated psychological evaluations.

piece work A system of compensation in which earnings are based solely on the number of units produced.

pitchfork effect *See* halo effect.

platinum rule "Do unto others as they would have you do unto them."

prioritize To rank tasks, by determining their degree of importance, to accomplish your goals on the job or in your life and in taking action accordingly—putting first things first.

profession An occupation requiring special training or advanced study in a specialized field. Physicians, lawyers, psychologists, and engineers all have to take advanced education and pass examinations to qualify for certification in their professions.

progressive discipline A systematic approach to correcting infractions of rules. A typical program has six steps, the first of which is an informal warning. If this step isn't successful, it's followed by (as necessary) a disciplinary interview, a written warning, probation, suspension, and, possibly, termination.

project manager A team leader assigned to head up a specific project, such as the design and manufacture of an electronic system or the development and marketing of a new product.

quality circles Groups of workers who voluntarily meet on a regular basis to discuss ideas about improving the quality of a product or service they produce.

real time What's going on here and now. The actual time in which a process occurs (for example, a computer can report real-time data or information about the status of a situation as of the time it's provided).

recruit To seek candidates to be considered for employment, usually done by personnel or human-resources departments.

reengineer To radically restructure the design of business processes (not just tinker with methods and procedures). When companies reengineer their processes, its managers must rethink everything they're doing in order to take advantage of the changes that will be made.

religious practices Practices that include, according to the EEOC, not only traditional religious beliefs but also moral and ethical beliefs and any beliefs an individual holds "with the strength of a traditional religious view."

results-oriented evaluation system A system in which performance expectations are agreed on at the beginning of a period and measured at the end of that period. At that time, new goals are developed to be measured at the end of the next period.

role playing A variation of case studies in which participants act out the parts of the characters involved. Used chiefly in studying problems in which interaction between characters is a major aspect.

satisfiers Also called maintenance factors; the factors—including working conditions, money, and benefits—employees must get from a job in order to expend even minimum effort in performing their work. After employees are satisfied with these factors, however, just giving them more of the same factor doesn't motivate them to work harder (*see* motivators).

selection A process of screening applicants to determine their suitability for a position. Preliminary screening is usually done by the human-resources department; subsequent screening, by supervisors or team leaders.

self-esteem The way you feel about yourself. If you think of yourself as a success, you will be a success; if you think of yourself as second-rate, you will always be second-rate—unless you change your self-perception. And it *can* be done.

self-directed team A team with no permanent team leader; team members are self-managed. Some teams have permanent administrative leaders to deal with the paperwork, but members rotate as project leaders. Team members schedule work, hire and train new members, budget funds, and monitor their own performance.

sexual harassment Any unwelcome sexual advances or requests for sexual favors or any conduct of a sexual nature when an employer makes submission to sexual advances a term or condition of employment, either initially or later on; or when submission or rejection is used as a basis of working conditions, including promotion, salary adjustment, assignment of work, and termination or has the effect of interfering with an individual's work or creating a hostile or intimidating work environment.

simulcast To bring together the audio and video so that they interact and intensify the message that's being communicated.

single-use plan A plan developed for a specific nonrecurring situation; for example, introducing a new product, moving to a new location, or opening a new facility.

SOPs (standard operating procedure) A set of standard practices in which company plans and policies are detailed (sometimes called "the company bible").

spontaneous termination A situation in which an employee is discharged without progressive discipline, usually precipitated by an egregious violation of company rules such as fighting, drunkenness, or gross insubordination (*see* progressive discipline).

stress or distress A chronic state of anxiety caused by unremitting pressures of job, personal, or societal problems.

synergy Two or more people or units working together so that the contributions of each enhances the results by more than the individual contribution by itself. "The whole is greater than the sum of its parts," or 2 + 2 may equal more than 4.

team A group of people who collaborate and interact synergistically in working toward a common goal.

telecommuting Technology that enables a person to perform work at home or at a location remote from a central office by receiving assignments and submitting completed work via computer.

total quality management A management system in which the focus of an entire company is placed on producing high-quality products or services. It involves statistical processes, training in both the technical and intangible aspects of quality management, and the commitment of all levels of employees to work toward continuous improvement.

training manuals Handbooks for teaching routine tasks; they make the training process easy for both trainer and trainees and can always be referred to when an employee is in doubt about what to do.

trait system of performance evaluation A system in which employees are rated on a series of traits, such as quantity and quality of work, attendance, and initiative. Ratings are usually measured on a scale from poor to superior.

upward communication The flow of ideas, suggestions, and comments from people in lower echelons of the organization to those in decision-making positions.

work sharing An alternative to layoffs in which all team members share the work that remains after some jobs are eliminated. The standard workweek is reduced by working fewer hours each day or fewer days each week. Another alternative is working full weeks, but fewer weeks each month. The hourly pay remains the same, but, because of reduced hours, the payroll is decreased.

WARN (Worker Adjustment and Retraining Notification Act) A law that applies to companies which have 100 or more employees when a mass layoff or plant closing occurs. Notice must be given to those employees at least 60 days before their final day of work. There are some exceptions to this rule, so check with your legal department to determine how it affects you.

Index

A

B

C

D

E

F

G

H

I

J

K-L

M

N

O-P

Q-R

U-V

W-Z